GOOD HOUSEKEEPING

EATING FOR A HEALTHY HEART

GOOD HOUSEKEEPING

EATING FOR A HEALTHY HEART

WITH

The Coronary Prevention Group

EBURY
PRESS

PUBLISHED BY EBURY PRESS
Division of the National Magazine Company Ltd
Colquhoun House
27–37 Broadwick Street
London W1V 1FR

ISBN 085223 614 X

SENIOR EDITOR Fiona MacIntyre
EDITOR Barbara Croxford
DESIGN Peter Bridgewater Design
PHOTOGRAPHY James Murphy
STYLIST Cathy Sinker
ILLUSTRATOR Annie Ellis
COOKERY Jacki Baxter

COVER PHOTOGRAPH: Provençal-Style Tart (page 34) and Ceviche (page 43)

Typeset by Textype Typesetters, Cambridge
Printed and bound in Hong Kong by Wing King Tong Co Ltd

Contents

Foreword

As a heart surgeon involved in the treatment of coronary heart disease, I believe in a preventive approach to the problem as well as a surgical one. This is because operations designed to relieve coronary heart disease are not in themselves the cure – they have to be combined with other measures, both to make the most of the operation and to reduce the risk of further disease.

This is where this book is unique. It gives the public the facts about coronary heart disease and details how to reduce the risks – not only through changes in lifestyle but also through sensible eating.

I strongly believe that this book serves as a guide to those who believe that the high risk of developing coronary heart disease can and should be reduced without interfering with the quality of life.

PROFESSOR MAGDI YACOUB
FRCS, MRCS, MRCP, MCH, DSC(HON)

Introduction

This book is all about healthy eating. By eating healthy food, not smoking, and taking regular exercise, you will give yourself the best chance of enjoying a fit and healthy life.

Experts are now sure, too, that good food reduces the risk of many common diseases: killers, notably coronary heart disease, stroke and some cancers; and disabling conditions, such as diabetes, gall stones and digestive disorders. The right kind of food also prevents tooth decay, constipation and weight problems.

But what is good food? The simplest guide to healthy eating is to eat plenty of whole cereal foods, especially whole grain bread, plenty of fresh vegetables of every variety, and fruit. Lean meat and fish of all kinds are a much better choice than fatty meat and meat products. If you fill up on whole, fresh food, you'll be less interested in unhealthy foods, most of them highly processed, heavy in fats, sugars, salt and additives. So go easy on alcohol, and enjoy the variety of good food that is now available.

In the last four or five years interest in nutrition has grown enormously. The health food shops of the 1970s used to be regarded as cranky. Today, that has all changed. Health foods or, more accurately, healthy foods, are now on sale in all supermarkets. Nutrition leaflets are produced by all the big retailers, and manufacturers are putting nutrition labels on their foods; even MPs are asking questions in Parliament about the nation's food.

Who can you trust? Much of the free information available on food and health is produced by food companies who also want to sell their products. Some of the scientists who are interviewed on TV and in newspapers and magazines are paid consultants to the food industry. They say what they believe to be true, but their views are often given exaggerated publicity by clever PR campaigns paid for by industry. Every year the food industry spends more than £500 million in advertising their products. In theory, advertising standards, overseen by bodies like the Advertising Standards Authority, should protect people from misleading information. But the Coronary Prevention Group and others believe that the existing advertising standards are not tough enough.

BUT WHAT DOES THE CORONARY PREVENTION GROUP ACTUALLY DO?

The Coronary Prevention Group works with government, political parties, industry, schools, hospitals and local authorities and provides information for the general public about the prevention of our number one killer: coronary heart disease.

The Coronary Prevention Group is not funded by food manufacturers, retailers or drug companies or, indeed, by anyone who could commercially benefit from the information we provide. In this respect this book is unlike many of the other sources of information on healthy eating.

This is our first book. We hope it will help you and your family to choose healthy foods, and to prepare delicious meals.

We would like you to write and tell us what you think of it, and what you would like us to do in our future work. Bon Appetit!

Anne Dillon – Director
THE CORONARY PREVENTION GROUP
60 Great Ormond Street
London
WC1N 3HR

WHAT'S GOOD FOR THE HEART

Before looking at healthy eating in detail it is important to put it into context. It is very important to remember that although unhealthy food is a major cause of coronary heart disease, it is only one of a number of inter-related factors. It is essential that the other factors are treated with equal importance.

YOU AND YOUR HEART

Your heart is a pump made of strong muscle. Each side is divided into two chambers: the atrium (upper) and the ventricle (lower). Blood is pumped from the right side of the heart to the lungs where it collects oxygen. It then returns to the left side of the heart where it is pumped out through the arteries to carry oxygen to the body tissues. To complete the cycle it returns through the veins to the right side of the heart. Arteries are long, narrow tubes through which the blood is pushed by the work of the heart to supply the body with oxygen.

In the average adult, the heart beats 60 to 90 times every minute, ie 100,000 beats every day, 3,000,000 beats every month. It pumps about half a teacup of blood with each beat. This works out at about 5 litres each minute, but during vigorous exercise it can increase to 20-25 litres per minute.

You can give yourself some idea of just how hard your heart works by opening your hand and then clenching your fist. Try doing that 75 times per minute and see how long you can keep going.

WHAT IS CORONARY HEART DISEASE?

Blood vessels spread through the whole body, delivering and collecting blood. The heart arteries, or coronary arteries, are the most important blood vessels in the body, providing the heart with a rich and continuous supply of oxygen. The heart cannot do its work unless it gets enough oxygen.

In a healthy person blood flows easily through the coronary arteries. But the inside of these arteries can become clogged up to such an extent that blood flow is impaired and finally stopped.

Coronary heart disease usually begins with atherosclerosis – the narrowing of the coronary arteries carrying blood to the heart. In the process of atherosclerosis, a fatty substance is deposited on the walls of the arteries. This fatty deposit is called atheroma and one of the main components of this substance is cholesterol (see page 9). If the artery becomes so narrowed with atheroma that it actually blocks the supply of blood to the heart muscle, a heart attack occurs. A heart attack can also be caused by the artery being blocked by a blood clot, known as a coronary thrombosis, or by a combination of atherosclerosis and thrombosis.

Sometimes a narrowing in the coronary arteries causes a severe pain in the chest which can spread to the neck and arms, and often occurs during a period of exertion or stress; it is usually relieved by resting. The pain is caused by a "cramp" in the heart muscles brought about by an inadequate supply of oxygen. This condition is called angina.

IS CORONARY HEART DISEASE REALLY A PROBLEM?

Well, here are just a few of the facts about coronary heart disease. They speak for themselves.

- Death rates from coronary heart disease are the equivalent of one jumbo jet crashing every day, and two each on Saturdays and Sundays.
- One person dies every three minutes from coronary heart disease.
- Between 50-60% of heart attacks occur without any prior warning.
- The UK has one of the highest death rates from coronary heart disease in the world for both men and women.
- One man in every five will have a heart attack before he reaches 65, and for half of them it will be fatal. Two thirds of deaths from heart attacks are sudden and take place before medical help can be reached.
- Of every 100 people under the age of 65 who have a heart attack, 45% die within the year. Over half of these, i.e. 25% of the total, die within 2 hours of the onset of the attack, without being seen by a doctor. Many survivors are disabled for life.

It is, in effect, a disaster. The facts are depressing, but the problem *can* be tackled. By understanding heart disease and taking the preventive action explained in this book, the picture will improve.

WHO IS AT RISK?

In 1985, these were the total numbers of men and women dying from coronary heart disease.

	MEN	WOMEN
England & Wales	91,626	71,478
Scotland	10,190	8,568
Northern Ireland	2,651	2,085
	104,467	82,131

Coronary heart disease death rates are spread over the whole of the UK. They are, though, worse in Scotland, Wales and Northern Ireland and the North of England. Death rates in the North of England are 30% higher than in the South East. More manual workers than non-manual workers die from coronary heart disease, as do their wives.

WOMEN AND CORONARY HEART DISEASE

Most people think of men, not women, as having heart attacks. Although women, overall, suffer fewer heart attacks than men, coronary heart disease is still a major problem for women. Coronary heart disease and strokes are second only to all cancers as the leading causes of death in women aged 35-54. Death statistics, however, ignore the thousands of women who are disabled by coronary heart disease. Coronary heart disease in women is more likely to take the form of angina than a heart attack.

To date, almost all the research on the causes and prevention of coronary heart disease has been conducted on men, and health education advice has tended to be geared towards them. If women are addressed, it is often in their role as mothers and wives, advising them what they could be doing to reduce their husband's, partner's or children's risk of coronary heart disease. But women's hearts need help, too. Until research focuses on women, the reason for the differences between the sexes in both the incidence and manifestations of coronary heart disease will probably remain unexplained. The facts, however, remain – women *are* at risk from coronary heart disease.

CHILDREN AND CORONARY HEART DISEASE

The seeds of coronary heart disease are usually sown in childhood. There is ample evidence for this, in particular from post mortem examination of the arteries of adolescents and young adults who died from other causes and were supposedly fit and healthy: many of these young people had layers of cholesterol in their arteries.

WHAT CAUSES CORONARY HEART DISEASE?

Medical research has identified the various factors most frequently associated with coronary heart disease. These are termed "risk factors". The most important risk factors are associated with things we do every day. The main risk factors are: unhealthy food, cigarette smoking, raised blood pressure, lack of exercise. Others include being overweight, stress and diabetes. In addition, there are risk factors over which we can have no control. These include, age, sex and family history.

Before we look at these risk factors, however, a word of advice. Many people ask about risk factor trade-offs. "I do smoke but I take a lot of exercise, so I'm alright", or perhaps, "Well I can't resist all those wonderfully rich foods and I know I need to lose some weight but I don't drink and I've given up smoking, so that's OK."

Self-deception is a wonderful thing. Most of the people asking these questions know perfectly well that the answer is an unequivocal "No – it isn't alright!" Obviously any efforts to make your lifestyle healthier will be beneficial and are better than nothing, but as we don't know what triggers a risk factor into a fatal event, there can be no cheating. You have to address *all* the risk factors. Other people and agencies, including government, can and should make lifestyle changes simple, palatable and even in some cases possible, but in the final analysis individuals must want to improve their lifestyle before successful action can be taken.

UNHEALTHY FOOD AND YOUR HEART

As we have already discussed, the underlying cause of coronary heart disease and heart attacks is narrowed or "furred up" arteries which have been blocked by atheroma or blood clots (see page 8). The central factor in both of these is cholesterol.

WHAT IS CHOLESTEROL?

Cholesterol occurs naturally in the cells of all animals, including ourselves. It is manufactured in the liver, and used to transport fatty acids around the body in the blood (this type of cholesterol is called plasma cholesterol, or blood cholesterol). The more fat and, in particular, saturated fats, you eat, the more cholesterol your liver produces to enable the fatty acids to be transported, stored or burned up as energy. Having delivered the fatty acids to the body organs, the cholesterol is left – a fatty, sludgy substance which often ends up in the inner walls of your arteries.

The quantity of cholesterol travelling around in the blood can be easily measured. The higher the level of cholesterol, the higher the risk of heart disease. In the UK, most adults have moderately raised or high levels of blood cholesterol in comparison with other countries.

If you have a blood cholesterol test, the chances are your doctor will look at the level of triglycerides too. These are also fats, and a high level can be an early warning sign of artery damage.

WHAT'S THE DIFFERENCE BETWEEN DIETARY CHOLESTEROL AND BLOOD CHOLESTEROL?

Many people are muddled about the difference between cholesterol in food, and cholesterol already in the body.

Most of the blood cholesterol is actually manufactured in the body (by the liver), and the body produces enough for its needs. Cholesterol in food is an extra, which for many people is an insignificant part of the total. However, people who have had a heart attack, have high blood cholesterol levels, or have heart disease in the family, are usually advised to watch the amount of cholesterol they eat.

SO WHERE DOES FAT COME INTO THIS?

If cholesterol is, as it seems, the villain of the piece, why have endless national and international committees recommended a reduction in the amount of fat in our diet and especially saturated fat?

The answers lie in substances called fatty acids. Chemists have discovered that all fats and oils are made of building blocks called fatty acids. There are more than 20 fatty acids, all with different names and chemical structures, and with different properties. Some fatty acids are saturated, some monounsaturated, and some polyunsaturated. The difference relates to their chemistry. All fats and oils contain both saturated and polyunsaturated fatty acids and it is the relative proportion or balance between different fatty acids that makes a fat or oil solid or liquid, smelly or odourless, easily stored or prone to rancidity, healthy or unhealthy.

Before we go any further it is important to know that some types of fat are essential for life. These essential fats are the building blocks of nerves, brain cells, and cell walls throughout the body; they also provide the essential vitamins A, D and E. And fat is a type of body fuel used for warmth, work, growth and repair. The problems occur, not from the existence of fats in our diet, but from an excess of them – too much of any kind of fat is harmful. The balance of saturated fats and polyunsaturated fats is also important.

WHAT KINDS OF FAT ARE THERE?

There are four main types of fats we need to look at to understand the health story. These are saturated fatty acids, polyunsaturated fatty acids, monounsaturated fatty acids and trans fatty acids.

SATURATED FATS contain a high proportion of saturated fatty acids. They tend to be solid at room temperature and have a good keeping quality. Crudely speaking, saturated fats can be described as unhealthy.

POLYUNSATURATED FATS contain a high proportion of polyunsaturated fatty acids. They tend to be liquid at room temperature, and in their natural state they are of poor keeping quality and tend to become rancid. Although some polyunsaturated fatty acids are regarded as more actively beneficial than others, all are benign.

MONOUNSATURATED FATS are those with a reasonable balance between saturated and polyunsaturated fatty acids. These fats will be liquid at room temperature but thicker and cloudier on a cool day. In the healthy versus unhealthy stakes they hold a balance and are generally regarded as benign.

TRANS FATS start off as unsaturated fats or oils but through a manufacturing process known as hydrogenation, change their chemistry to become trans fats. In health terms, these should be regarded as a sort of saturated fat.

WHAT'S SO BAD ABOUT SATURATED FATS?

Eaten in large amounts, saturated fat damages the heart. To begin with, saturated fats thicken your blood, making it more likely to clot. In addition, an excess of saturated fat stimulates your liver to produce far more cholesterol than your body needs or can cope with.

WHAT'S SO GOOD ABOUT POLYUNSATURATES?

Some polyunsaturated fatty acids are rather like vitamins. They are essential for the brain and nerves to grow and develop properly, and for their maintenance. They also help to keep your blood less sticky and therefore less likely to deposit atheroma in your arteries. They also make the blood less likely to clot.

WHAT ABOUT MONOUNSATURATES?

Monounsaturated fats were believed, until recently, to have a neutral effect on blood. However, some recent research indicates that these fats are actually beneficial and that they behave rather like polyunsaturates.

SMOKING AND YOUR HEART

Smoking is a disaster! There are no redeeming features, the only answer is to stop. Fortunately people are now more sympathetic and sensitive in dealing with what is a national addiction.

HOW GREAT IS YOUR RISK?

In 1985 smoking killed over 100,000 people in the UK. Of these deaths, 36,800 (35%) were from lung cancer, but 37,300 (36%) were from coronary heart disease. A cigarette smoker has about twice the risk of having a heart attack as a non-smoker. A combination of hypertension and raised blood cholesterol increases the risk four-fold, and the combination of all three risk factors multiplies the chances of having a heart attack by more than eight. One major study has shown that male heavy smokers (twenty-five or more cigarettes per day) under the age of forty-five have fifteen times the risk of a fatal heart attack compared with that of non-smokers. Smoking is thought to be responsible for about eight out of ten deaths from coronary heart disease in young men.

From 1972 to 1984, the percentage of adult men in the United Kingdom who smoked went down from 52% to 36% and the percentage of women smoking went down from 41% to 32%. Worryingly, though, smoking among young women is now showing a marked increase. Women smokers are at special risk of coronary heart disease if they also take the contraceptive pill; a woman over 35 years old who smokes has a relative risk of arterial disease 3 times greater than that of a woman of the same age who neither takes the pill nor smokes.

HOW DOES SMOKING AFFECT YOUR HEART?

There are several thousand chemicals in cigarette smoke, two of which, in particular, are thought to cause coronary heart disease. Carbon monoxide is the poisonous gas (also present in car exhaust fumes) which constitutes 4% of cigarette smoke. Haemoglobin, which carries oxygen in the blood, picks up carbon monoxide much more readily than it does oxygen. Therefore, when carbon monoxide is present there is less room for oxygen. In cigarette smokers the oxygen-carrying capacity of the blood may be cut by up to 15%. Nicotine, which causes addiction, stimulates the production of adrenalin which makes the heart beat faster and causes blood pressure to rise. Nicotine, like carbon monoxide, also causes blood in the coronary arteries to clot more readily.

WHAT ABOUT LOW TAR CIGARETTES?

Those who change over to low tar cigarettes tend to inhale more to keep up their nicotine intake. This has the effect of increasing the amount of carbon monoxide absorbed. So, although the low tar smoker may reduce the risk of lung cancer, his/her risk of heart attacks may even increase.

IS IT TOO LATE TO GIVE UP?

It's never too late to stop. Ex-smokers have a much lower risk of coronary disease than those who continue to smoke. In fact, within just a year or two the risk is greatly reduced, and after five years it approaches that of the non-smoker. So give up now!

BLOOD PRESSURE AND YOUR HEART

Raised blood pressure (hypertension) is a major risk factor associated with coronary heart disease.

A blood pressure level of below 140/90 is usually considered normal – 140 being the pressure in the vessels when the heart relaxes between beats. About a quarter of middle-aged adults in Britain have blood pressure over 140/90. Medical treatment with drugs for hypertension usually starts when the blood pressure is persistently at least 150/105 but there is no hard and fast rule, and the decision to treat it is made according to a patient's age and general health.

The only way for a person to know if he/she has hypertension is to have his/her blood pressure checked, because there may not be any obvious symptoms. For some people, the first they know about high blood pressure is when they have a stroke or heart attack. Severe hypertension is very rare in young people (under the age of about 25) and is usually caused by kidney problems. So if high blood pressure is detected in children, doctors are always careful to investigate thoroughly.

CONTROLLING YOUR BLOOD PRESSURE

The Royal College of General Practitioners recommends that all adults should keep a regular check on their blood pressure: once every five years from the age of 25 onwards. The check is very simple and takes about three minutes. Women are more likely to receive regular checks through attendance at family planning and ante-natal clinics; men are more likely to have to request them.

EXERCISE AND YOUR HEART

Regular exercise helps the heart work more efficiently. The heart is able to pump more blood with each beat, so its maximum output is increased and its output can be maintained when it is beating more slowly during periods of inactivity and rest.

There are three main ways in which exercise seems to help reduce the risks of coronary heart disease:

- It helps reduce blood pressure. When exercised regularly, muscles become larger and stronger, and the number of blood vessels running through them increases. This increased number of vessels makes it easier for the heart to pump blood around the body without having to generate such a head of pressure.
- When a coronary artery becomes blocked, the amount of oxygen available is reduced. A heart which has been exercised regularly will be more able to cope with this reduction than one which has not. Exercise lowers the level of blood cholesterol and it therefore helps to prevent the laying down of the fatty deposits which block coronary arteries and cause heart attacks.
- As well as protecting against coronary heart disease, exercise may improve the ability of the lungs to put oxygen into the blood. This helps the heart, healthy or not, to work to its full potential.

Any exercise which makes us breathless and puts our heart rate up is beneficial and will help tone up the heart and lungs; there is no reason why a healthy amount of exercise should hurt. Everyday activities can help you keep fit – climb the stairs instead of taking the lift, walk instead of taking the bus or driving. Walk a bit faster.

Aim to do 30 minutes' exercise two or three times a week, but build up to it gradually. Sudden strenuous exercise can do more harm than good. Make sure you choose an exercise that you enjoy. Don't feel you're too old or too unfit to take up exercise, but the less fit you are to start with, the sooner you'll notice the benefits.

WEIGHT AND YOUR HEART

Carrying around extra weight puts an added strain on your heart. It does not do too much good to the rest of your body either. More than one-third of adults are overweight. The more overweight you are, the higher the chance of early illness and death. In terms of heart disease, being overweight is associated with raised blood pressure and raised fat levels in your blood.

STRESS AND YOUR HEART

What is stress? Once you start thinking about it, you realize it is very difficult to define. Consequently, medical experts can't agree on exactly what part it plays in heart disease. However, most experts now believe that stress contributes in some way, not only to heart disease, but also to illnesses such as stomach ulcers, asthma and eczema.

When you are under stress the blood is rapidly pumped round your body and your blood pressure rises. Your blood becomes stickier and better able to clot (preparing the body in case of accident) and the liver releases sugar and fats into your bloodstream to give you instant energy. The raised blood pressure caused by stress can mean more wear and tear on the arteries. The stickiness of blood increases the likelihood of blood clots forming.

And, if the extra supplies of sugar and fats released from the liver are not used up in energy, then they're available to form more atheroma, causing the arteries to fur up even more.

There's no easy way to beat stress, but it helps if you tackle the problem in two ways: reduce the physical effects of stress and reduce the causes of stress.

Generally, it is best to reduce the physical effects of stress by learning how to relax. This may be through meditation techniques or special breathing; it may be through yoga or it may be through regular exercise sessions. What you must try to avoid are the instant calmers – cigarettes and alcohol. It's more sensible to build regular relaxation techniques into everyday life than to lurch from one bout of stress to another relying on cigarettes and bottles to see you through.

OTHER RISK FACTORS AND YOUR HEART

There are four other factors which can influence the occurence of coronary heart disease.

AGE

Atherosclerosis begins in childhood and continues throughout life. Hence, the older you are the more common heart attacks become, but they are not inevitable. It is never too late to make sure your lifestyle is healthy, and to maintain it through old age.

SEX

Coronary heart disease is a major killer for both men and women, but premature death from coronary heart disease, ie before 65, is a particular problem for men. A man in his forties is five times as likely to have a heart attack as a women of the same age. Before women get too complacent, though, it must be pointed out that they catch up when female hormones decline during the menopause.

FAMILY HISTORY

Coronary heart disease often runs in families. If either of your parents, brothers, sisters or grandparents died prematurely of heart disease, you are more likely to suffer from the disease yourself, although it is in no way inevitable. Family history simply means that you need to take more care. It's worth saying a word here about a hereditary (genetic) condition called familial hypercholesterolaemia. This can be diagnosed from a blood test. People with this condition have very high blood cholesterol levels which puts them at very high risk of early heart attacks, so they have to live extra-healthy lives, and must be especially careful with diet. Extremely high blood cholesterol can be lowered with drugs. About one in every five hundred people suffers from this condition. If there is a history of heart disease in your family it is worth discussing it with your doctor and having your blood cholesterol checked.

DIABETES

Diabetics are more likely to have heart attacks. The reason for this is not fully understood, but the process of atherosclerosis seems to be accelerated. Diabetics, too, have to live extra-healthy lives.

BACKGROUND TO THE HEALTHY EATING REVOLUTION

'Western' diseases, such as heart attacks, *can* be prevented. That's the message from sixty-five reports published in the last 25 years by national and international medical committees around the world. These independent committees, sponsored by government and the medical profession, examined the links between food and health, and the overwhelming majority came to a positive conclusion. The key to good health is a healthy national food supply.

Many western governments took these reports seriously, and by the mid 1970s several nations had embarked on enthusiastic heart disease prevention campaigns. The USA, Finland and Australia have all had successful programmes, and the heart attack rates have come down.

In the UK, though, nothing happened. The Royal College of Physicians and the British Cardiac Society, and the Department of Health and Social Security, produced several reports between 1974 and 1983 detailing the links between ill health and fatty, sugary, low-fibre foods.

Of these, the message about fibre caught the public attention. But the rest largely fell on deaf ears. Then came NACNE. In 1983, the Sunday Times revealed that a report on food and health commissioned by government had been suppressed. The National Advisory Committee on Nutrition Education (NACNE) had been asked to draw up guidelines for the teaching of nutrition in the community, in schools, hospitals, local authorities, industry. Their message, that the food typically consumed in the UK is a major cause of the diseases we mostly suffer and die from, turned out to be unpalatable both to the food industry and to government. They tried to stop its publication. In doing so, they created a scandal which led to massive publicity for the NACNE report, and to a fundamental shift in eating habits in the UK which continues to this day.

THE 1983 NACNE REPORT

But what did NACNE say to upset the Government, incense the food industry and interest the public?

The report collected all the important medical reports on food and health produced since 1974 by the DHSS and the Royal College of Physicians, the World Health Organization and others. It summarized previous medical findings, establishing the links between fats and heart diseases, sugars and tooth decay, insufficient fibre and intestinal problems, salt and blood pressure, alcohol and its disorders, and vitamin shortages and problems in pregnancy. For the first time since the Second World War, when healthy food was a national priority, the fragmented medical statements about food and different diseases were put together to give a clear message about overall diet. When examined in its entirety, the British food supply contained too much fat, particularly saturated fat, too much salt and refined sugars, and not enough fibre.

THE 1984 COMA REPORT

The NACNE findings were backed by the 1984 report from the Department of Health's Committee on Medical Aspects of Food Policy (COMA). The committee, having reviewed all the different types of evidence linking food with heart disease, concluded that a decrease in the amount of saturated fat eaten in the UK would be likely to reduce the high rates of heart disease. It recommended that:

- Health educators should tell the public about the need to eat healthy food, and that this must be tackled vigorously.
- Manufacturers and retailers should ensure that wrapped foods are properly labelled with their fat content, so that the public can easily identify foods which are less fatty, and which foods contain less of the unhealthy saturated fats, and more of the healthier polyunsaturated fats. Foods sold unwrapped should be displayed alongside information about their fat content.
- Foods which are low in salt should be made more widely available for general sale.
- Nutrition education should start in schools.
- Doctors should identify people who have a high family risk of heart attacks, and advise them about the importance of healthy food.
- Government ministries should start discussions with the producers, manufacturers and distributors of foods in order to both improve legislation, and draw up industrial Codes of Practice that would lead to the production of healthier foods.
- Production of leaner meat carcasses should be encouraged by the Ministry of Agriculture, Fisheries and Food.
- Some parts of the Common Agricultural Policy make it difficult for people to buy healthy foods. Government needs to consider how these difficulties can be overcome.

THE 1985 JACNE REPORT

The NACNE committee was abolished by government in 1984, and reconvened under the title Joint Advisory Committee on Nutrition Education, or JACNE.

The work of the JACNE Committee was no less controversial than its predecessor NACNE. Having produced a draft publication for the public on 'Healthy Eating', the draft was altered by the Ministry of Agriculture, Fisheries and Food via the DHSS. The Chairman of the Committee threatened to resign if there was any further government interference and eventually the publication "Healthy Eating and Your Heart" limped on to the presses. Only limited copies were made available and in 1987 the JACNE Committee was abolished along with the Health Education Council. The new Health Education Authority has not as yet organized a successor.

At the time of writing, there is no concerted government effort to improve the quality of the national food supply, or to ensure changes for the better in hospitals, schools and other institutions which most need to change their catering.

CHOOSING HEALTHY FOOD

The healthy eating message is pretty straightforward. Basically it is a question of eating less fat, in particular saturated fat, less sugar, less salt and more fibre. Loosely translated, this means more fruit and vegetables, more whole grain bread and cereals, more fish, lean red meat or game and poultry.

Is healthy food a punishment to eat? Much has been made of the stringency of the NACNE and COMA guidelines by those who oppose them. They point out that food containing less fat, salt and sugar, and more fibre is heavy, tasteless and dull. But as most people know by now from the new recipe books and television cookery series that have appeared in the last few years, that simply is not true. Healthy meals don't have to be dull. They can, and should, be delicious, a pleasure to cook and a joy to eat.

PACKETS OF FOOD CHOICE

There are over 70,000 foods on sale in the UK. The bigger supermarkets become, the more variety they offer. Amongst these 70,000 packets, tins, frozen dinners, delicatessen goods, jars, and fresh foods on offer, which are the best bet for keeping you and your family healthy?

Always check the list of ingredients on packaged foods. Ingredients are given in order of amount, with the largest first. However, the ingredients list alone won't mean much to people who have not studied food chemistry: although some of the ingredients named are straightforward, others make foods sound like chemistry sets.

Following is a simple guide to help you identify the

healthiest foods. It will show you which foods contain most fats, sugars, salt, and least fibre, which foods to avoid and which to choose.

FATS IN FOOD

In Britain we eat on average 100 g (4 oz) of fat every day. By world standards, that is a great deal; few countries eat as much or more fat than we do. In addition, the fat we eat is of poor quality, at least in terms of our health, for about half of all the fat we eat is saturated fat. One-third of all the fat we eat comes from dairy foods (milk, cream, butter, cheese), one-third from meats and pies, one-quarter from oils, margarines and cooking fats, and the rest comes from cakes, biscuits, sweets, chocolates, crisps and other snacks. So most of our fat comes from animal foods – meats and dairy products. But remember that nobody is an 'average'. We all choose different foods. Some people eat enormous amounts of fat from snacks, puddings, biscuits and take away meals, and little from meats.

ANIMAL FATS AND VEGETABLE OILS

For years, many doctors have managed to create a great deal of confusion by persistently referring to saturated fats as animal fats. This is because much of the saturated fats we eat comes from meat and dairy products. However, some plant fats, such as palm and coconut oil, are also saturated and they are frequently used in making biscuits, sweets, chocolates, cakes, sauces and ice creams. Other vegetable oils, often benign to begin with, go through a process of hydrogenation during manufacture which turns some of their fat into unhealthy saturated fats, or into 'trans' fats. Hydrogenation is the process whereby hydrogen is added to fats to harden them. So don't be fooled. If a product states it contains vegetable oil but doesn't state that it is polyunsaturated, it probably isn't a healthy oil. And next time someone mentions animal fats, ask them if they really mean animal fats, or saturated fats, instead.

MEATS

The list, below, will help you avoid the produce higher in saturated fats.

BEEF, LAMB, MUTTON AND PORK

These all contain saturated fats. First of all, the actual meat is usually fatty, both around the carcass and organs, and in between the muscle fibres themselves. Even lean meat contains fat hidden between the muscle fibres. The fat, wherever it occurs, is quite highly saturated. Beef and lamb fat are more saturated than pork and bacon fat because cows and sheep are ruminants. The bacteria in the rumen saturate the fat in the stomach before it is absorbed into the animal's bloodstream.

The way that animals are bred and fed in Britain also encourages deposition of large amounts of fat, both in the muscle tissue and under the skin. Their lifestyle, which involves little exercise, is designed to produce meat that satisfies the Ministry of Agriculture Fisheries and Food's carcass grading standards, which have in the past encouraged over-production of fat.

Since the 1984 COMA report, government has announced new, leaner carcass grading standards, and many butchers and supermarkets now promote leaner cuts of meat. There is still a long way to go, however, before most of the meat sold in the UK can be truly classed as lean.

POULTRY

Chicken and turkey should contain less fat than the red carcass meats, especially when the skin is removed (the majority of the fat is stored just below the skin). Poultry fat is also less saturated than that of beef, lamb and pork.

GAME

Venison, rabbit, pheasant and other forms of game are the leanest of all meats. The little fat they contain is less saturated than beef, lamb and pork. The fat in this meat is a rich source of polyunsaturated fatty acids.

DUCK AND GOOSE

These are fatty, but the fat is nevertheless less saturated than that of red meats and intensively reared poultry.

DAIRY FOODS

Milk fat is saturated. Unless milk contains a certain quantity of fat, it is rejected by the Milk Marketing Board which purchases all milk in Britain from the farms. Such regulations actively encourage the production of fatty milk. Because milk fat is saturated, the butter, cheese and cream products produced from it also contain saturated fat. Dairy foods supply about a third of all the fat we eat, and about 40 per cent of all the saturated fat in the British diet. Milk alone supplies a substantial proportion of this fat.

Dairy foods are listed below in approximate order of fat content, starting with the most fatty, and ending with the least fatty.

HIGH FAT CONTENT • Butter • Double cream • Cream cheese • Lymeswold cheese • Stilton cheese • Cheddar, other hard yellow cheeses • Danish blue cheese

MEDIUM FAT CONTENT • Brie, Edam, Camembert and Melbury cheese • Feta cheese • Mozzarella • Shape Cheddar cheese • Smetana • Single cream • Tendale cheese • Greek yogurt • Curd cheese, Ricotta • Channel Islands milk • Goats milk • Silver top milk • Full-fat yogurt • Semi-skimmed milk

LOW FAT CONTENT • Cottage cheese • Low-fat curd or soft cheese • Skimmed milk • Low-fat yogurt • Low-fat crème fraîche

MILK

Most milk drunk in Britain is bought from the doorstep

delivery float, and most of it is full fat. Until recently, most of us had no choice. Full-fat silver, gold or red top was all that was on offer. However, since the more enterprising supermarkets launched their skimmed and semi-skimmed fresh milks, the doorstep dairies have caught on to the idea that most of us would like to have a choice. Since the summer of 1984, the National Dairy Council has been advertising fresh skimmed and semi-skimmed milk for doorstep sales. Most other Europeans and the North Americans have been drinking low-fat milks for years.

Ask your milkman for fresh, skimmed or semi-skimmed milk. Low-fat milks contain all the protein, minerals and important water-soluble vitamins that are found in full-fat milk. Some have added powdered milk solids to give more 'body' to the milk; some have extra vitamins. Using low-fat milk instead of full-fat milk is an easy way to cut out some of the saturated fat from your food. If you make sure it is pasteurised, and not sterilised, it will taste fresh and will not have that 'boiled' flavour which many people dislike.

MILK LABELLING

Milk sold in cartons has nutrition information telling you the amount of fat. Bottled milk has different coloured tops which are controlled by law, and by a Code of Practice within the dairy industry.

PLAIN SILVER pasteurised, full-fat milk, (3.8% fat).

PLAIN GOLD pasteurised, full-fat Channel Islands milk (4.8% fat).

PLAIN RED pasteurised, homogenised, full-fat (3.8% fat) milk. (All the fat is mixed into the milk).

RED/SILVER STRIPED pasteurised semi-skimmed milk (1.5–1.8% fat).

BLUE/SILVER CHECKED pasteurised, skimmed milk containing almost no fat (less than 0.1% fat).

BLUE/SILVER STRIPED labelled 'Channel Islands', pasteurised, full-fat (4.8% fat), Kosher milk for Passover.

PURPLE TOP, SILVER STRIPE pasteurised, full-fat (3.8% fat) Kedassia milk (Kosher for Orthodox Jews).

CLAMPED BLUE METAL TOP sterilised, full-fat (3.8% fat) milk.

CLAMPED PINK METAL TOP UHT, full-fat (3.8% fat) milk.

POWDERED MILK

Make sure it is skimmed. Avoid the non-dairy coffee whiteners because many of them contain a lot of saturated fat, and glucose.

YOGURT

Low-fat yogurts made from skimmed milk contain less than 1% fat by weight. (Some manufacturers add extra cream to yogurt to give a more creamy taste, so be sure to read the list of ingredients to see what has been added). Eat more plain and less sweetened fruit yogurts.

CREAM

Double cream is high in saturated fat; single cream is medium high in saturated fat. Some dairies now produce half and half cream which tastes good but is comparatively low in fat. Try to use low-fat plain yogurt instead of cream on puddings; even the thick Greek style yogurt is still better than cream. Yogurt is also a good substitute for creams in cooking. It will not curdle if it is first heated with a teaspoon of cornflour, or added at the last minute after the food has been allowed to cool slightly.

CHEESE

Eat more of the low- and medium-fat cheeses (see page 14). When you buy full-fat cheese, look for the mature or strong-flavoured varieties. Because they have far more flavour, you will not need to use as much, particularly in cooking. Try some of the medium-fat cheeses such as Mozzarella, Brie, Camembert, Ricotta and Melbury.

BUTTER

Try to reduce the amount of butter you use gradually, spreading butter thinly on bread and cooking with oils whenever you can.

FATS AND OILS

Fats are solid at room temperature, whereas oils are liquid. Oils can be turned into solid fats by processing methods. Many people believe that all fats are unhealthy and all oils are healthy but this simple distinction is misleading.

MARGARINES

Margarines are of very variable nutritional quality. All of them are made from vegetable, fish or animal fats. The proportions of particular ingredients may be varied from time to time by the manufacturers, but the level of saturation will remain more or less consistent within a particular brand. All margarines contain some saturated fat. Some are even more saturated than butter because of the way in which they are produced, but the labels do not always help you to distinguish between them. The best advice, therefore, is to look for margarines labelled 'high in polyunsaturates'. These contain at least 45 per cent polyunsaturates.

LOW-FAT SPREADS

Margarine, by law, must contain at least 80 per cent fat, and less than 16 per cent water. So the low-fat spreads cannot be called 'margarine' because they contain half, or less than half, the fat of butter or margarine. These products are useful for those who want to cut down the fat they eat, but cannot get along with thinly spread butter or margarine. However, look for the nutrition label and check the amount of saturated fat; the less the better.

COOKING FATS

Lard, dripping and other solid cooking fats are usually highly saturated fats. Many cooking fats are made from liquid oils, which are saturated (hydrogenated) during processing. The degree of saturation depends on which oil is used. A healthy polyunsaturated oil can therefore be turned into a harmful saturated fat during processing.

So, just because a food label tells you that the food 'contains vegetable oils', it does not necessarily mean it is free from saturated fat. Look for those with 'high in polyunsaturated' on the label.

COOKING OILS

Most people in Britain now cook with oils rather than solid fats because they have heard that oils are healthier. Which ones are the best? The following oils are all low in saturated fats, and most of them are high in polyunsaturates. Use these oils for cooking and for salads:

soya • sunflower • corn (maize) • safflower • olive • walnut • sesame

Some of the blended or own-label vegetable oils may be high in polyunsaturates, but because they are not labelled, you cannot be sure what they contain and they should therefore be avoided.

LARD, DRIPPING, BUTTER AND SUET

These are all highly saturated fats which are best avoided whenever possible. Some manufacturers have recently invented hard cooking fats which are high in polyunsaturates. These are preferable to other types of hard, processed fat.

CAKES AND BISCUITS

Most cakes and biscuits are made with hardened (hydrogenated) oils. Filled and wafer biscuits are often made with palm and coconut oils, which are highly saturated. Home-made cakes and biscuits made with butter and saturated margarines are, of course, no healthier.

SWEETS AND CHOCOLATES

Many people don't realize that sweets and chocolates are often very fatty. Most sweets nowadays contain more than just sugar – hydrogenated fat is one of the main ingredients. Chocolates often have added vegetable fat (saturated), and cocoa fat itself is saturated.

CRISPS, SAVOURY SNACKS, DEEP FRIED FOODS

The quality of the oils used is very variable. Most crisps are made with polyunsaturated oils (such as soya oil) but some are made with more highly saturated oils. It is often difficult for the consumer to know which oils are being used in a particular product, so they are best avoided altogether. The ingredients list will say if 'hydrogenated oils' have been used.

ICE CREAM

Most ice cream is made without real cream. Ingredients are often hardened (hydrogenated) vegetable fats, sugars, milk powder, potato starch, flavouring and colouring.

BALANCING THE FATS

To avoid any unnecessary saturated fats, choose game, poultry and very lean cuts of red meat. Cut off any visible fat before you cook it, and grill or roast meat (unlarded) rather then frying it. You can cut down the amount of meat you use by mixing lean cuts with vegetables, beans or pasta. The Meat and Livestock Commission have recently been very active in encouraging the production of leaner meat, and changes in butchering practices to produce leaner cuts.

Avoid buying fatty (and often salty) meats like sausages, frankfurters, liver-sausage, black pudding, haggis, pies, pasties, corned beef, spam and haslet. The more enterprising manufacturer nowadays indicates the quantity of fat in meat products on the label. Compare different varieties.

Use polyunsaturated margarines and oils (see page 15) and use yogurt as a thickener in sauces instead of cream, or to serve with puddings. Use skimmed and semi-skimmed milk in preference to full-fat milk, and choose low-fat cheeses. Below, are other sources high in polyunsaturates.

FISH

Fish fat is healthier than that of meat and dairy products because it is rich in polyunsaturated oils. Fatty fish such as herring, mackerel, sprats, sardines, salmon and tuna contain large amounts of polyunsaturated fats; white fish (cod, plaice, haddock) contains hardly any fat.

Shellfish are generally high in polyunsaturates; the main problem is likely to be one of pollution, so choose your fish shop carefully, and report any ill-effects. Eating raw shellfish is inadvisable unless you are sure they are clean and fresh.

Avoid smoked, salted fish. Choose sardines tinned in named oils (olive or soya, for example).

CEREALS

Whole grain cereals contain appreciable amounts of oil in the germ (the bit of the seed from which a new plant grows). Cereal oils are high in polyunsaturates, and low in saturates. Foods made with whole grain cereals therefore contain more essential oils than those made with refined cereals from which all or most of the germ has been removed.

FRUIT AND VEGETABLES

Fresh green vegetables and fruits all contain minute quantities of polyunsaturated oils, particularly in the growing tips (like broccoli), skin and seeds.

NUTS

Nuts are usually high in fats, and much of the fat is of the polyunsaturated variety. Coconuts are the exception, having highly saturated oil in the flesh. Walnuts are particularly high in polyunsaturates.

CARBOHYDRATES

There are two types of carbohydrate: digestible carbohydrates (also known as simple carbohydrates or sugars), and complex carbohydrates such as starch and fibre.

Smoked Salmon Kedgeree (PAGE 30)

During the twentieth century the UK population has eaten less complex carbohydrates, and more simple ones. We eat notably fewer oats and bread, and less starchy vegetables such as potatoes. Instead, we eat more meat and dairy products and more foods made with refined cereals (for example, cakes, biscuits and crunchy snacks). The overall result is that many of us are constipated (over 15 per cent of adults in Britain use laxatives). Intestinal disorders of later life (piles, diverticular disease, even colon cancer) are probably all related to the deficiency of dietary fibre in our meals.

Dietary fibre is the substance that reaches the large intestine and is turned into faeces. In the early days of research on fibre, the whole process of digestion and elimination was thought to be rather simple. It was believed that roughage in food could not be digested or absorbed into the bloodstream; instead, it was all sent to the bowels, the water was absorbed from it and the residue excreted. Fibre was therefore pretty useless as 'food'.

All that has now changed. The few single-minded doctors who stimulated research in the 1970s into the effects of dietary fibre were convinced that wholemeal bread and other cereals, beans, fruit and vegetables are all actively essential for keeping the intestine healthy. Furthermore, such foods may actually prevent the chronic 'Western' disorders and diseases that are common in industrialized nations – heart disease, colon cancer, constipation, diabetes, gallstones, varicose veins and a host of other common problems. Until about 15 years ago, such ideas were rejected by the medical profession at large as eccentric nonsense. How could inert fibrous material possibly affect such a host of different organs?

Recent research on dietary fibre reveals a much more complex picture. A summary of the findings to date is as follows: dietary fibre speeds the passage of food through the intestine. It increases the bulk of the faeces, and the frequency with which they are produced. A high fibre intake produces softer faeces, containing a little more fat. It is thought that fibre, while speeding the passage of food material through the intestine, also speeds up the passage of toxins and that this prevents them from lurking around causing damage to the intestinal walls. Fibre also changes the chemistry of many food compounds in the large bowel. Fibre is therefore a much more complicated materal than the early researchers realized.

Fibre of itself is not slimming; it does not contain a magic ingredient. What it does do is provide a feeling of satiety and fullness. For example, two slices of wholemeal bread are usually more satisfying than two slices of white.

STARCH

Starch is a type of complex carbohydrate. It is found in largest quantities in cereals – rice, wheat, barley, oats, rye – and in starchy root crops – potatoes, yams and cassava.

The interesting thing about starch is in its comparison with refined sugars. Refined sugars rot the teeth; they can upset the blood sugar level when they are absorbed too quickly into the bloodstream and can produce cravings for sugar which can lead to obesity. It is easy to overeat sugary foods.

Starch, on the other hand, has no effect on teeth (in the absence of refined sugars). It is absorbed slowly into the bloodstream, and satisfies the appetite as opposed to increasing it.

But there has been a great deal of confusion between the different kinds of carbohydrates. Starch, eaten as wholemeal bread, porridge, pasta, rice or potatoes is a healthy food. Foods containing refined sugars, on the other hand, are foods of little nutritional value. Whole cereals and root vegetables contain the starch, vitamins, minerals and proteins necessary for health; refined sugars supply only quick-release energy.

We have been taught that carbohydrates are fattening. Starchy, fibrous foods are not especially fattening; they only become fattening if cooked and eaten with too much fat and sugar.

BREAD

Wholemeal bread is the healthiest bread of all, because it contains all of the fibre, vitamins and minerals present in the wheat grain. Brown bread contains less of these valuable nutrients, and white contains even less. Bread by itself is not especially fattening. The trouble starts when you reach for the butter or margarine, both high-energy foods with a high saturated fat content. But better bread needs less butter, and if we as a nation had access to really good quality, delicious, fresh bread all the time – as was the case in the past and still is to a large extent in Europe – there is little doubt that we would eat more of it, and our health would improve.

Recently, the quality of much of the bread in the UK has improved, although the way in which manufacturers label their bread can be confusing. In general, try to eat more wholemeal or wholewheat bread.

WHOLEMEAL/WHOLEWHEAT

By law, this must contain 100 per cent of the wheat grain. Wholemeal/wholewheat bread cannot be made using all the chemical improvers that are permitted in white and brown breads, and it naturally contains more vitamins and minerals and oils than other types of bread.

BROWN

Brown bread contains about 85 per cent of the wheat grain (the outside 15 per cent is removed in milling); it is not wholemeal. This bread is sometimes coloured.

GRANARY

Although this is the registered trade mark of Rank Hovis McDougall Ltd., many bakeries produce their own granary loaves. They are made of brown flour to which malted whole grains of wheat are added. Granary is not wholemeal.

Autumn Barley Soup (PAGE 34)

GRANARY WHOLEMEAL
Again, the registered trade mark of Rank Hovis McDougall Ltd., this time made with wholemeal flour, with malted whole grains added.

HOVIS AND OTHER WHEATGERM BREADS
Hovis (trade mark of Rank Hovis McDougall Ltd.) and Vit-Be (trade mark of Allied Bakers Ltd. and Allied Mills Ltd.) are made of flour to which wheatgerm has been added. They are not wholemeal, although wholemeal varieties have recently been produced.

HIGH-FIBRE BREADS
There are now several 'high-fibre' brown and white breads available. The brown ones are made with added wheat bran, the white ones with added vegetable fibre. They are unlikely to have the same vitamin and mineral content as wholemeal bread.

WHITE BREAD
Factory-made and bakery-made white bread is made with white flour. By law this is 72 per cent extraction with the outside 28 per cent of the grain removed in milling. White breads, and white flour, are deficient in most of the vitamins, minerals and fibre found in wholemeal products.

POTATOES, RICE, PASTA, NOODLES

Like bread, these types of food are not likely to be fattening if eaten with little added fat or highly saturated sauces. In general we should try to eat more of them.

Boiled, mashed and jacket potatoes are all healthy. Try some of these fillings with jacket potatoes: curd cheese with herbs, smoked mackerel and lemon juice, plain yogurt. Mash potatoes with a little olive oil and herbs instead of butter; or add yogurt, parsley and chives to them.

Have fried potatoes and chips less often, if at all. If you are going to fry, use a good quality oil. But bear in mind that repeated heating and cooling of oil will in time make it more saturated and less polyunsaturated. Use less oil, and shallow-fry rather than deep-fry. Cut the potatoes into bigger chunks so that they soak up less fat.

Brown rice is easier to cook than white, although it tends to take longer. Fresh pasta is quick and simple to cook and is particularly delicious. Wholemeal pasta can be rather heavy so a mixture of ordinary white and wholemeal pasta is an alternative.

VEGETABLES AND FRUIT

Fresh foods are vital for health, and contain essential nutrients which protect against disease. Many people in the UK eat worryingly little of them, leaving themselves vulnerable to vitamin and mineral deficiencies. Eat more fresh fruit and vegetables of all types. Have a fresh salad at least once a day.

The British diet is relatively low in folic acid, a vitamin found in green leaves. Deficiency of folic acid (in pregnant women, and in early pregnancy,) has been linked with spina bifida and other birth defects, for which some parts of Britain (Northern Ireland, Scotland, South Wales, the north of England) have the highest rates in Europe. Choose green vegetables which look crisp and fresh. Flabby leaves have an inferior flavour as well as containing fewer vitamins.

If you can't get fresh vegetables, use frozen rather than tinned. Tinned vegetables often contain added salt or sugar, although some manufacturers have started selling low-sugar, low-salt varieties.

Vegetables have most flavour when undercooked; they will also retain more vitamins and minerals. Cook vegetables for as short a time as possible in very little boiling water. Alternatively, use a steamer or cook in a wok. Some vegetables, such as spinach and leeks, require no cooking water as they cook in their own juice.

BEANS

Eat more beans of all types. When cooking, throw away the first lot of boiling water after about 15 minutes. The beans will then be less likely to give you indigestion. Lentils and black-eyed beans can be cooked in under an hour, and if you have a pressure cooker, they can be cooked even faster.

Most baked beans contain 3 to 15 per cent added sugar, and also salt. They are many children's favourite food, and are much healthier than fatty sausages and hamburgers. If children ate far less sugar (in sweets, soft drinks and biscuits) the amount in baked beans would be less important. Some manufacturers now produce low-sugar versions; buy these where possible.

SUGAR

In Britain we get through 1 kg (2 lbs) of sugar per head per week. Two-thirds of that comes in sweets and processed foods. We buy the other third of sugar in packets. The actual amount of sugar purchased in packets has been falling over the last 20 years, yet while we have been putting less in our tea and coffee or using artificial sweeteners, the food manufacturers have been busy putting it back into our food at the manufacturing stage.

So we now have a situation where nearly all packeted and tinned foods contain sugars in one guise or another. Sugar can be called sugar, sucrose, glucose, dextrose, fructose, maltose, syrup or invert sugar. All these are variations of the same refined, sickly sweet sugar. So next time you pick up a packet of 'savoury' food, just check the label to find out whether you are buying sugars with it!

Everyone knows that sugar is bad for teeth: refined carbohydrates and sugar stick between the teeth and encourage the formation of plaque resulting in dental decay.

It is also generally agreed that eating a lot of sugary food causes weight problems. Sweet foods are easy to eat, low in bulk, and a lot slips down easily. They are also generally low in essential minerals, vitamins and oils. The amount of sugar typically eaten in the UK is considered by most doctors to be excessive, and to lead to ill health.

The general recommendation is to eat half as much – not more than one pound per person per week. Some people will not find this difficult. Others, who already eat much more than 1 kg (2 lbs), will find it harder.

BROWN SUGAR
Most brown sugar is white sugar dyed with caramel (burnt sugar). It is no healthier than white. Raw, unrefined cane sugar contains more minerals, and has a distinctive taste. However, the minerals in your food are much better provided by fruit and vegetables.

BREAKFAST CEREALS
Most are sweetened, although manufacturers have started to produce some without added sugars. Read the label of your favourite cereal: the higher up sugar comes on the list of ingredients, the more it contains. If you enjoy muesli, try making your own. Wholefood shops usually sell muesli base, to which you can add your own selection of dried fruit and nuts. And if you start children off with unsweetened cereals, they are less likely to develop a taste for the sweet varieties. Porridge is an excellent breakfast, especially on cold mornings.

TINNED VEGETABLES AND FRUIT
Choose unsweetened varieties canned in natural juice.

YOGURTS AND DESSERTS
Have more plain, low-fat yogurt and mix it with fresh or dried fruit. 'Fruit flavour' yogurt contains no fruit at all! Try mixing one fruit yogurt with a plain one to spread the sugar out. Eat fewer sweet desserts.

CAKES, PUDDINGS, BISCUITS
Nearly all are very sweet. Some are 50 per cent sugar, or more. Eat them less often. Have cakes at the weekends rather than every day.

JAMS
Look for the low-sugar jams and preserves. Ordinary jam must have 60 per cent sugar (minimum, by law) but most have more. Low-sugar jams contain 30-40 per cent sugar by weight.

SWEETS AND CHOCOLATES
Eat fewer sweets, and chocolates, and do not eat them between meals.

SUCROSE, GLUCOSE, FRUCTOSE
Refined sugar comes in many guises. On food labels you may find the words glucose (or dextrose), fructose (fruit sugar), sucrose, sugar, syrup, maltose, lactose (milk sugar) or dextrose. All of them are processed sugars and all of them are best avoided.

LOW SUGAR FOODS
Since the NACNE report was published, manufacturers have been falling over themselves to cash in on consumer awareness about the damage sugar does to health, particularly to children. 'No added sugar' or 'low sugar' products are usually sweetened with concentrated apple or grape juices, or with dextrose, glucose or fructose. The total amount of sugar in the new product may not be much lower than in the original, and may rot teeth just as much, so look at the label before buying.

SALT

Before the invention of canning and refrigeration, salt was used to preserve foods. The salt helped to draw the water out of the food, and prevented bacteria from growing. Fish, vegetables and meat were salted and dried. Bacon, cheese and kippers are all relics of the days of salting food for the winter months.

Salt is thought by some scientists to increase blood pressure, and high blood pressure is known to cause strokes, and also heart attacks. Human requirements for salt are very small indeed. There is enough salt in natural food to cater for our requirements. Yet on average we eat about 10 times as much as we need. All fruit, vegetables, milk, meats and cereals contain small amounts of salt, and adding extra to food is unnecessary. It is sometimes said that in hot weather extra salt in food is needed to make up for the salt losses in sweat. But, except in exceptional circumstances such as very vigorous exercise in the heat, extra salt is not needed. The human body adapts to hot temperatures by reducing the level of salt in sweat.

About three-quarters of the salt we eat comes from manufactured foods. Salt added in the home during cooking and at the table accounts for the rest of our salt intake. Read the labels of *all* the foods you buy. If salt is included, consider whether you could use fresh or frozen food instead. Below are a few guidelines:

BREAKFAST CEREALS Most packet varieties contain added salt. Shredded Wheat, Puffed Wheat, and some mueslis are among the few without. Many of the bran cereals are high in salt and sugar.

BREAD Nearly all British bread has some salt added. If you bake your own bread, try gradually reducing the amount of salt you add.

TINNED VEGETABLES Many are prepared in salty water. Use fresh vegetables.

SAUSAGES, BACON, HAM Some supermarkets now sell less salty bacon and ham, but they do not usually label them distinctively. Ask, if you want less salty foods. Smoked bacon is usually more salty than unsmoked.

CRISPS, SNACKS Most are very salty. Have them less often.

CAKES, PASTRIES, BISCUITS Most are made with salt. Use less salt when baking at home; it will not affect the baking quality.

SOFT DRINKS Many contain added sodium. Avoid soda water.

MEAT AND VEGETABLE EXTRACTS, STOCK CUBES All are very salty. Use them less often in cooking, or try using the new low-salt varieties.

Reduce the amount of salt you use gradually. Lemon juice is a good substitute for salt; used in meat dishes, it provides a delicious flavour. After eating less salt for a few months, you will find that food has more flavour, not less. Pepper, too, is a good alternative.

TABLE SALT
Use less with the aim of stopping it altogether. Throw away your salt pot, or keep it as an interesting antique.

SEA SALT
Sea salt does contain more minerals than ordinary salt. However, it is still mostly sodium chloride, and in that respect is just as bad for your blood pressure as the cheaper varieties.

SALT SUBSTITUTES
Some shops now sell salt substitutes. They are usually a mixture of sodium chloride and potassium chloride; a few are potassium chloride alone. Potassium chloride develops a bitter flavour in cooking and can be very expensive. There is no reason to advise the use of these alternatives to salt. The best advice is simply to use less salt.

SALT AND CHILDREN
Never give salt to babies and young infants. Their kidneys are not mature enough to deal with it. If you do not introduce children to salty food, they will be less likely to develop a taste for it, so don't cook your children's food with salt, and don't let them add salt at the table.

ALCOHOL

Heavy drinking can damage your health. Alcoholic drinks are usually high in calories and low in nutrients. In addition, heavy drinkers often lose their appetites and as alcohol can alter the absorption of some essential nutrients, vitamin and mineral deficiencies can result. Alcohol can also increase your blood pressure, and is therefore another factor in the incidence of heart attacks and strokes.

WHAT ABOUT LIGHT DRINKING?
It has been suggested that a little alcohol protects against heart attacks. The evidence for this, however, is controversial, and we certainly would not encourage a teetotaller to start drinking. To make sure you stick to light drinking, try not to drink more than 21 standard drinks a week if you are a man or 14 if you are a woman. Half a pint of beer, a single measure of spirits, a small glass of sherry or port and a glass of wine have about the same alcoholic content and are classfied as a standard drink.

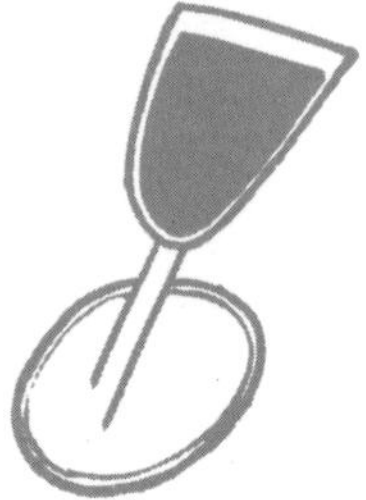

WHO IS THIS INFORMATION FOR?

The sort of information and advice given in this book is suitable for everyone unless you have been prescribed a particular diet by a doctor.

CAN I USE THE RECIPES IF I'M RECOVERING FROM A HEART ATTACK?

The food described in this book is ideal for anyone recovering from a heart attack. Your doctor may have given you a diet sheet for weight loss, or for low-cholesterol, low-saturated fat foods, but the advice is likely to be very similar to the advice in this book. It is always advisable to check with your doctor first, but the recipes in this book are designed to be low in saturated fat, and are therefore ideal for people in your position.

WHAT IF I AM OVERWEIGHT?

More than one-third of British adults are overweight. An even greater proportion of us say that we are too fat. Those who are the right weight for their height, but claim to be too fat, are more than likely correctly identifying themselves as being overfat: too much fat with too little muscle. Until very recently, slimming was only concerned with counting calories. But anyone who has been a persistent dieter knows that not only is dieting very difficult, it is also well nigh impossible to keep the fat off.

To lose weight, eat the kind of food described in this book. Avoid sugars like the plague. Avoid all visible fat, except for tiny amounts of healthy oils. Eat very little fatty cheese; have poultry or fish instead of meat and use skimmed milk. Fill up on boiled and jacket potatoes and other starchy foods. Eat lots of fruit and vegetables. If you are on a calorie-controlled diet, use the calorie totals for each dish to work out a menu plan. If you are severely overweight, ask your GP if you can see the local community dietician or consider joining a weight-losers group.

In addition to eating healthy food, take more exercise. But start exercise gradually. Swimming, cycling, brisk walking and gentle keep-fit exercises are good for the overweight. You might even take up gentle jogging and running, but buy a good pair of shoes at a reputable sports shop beforehand.

FOOD FOR CHILDREN

All parents want to do the best for their children, and few things are more important than their daily meals. The foods recommended in this book are ideal for children, and will give them a healthy start in life. Children need particularly high quality food to give them the vitamins, minerals, oils, proteins and energy they need for growth of all the vital organs. Children also need plenty of fresh foods.

BABIES AND SMALL CHILDREN

The best food for babies is breast milk. And breast-feeding mothers should know that the nutritional quality of their milk depends on the quality of their own meals. If the mother has eaten food high in saturated fat, then her milk will be more saturated. Pregnant and lactating women need plenty of whole, fresh foods to produce healthy milk.

Some time after three months, babies will begin to get hungry for extra foods. Ask your health visitor for advice if you don't know what to do. Never give a baby under 6 months ordinary doorstep milk, but always use a special baby formula. From 6 months to two years, the DHSS recommends that babies and toddlers have whole (full-fat) milk. After two years, semi-skimmed milks are fine for most children. Introduce your baby to low sugar, no salt food (salt is very bad for small babies), and watch the amount of saturated fat.

Small babies and toddlers with little appetites may need feeding more often, and will need extra care to see that they get enough food for growth. Don't go overboard on the fibre for young children. Never give them bran by itself, or bran products, because they can stop minerals being absorbed. Wholemeal bread, fruit and vegetables are fine.

Low fat meals, as shown in the recipes in this book, are fine for most toddlers. But if your child seems to be very thin, or is growing more slowly than others of his/her age, always check with your doctor, health visitor or community dietician. Some small children, for example, may need a bit more fat and/or oil in their meals to increase their weight.

FOOD FOR ELDERLY PEOPLE

Anyone who has reached the age of seventy or more is of course a survivor! While scientists in the USA now talk of living to 120 or more in years to come, the rest of us just want to get on with keeping fit and active for as long as possible.

The food described in this book is ideal for elderly people. Old people often become undernourished, either beause they lose their appetites, live alone and don't enjoy their meals, or because they find shopping and cooking difficult. Badly fitting dentures make it difficult to eat fresh fruit and vegetables, and other 'chewy' foods. Stiff joints makes it difficult to cut up vegetables. Particular problems to watch for are lack of fresh fruit and vegetables, too many cakes and biscuits and cups of sweet tea.

Invaluable aids for elderly people are a freezer, a blender, or other easy-chopping gadgets, and a microwave oven. These can be relatively expensive items, sadly out of many pensioners reach, but all of them make cooking much easier. It may be an idea for other family members to club together to buy such aids as a present.

CONCLUSION

The healthy eating revolution is underway, but there is a long way to go before healthy food is available to all people at a price they can afford.

What needs to be done? The Coronary Prevention Group has been working behind the scenes in parliament with all the political parties, schools, local authorities, hospitals and in industry to make sure that the people who take the decisions understand how coronary heart disease can be prevented.

We work with scientists of international standing who have devoted their working lives to research into the causes and prevention of heart disease. With their help, the Coronary Prevention Group has drawn up a list of things that need to be tackled to lower the UK's appalling rates of premature illness and death. These include:

NATIONAL FOOD POLICY

We need a clear, national food policy which cares for conservation of the countryside, as well as people's health, which produces healthy food that people want to eat, at prices they can afford, which does not result in over-production.

CLEAR NUTRITIONAL GUIDELINES

The government should issue, as a matter of urgency, high nutritional standards against which to judge the quality of the national food supply. Present standards are fragmentary; the UK has some of the lowest official nutritional standards in the Western world. In 1987, the DHSS announced a new committee to look at nutrition standards and said it would take *ten years* to complete its task! This is ridiculously slow.

SCHOOL MEALS, HOSPITAL MEALS, LOCAL AUTHORITY MEALS

Nutritional standards, set by law, are urgently needed. Parents want to know their children are being properly fed. Healthy food is an essential part of treatment and recovery from illnesses and operations in hospital.

NUTRITION LABELLING OF FOODS

The Government has put forward draft legislation for nutritional labelling of foods. It does not go far enough, and is too complicated for shoppers who lack scientific training. Simple labels telling us if foods are high, medium or low in fats, saturated fats, sugars, salt and fibre are needed.

INGREDIENT LABELLING OF FOODS

The ingredients list of foods should be reformed. The percentage by weight of main ingredients should be given. For example, **biscuits**: Flour (30%), sugar (25%, vegetable fat (25%), dried fruit (18%), salt, raising agents.

COMPOSITIONAL STANDARDS FOR BASIC FOODS

The government has lowered the legal standard of many staple foods such as meat pies (they now contain less meat). High standards must be set, by law, to protect consumers from disreputable manufacturers, and to compel all manufacturers to use high-quality ingredients. Not all foods can be controlled by law, but basic ones can.

OFFICIAL SECRETS ACT

The advisory committees which make recommendations to government on future legislation, and on the need for new health programmes in the UK, are covered by the Official Secrets Act. Food should be an area of maximum publicity, not maximum secrecy. We will not be able to have proper, constructive discussions with government until consumers are given all the facts. Discussions on the contents of a fish finger by government committees for example, should not be covered by the Official Secrets Act.

NUTRITION TEACHING

The new curriculum for schools announced in 1987 may not include home economics, nutrition or, indeed, health. All children should be taught the basic principles of healthy eating, and cooking, and should be given practical classes.

Teaching materials used in schools are often supplied free of charge by food manufacturers. The British Dietetic Association (the professional body of dieticians) should be asked to pass all teaching material before it is distributed to schools. All doctors, nurses and other health professionals should be adequately taught about nutrition.

The writing is on the wall for the dominance of food issues by civil servants, government committees, and the food industry. Increasingly, consumers are demanding and winning a say. Food and health are rapidly becoming vote-catching issues. But if we are to ensure that the present progress towards the production and availability of healthy foods continues, it is essential that our MPs and MEPs are left in no doubt of what you, the public, want.

RECIPE ANALYSIS AND NUTRITION LABELLING

Each recipe in the following section is accompanied by a simple nutritional analysis. A serving of each recipe has been computer-analysed for its calorie (kilojoule), protein, fat, saturated fat, fibre, added sugar and salt content. Our star guide shows you, at a glance, just how healthy a recipe is. The more stars a recipe has, the better it is for you. This is what the star system means:

★★★★ High fibre, low fat, low saturated fat, low added sugars, low salt
★★★ Medium-high fibre, medium-low fat, medium-low saturated fat, medium-low added sugars, medium-low salt
★★ Medium-low fibre, medium-high fat, medium-high saturated fat, medium-high added sugars, medium-high salt
★ Low fibre, high fat, high saturated fat, high added sugars, high salt

For example, Fruity Muesli in the breakfast chapter would be labelled per portion in this way

Fruity Muesli (per portion)	
287 kcals/1202 kj	
5.5 g Protein	
50 g Carbohydrate	
8.7 g Fat	★★★
1.1 g Saturated fat	★★★★
6.8 g Fibre	★★★★
No Added Sugar	★★★★
61 mg Salt	★★★★

FAT AND SATURATED FAT The average UK consumer eats about 100 grams of fat and 50 grams of saturated fat a day. A healthier amount is about 85 grams of total fat, and 35 grams of saturated fat.

The amount of fat, particularly saturated fat, used in the recipes for this book has been kept to the minimum, without detracting from the overall flavour. Some recipes, such as salads, are labelled high in fat because we have assumed that all the salad dressing will actually be used. If you use less, the amount of fat you eat will be less. Any recipes labelled high in fat are usually low in saturated fats. The high level of overall fat comes from the healthier unsaturated fats. If you combine a recipe high in fat with one containing hardly any fat, the meal will be healthier overall. Remember, it is the *overall* total that counts in the end.

FIBRE The average UK consumer eats around 20 grams of fibre a day. For adults, and any teenager who has an adult appetite, it has been suggested that 30 grams would be healthier, with the extra fibre coming from whole, fresh foods where possible. Do not expect a child under 12, particularly one with a small appetite, to reach 30 grams. They should get adequate amounts of fibre if they eat small portions of your healthy meals.

Some of the dishes in the book, particularly in the main meal and barbecue sections, are low or medium fibre. However, if you combine them with vegetable dishes or whole grain cereals, and follow them with fruit, then the overall fibre content of the meal will be higher.

ADDED SUGARS The average UK consumer eats around two pounds (900 grams) of added sugar per week. That's the equivalent of 25 teaspoons of sugar a day, or 130 grams. A healthier amount is around 10 teaspoons, or 50 grams a day.

The recipes in this book have been analysed to show the added sugars as opposed to those occuring naturally within a given ingredient. These added sugars include white and brown sugars and honey.

All the recipes are low in added sugar, with the exception of some of the puddings. A sweet tooth is an acquired habit; it also takes time to lose the craving for sweetness.

SALT The amount of salt eaten in the UK comes to around 7 to 10 grams per person, per day. That's 7000 to 10,000 milligrams. There is no agreement on the exact amount we should eat, but you should aim to reduce intake to around 5 grams (5,000 milligrams) a day.

All recipes have been analysed without added salt. The salt levels shown are those that occur naturally in food, or have been added by manufacturers to items such as tinned tomatoes, tuna in brine, smoked foods and cured meats.

Food cooked without salt may at first taste very bland if you are usually heavy handed with the salt pot. With time, however, most people find the natural flavours of food actually stronger without salt, rather than weaker, but be prepared for this to take several months.

1

Breakfast and Brunch

With today's busy lifestyles and the problem of getting the family out of the house quickly, breads and cereals tend to be the most obvious choice for breakfast. And yet it is just as quick and easy to make one of the alternatives given in the following chapter – especially if you are preparing a celebration brunch. If you want a refreshing start to the day, why not try a fruit-based dish like Fresh fruit with raspberry and yogurt purée, (page 26), or give the children a treat and let them help themselves to a plate of freshly made waffles (page 27). If you feel that you need the commercial cereals as a standby, choose wholemeal varieties and read the labels carefully to avoid those with added sugar and salt.

Sunshine Citrus Juice

This can be made with either commercial fruit juices or freshly squeezed fruit.

NUTRITIONAL ANALYSIS
26 kcals/110 kJ
0.4 g Protein
6.3 g Carbohydrate
0 g Fat ★★★★
0 g Saturated Fat ★★★★
0 g Fibre ★
No Added Sugar ★★★★
3 mg Salt ★★★

SERVES 4

juice of 2 grapefruit
juice of 2 oranges
juice of 2 lemons
juice of 2 limes
chilled mineral water
limes slices, to decorate

FOR THE LEMON AND ORANGE ICE CUBES

1 lemon
1 orange

1 Make the ice cubes in advance. Cut the lemon and orange into slices, then into small sections. Put one into each division of an ice cube tray and fill up with water in the usual way. Freeze.
2 Mix together all the fruit juices and pour into 4 tumblers. Top up with mineral water, decorate with lime slices and add the flavoured ice cubes.

Orange and Apple Fizz

There are many mineral waters to choose from today, either still or carbonated. Here, carbonated mineral water is combined with fruit juices for a refreshing start to the day.

NUTRITIONAL ANALYSIS
58 kcals/241 kJ
0.5 g Protein
14.9 g Carbohydrate
0 g Fat ★★★★
0 g Saturated Fat ★★★★
1.2 g Fibre ★★★★
No Added Sugar ★★★★
15 mg Salt ★★★★

SERVES 1

45 ml (1¾ fl oz) unsweetened apple juice, chilled
25 ml (1 fl oz) unsweetened orange juice, chilled
75 ml (3 fl oz) carbonated mineral water, chilled
1 orange slice
1 apple slice
1 mint sprig, to decorate

1 Measure the juices into a tall glass and top up with the mineral water.
2 Decorate the drink with orange, apple and mint. Serve immediately.

Strawberry Yogurt Drink

Do not confine this refreshing quick breakfast drink to summer. It is equally good made with frozen strawberries and will provide vitamin C during winter months. The natural flavour of the fruit will provide the necessary sweetness.

NUTRITIONAL ANALYSIS
77 kcals/321 kJ
6.6 g Protein
11.5 g Carbohydrate
0.8 g Fat ★★★★
0.5 g Saturated Fat ★★★★
1.1 g Fibre ★★★★
No Added Sugar ★★★★
246 mg Salt ★

SERVES 4

200 g (7 oz) fresh or frozen strawberries
300 ml (½ pint) low-fat natural yogurt, chilled
300 ml (½ pint) skimmed milk, chilled

1 Purée all the ingredients in a blender or food processor until smooth.
2 Pour the drink into 4-6 glasses and serve immediately.

Winter Breakfast Fruit Salad

The natural sugars in these dried fruits sweeten the juice as it is left to stand for several days before serving. Serve the fruit salad on its own, with yogurt or muesli.

SERVES 4-6

225 g (8 oz) dried apricots

100 g (4 oz) dried prunes

50 g (2 oz) raisins

25 g (1 oz) flaked almonds

15 ml (1 tbsp) orange flower water

1 Put the fruit into a glass bowl with the almonds and orange flower water. Add enough water to just cover the fruit.
2 Cover the bowl and refrigerate for at least 2 days before serving.

NUTRITIONAL ANALYSIS
139 kcals/582 kJ
3 g Protein
28.5 g Carbohydrate
2.2 g Fat ★★★★
0.2 g Saturated Fat ★★★★
12.9 g Fibre ★★★★
No Added Sugar ★★★★
70 mg Salt ★★★★

Fruity Muesli

Some shop-bought mueslis contain as much as 20 per cent extra sugar. The fruits in this recipe provide all the necessary sweetness.

SERVES 4

100 g (4 oz) porridge oats

50 g (2 oz) raisins

50 g (2 oz) sultanas

50 g (2 oz) nuts, chopped

fresh fruit such as apples, pears or peaches, chopped, to serve

skimmed milk, to serve

1 Mix together the oats, raisins, sultanas and nuts. The dry muesli will keep fresh for several weeks if stored in an airtight container.
2 Serve the muesli in individual bowls with the fresh fruit and milk.

NUTRITIONAL ANALYSIS
287 kcals/1202 kJ
5.5 g Protein
50 g Carbohydrate
8.7 g Fat ★★★
1.1 g Saturated Fat ★★★★
6.8 g Fibre ★★★★
No Added Sugar ★★★★
61 mg Salt ★★★★

Date and Banana Yogurt

Make the day before serving, for the natural sweetness of the dates and bananas to be absorbed by the yogurt.

SERVES 4

100 g (4 oz) dried dates, stoned and chopped

2 bananas, peeled and sliced

300 ml (½ pint) low-fat natural yogurt

1 Place the dates and bananas into a small serving dish. Pour over the yogurt.
2 Cover the dish and refrigerate overnight.

NUTRITIONAL ANALYSIS
142 kcals/594 kJ
4.9 g Protein
30.6 g Carbohydrate
0.9 g Fat ★★★★
0.5 g Saturated Fat ★★★★
3.9 g Fibre ★★★★
No Added Sugar ★★★★
150 mg Salt ★★★

NUTRITIONAL ANALYSIS
120 kcals/503 kJ
3.8 g Protein
27.1 g Carbohydrate
0.4 g Fat ★★★★
0.2 g Saturated Fat ★★★★
8.6 g Fibre ★★★★
No Added Sugar ★★★★
85 mg Salt ★★★★

Fresh Fruit with Raspberry and Yogurt Purée

Dip the fresh fruit into the raspberry and yogurt purée for an interesting breakfast. Vary the fruits to suit your taste.

SERVES 4

225 g (8 oz) fresh raspberries
150 ml (¼ pint) low-fat natural yogurt
12 large strawberries, hulled and halved
8 ripe apricots, halved and stoned
12 black grapes, halved
1 large pink grapefruit, peeled and segmented
1 ripe pear, cored and cut into sections
90 ml (6 tbsp) apple juice
fresh mint leaves, to decorate

1 Purée the raspberries, yogurt and sugar in a blender or food processor. Turn into a serving bowl.
2 Sprinkle the prepared fruit with apple juice and arrange on a serving platter. Decorate with mint leaves and accompany with the raspberry and yogurt purée.

NUTRITIONAL ANALYSIS
110 kcals/459 kJ
1.4 g Protein
20 g Carbohydrate
3.2 g Fat ★★★
2.6 g Saturated Fat ★★
2.7 g Fibre ★★★★
No Added Sugar ★★★★
25 mg Salt ★★★★

Fresh Fruit and Coconut in Grapefruit

This tangy, exotic fruit mix makes a refreshing new way to serve grapefruit.

SERVES 4

2 grapefruit
100 g (4 oz) fresh dates, stoned and chopped
175 g (6 oz) fresh pineapple rings, cut into 1 cm (½ inch) chunks, or canned unsweetened chunks
50 g (2 oz) seedless grapes
25 g (1 oz) unsweetened coconut flakes
4 fresh mint sprigs, to garnish

1 Cut each grapefruit in half and cut around each half, loosening the flesh from the outer skin. Cut between the segments to loosen the flesh from the membranes. Reserve the grapefruit shells.
2 Put the grapefruit flesh into a bowl with the dates, pineapple, grapes and coconut and mix well. Place the fruit in the grapefruit shells and garnish each with a sprig of mint.

Quick Muffins

Split the warm muffins and lightly spread with polyunsaturated margarine. Or allow to cool, then split and toast them before serving.

MAKES 12
225 g (8 oz) plain flour
30 ml (2 tbsp) caster sugar
15 ml (1 tbsp) baking powder
1 egg
225 ml (8 fl oz) skimmed milk
50 ml (2 fl oz) sunflower oil

NUTRITIONAL ANALYSIS
128 kcals/535 kJ
3.1 g Protein
19.1 g Carbohydrate
4.9 g Fat ★★★
0.8 g Saturated Fat ★★★★
0.6 g Fibre ★★
2.6 g Added Sugar ★★★
42 mg Salt ★★★★

1 Put the flour, sugar, baking powder and salt into a large bowl and stir to mix well.
2 Beat the egg lightly with a fork in a small bowl, then stir in the milk and oil.
3 Add the egg mixture to the dry ingredients all at once and stir lightly until the flour is just moistened. Do not overbeat: the mixture should still be slightly lumpy.
4 Spoon the mixture into twelve lightly greased 6.5 cm (2½ inch) patty tins. Bake at 200°C (400°F) mark 6 for 20-25 minutes or until well risen. When cooked, a skewer inserted in the centre should come out clean.
5 Turn out the muffins on to a wire rack and serve immediately.

Buttermilk Waffles

Buttermilk is the low-fat liquid left after butter-making to which bacteria are added; the lactic acid produced by the bacteria helps the waffles to rise. Buttermilk is also ideal to use when making scones and soda bread.

MAKES 6
100 g (4 oz) self-raising wholemeal flour
2.5 ml (½ tsp) ground cinnamon
15 ml (1 tbsp) sugar
1 egg, separated
30 ml (2 tbsp) sunflower oil
300 ml (½ pint) buttermilk

NUTRITIONAL ANALYSIS
136 kcals/567 kJ
4.9 g Protein
15.6 g Carbohydrate
6.4 g Fat ★★
1.1 g Saturated Fat ★★★★
1.7 g Fibre ★★★★
2.6 g Added Sugar ★★★
88 mg Salt ★★★★

1 Lightly grease and heat a waffle iron. Mix together the flour, cinnamon and sugar in a bowl. Make a well in the centre and add the egg yolk, oil and buttermilk. Whisk gently to form a smooth batter. Whisk the egg white until stiff and gently fold into the batter.
2 Pour the batter into the waffle iron, leaving 2.5 cm (1 inch) around the edges. Cook the waffle for 2-3 minutes, turning once if using a hand waffle iron.
3 Remove the waffle using a palette knife and keep warm. Cook the remaining waffles, reheating the iron each time. Serve warm, lightly spread with polyunsaturated margarine, if liked.

NUTRITIONAL ANALYSIS
159 kcals/663 kJ
3.8 g Protein
27.3 g Carbohydrate
4.6 g Fat ★★★
0.9 g Saturated Fat ★★★★
1.5 g Fibre ★★★
2.8 g Added Sugar ★★★
298 mg Salt ★★★

Cinnamon Buns

These spicy rich buns freeze well, so make double the quantity and freeze half. Reheat from frozen in the oven.

MAKES 9

225 g (8 oz) unbleached strong white flour

1.25 ml (1/4 tsp) salt

5 ml (1 tsp) easy mix dried yeast

15 g (1/2 oz) polyunsaturated margarine

75 ml (3 fl oz) skimmed milk, warmed

1 egg

FOR THE FILLING

25 g (1 oz) polyunsaturated margarine

25 g (1 oz) brown sugar

5 ml (1 tsp) ground cinnamon

50 g (2 oz) raisins

1 Mix together the flour, salt and yeast in a bowl and rub in the margarine. Beat the milk and egg together, then stir enough into the flour mixture to make a soft dry dough.
2 Turn out the dough on to a lightly floured work surface and knead for 5 minutes.
3 Place the dough in a lightly oiled bowl, cover with polythene and leave to rise in a warm place until doubled in size.
4 Knead the dough then roll out into a rectangle 30×23 cm (12×9 inches). Spread with 15 g (½ oz) of the margarine. Mix together the sugar, cinnamon and raisins and sprinkle over the dough.
5 Starting with the longer side, roll up the dough like a Swiss roll, then cut into 9 even slices. Arrange, cut sides down, in a lightly oiled 18 cm (7 inch) square shallow cake tin. Cover with greased polythene and leave to prove in a warm place for 30 minutes or until doubled in size.
6 Bake at 190°C (375°F) mark 5 for 30-35 minutes. Brush with the remaining melted margarine and serve warm.

NUTRITIONAL ANALYSIS
102 kcals/426 kJ
3.6 g Protein
19.8 g Carbohydrate
1.5 g Fat ★★★★
0.2 g Saturated Fat ★★★★
3.5 g Fibre ★★★★
2.1 g Added Sugar ★★★
168 mg Salt ★★★

Granary Prune Loaf

This fibre-rich, sweet crunchy loaf can be made into buns. This recipe freezes well.

MAKES 1 SMALL LOAF

250 g (9 oz) granary flour

1.25 ml (1/4 tsp) salt

10 ml (2 tsp) easy mix dried yeast

15 g (1/2 oz) polyunsaturated margarine

25 g (1 oz) brown sugar

150 ml (1/4 pint) skimmed milk, warmed

100 g (4 oz) no-soak stoned dried prunes, chopped

1 Mix together the flour, salt and yeast in a bowl and rub in the margarine. Stir in the sugar, reserving 15 ml (1 tbsp) for glazing the loaf. Add enough milk to the flour to make a soft dry dough.
2 Turn out the dough on to a lightly floured work surface and knead for 5 minutes. Knead in the prunes.
3 Place the dough in a lightly oiled bowl, cover with polythene and leave to rise in a warm place until double in size.
4 Knead the dough for a further 2 minutes. Put into a lightly oiled 450 g (1 lb) loaf tin.
5 Bake at 200°C (400°F) mark 6 for 25-30 minutes or until the loaf sounds hollow when tapped on the base.
6 Dissolve the sugar in 15 ml (1 tbsp) boiling water and brush over the top of the loaf to glaze. Serve cut into thick slices and spread very sparingly with polyunsaturated margarine.

Wholemeal Bread

Wholemeal bread is often slightly heavier than many shop bought loaves because commercial bakers usually use 'improvers' which lighten the loaf. If your first efforts are too heavy, try making a fifty-fifty loaf, using half wholemeal flour and half unbleached strong white flour.

MAKES ONE 1.1 KG (2½ LB) LOAF, TWO SMALL LOAVES OR 20 ROLLS	5 ml (1 tsp) salt
	1 sachet easy mix dried yeast
750 g (1½ lb) wholemeal flour	15 ml (1 tbsp) sunflower oil

1 Mix together the flour, salt and yeast in a bowl. Mix the oil with 150 ml (¼ pint) boiling water and 350 ml (½ pint) cold water. Stir enough water into the flour to make a soft dry dough. (Flours vary as to how much water they will absorb.) Alternatively, if you have a food processor, insert the plastic blade, place the dry ingredients into the bowl, start the machine and pour in the liquid through the lid. When the mixture forms a ball, continue to process for 1 minute.
2 Turn out the dough on to a lightly floured work surface and knead for 5 minutes.
3 Place the dough in a lightly oiled bowl, cover with polythene and leave to rise in a warm place until doubled in size.
4 Knead the dough for a further 2 minutes. Divide between 2 lightly oiled 450 g (1 lb) loaf tins or use a 900 g (2 lb) loaf tin. If making rolls, divide the dough into 50 g (2 oz) portions, shape into rolls and arrange on lightly oiled baking sheets, allowing room between each for rising. Cover with greased polythene and leave to prove in a warm place for 20 minutes or until doubled in size.
5 Bake at 230°C (450°F) mark 8 for 35 minutes for a large loaf, small loaves for 25-30 minutes and rolls for 15-20 minutes or until the bread sounds hollow when tapped on the base.

NUTRITIONAL ANALYSIS
127 kcals/530 kJ
5.1 g Protein
24.7 g Carbohydrate
1.5 g Fat ★★★★
0.2 g Saturated Fat ★★★★
3.7 g Fibre ★★★★
No Added Sugar ★★★★
253 mg Salt ★★★

Wholemeal Apple Rolls

Make a batch of these rolls the day before and warm them in the oven before serving for a speedy breakfast.

MAKES 8	225 g (8 oz) plain wholemeal flour, plus 5 ml (1 tsp) for dusting
15 g (½ oz) fresh yeast, or 7.5 ml (1½ tsp) dried yeast and 5 ml (1 tsp) clear honey	225 g (8 oz) strong white flour
	75 g (3 oz) eating apple, peeled, cored and grated

1 Crumble the fresh yeast into 150 ml (¼ pint) tepid water and stir until dissolved. If using dried yeast, sprinkle it on to the tepid water mixed with the honey. Leave in a warm place for about 15 minutes until frothy.
2 Mix together the flours in a bowl. Add the yeast liquid, apple and 150 ml (¼ pint) tepid water, then mix to a soft dough.
3 Turn out the dough on to a lightly floured work surface and knead for about 5 minutes or until smooth and no longer sticky.
4 Place the dough in a bowl, cover with a clean tea-towel and leave to rise in a warm place for about 1 hour or until doubled in size.
5 Turn out the dough on to a lightly floured surface and knead for a few minutes. Divide the dough into 8 pieces. Shape into rolls, about 7.5 cm (3 inches) long. Place on a lightly greased baking sheet, cover and leave to prove in a warm place for 30 minutes or until doubled in size.
6 Dust the rolls with wholemeal flour. Bake at 230°C (450°F) mark 8 for 15-20 minutes or until the rolls sound hollow when tapped on the bases. Serve warm.

NUTRITIONAL ANALYSIS
193 kcals/806 kJ
7.3 g Protein
41.3 g Carbohydrate
0.9 g Fat ★★★★
0.1 g Saturated Fat ★★★★
4 g Fibre ★★★★
0.5 g Added Sugar ★★★★
6 mg Salt ★★★★

NUTRITIONAL ANALYSIS
224 kcals/935 kJ
10.7 g Protein
18.8 g Carbohydrate
12.3 g Fat ★★
3.1 g Saturated Fat ★★★
3.8 g Fibre ★★★★
No Added Sugar ★★★★
940 mg Salt ★

Baked Eggs with Yogurt Sauce

The flavour of the sauce in this recipe can be varied by using only one herb, such as tarragon.

SERVES 4

4 large thin slices wholemeal bread

25 g (1 oz) polyunsaturated margarine

4 eggs

FOR THE YOGURT AND HERB SAUCE

15 ml (1 tbsp) finely chopped fresh mixed herbs or 7.5 ml (1½ tsp) dried

150 ml (¼ pint) low-fat natural yogurt

pepper, to taste

1 Cut the crusts off the bread slices and spread the slices with the margarine.
2 Place a slice of bread, margarine side down, in 4 lightly greased individual ramekins, pressing down so the egg cannot escape underneath. Crack an egg into the centre of each slice. Bake at 190°C (375°F) mark 5 for about 10 minutes or until the eggs are just set but not hard.
3 Meanwhile for the sauce, stir the herbs into the yogurt and season to taste. Serve the baked eggs in their bread cases at once, accompanied by the sauce.

NUTRITIONAL ANALYSIS
326 kcals/1364 kJ
17.4 g Protein
48 g Carbohydrate
8.6 g Fat ★★★
3.6 g Saturated Fat ★★★
2.5 g Fibre ★★★
No Added Sugar ★★★★
1893 mg Salt ★★

Smoked Salmon Kedgeree

This luxurious kedgeree makes a very special brunch dish. Economise by buying smoked salmon offcuts or trimmings. Cook the rice the night before for a quick start in the morning. Reheat in a steamer or microwave cooker.

SERVES 4

225 g (8 oz) brown rice

4 spring onions, trimmed and chopped

2 large pickled sour sweet gherkins, finely chopped

150 ml (¼ pint) low-fat crème fraîche

150 g (5 oz) smoked salmon offcuts, cut into thin strips

pepper, to taste

1 hard-boiled egg, sliced, to garnish

1 Put the rice in a saucepan of boiling water and cook for 30-35 minutes or until just cooked. Drain.
2 Stir in the onions, gherkins, crème fraîche and smoked salmon, reserving a few slices for garnish. Season to taste.
3 Garnish with egg slices and reserved pieces of smoked salmon.

2

Soups

Homemade soups taste infinitely better than commercially prepared ones. The recipes included here make the most of fresh ingredients to provide a versatile range of soups that can be served just as successfully at elegant dinner parties or wholesome family lunches.

Most soups can be prepared ahead of time then reheated when required; they can also be frozen unless the recipe includes eggs or cornflour. Always make soups with homemade stock. They not only have a better flavour, but are substantially lower in salt content than commercial stock cubes. Stock can be made in advance and then kept in the freezer for up to 6 months.

NUTRITIONAL ANALYSIS
38 kcals/157 kJ
2.4 g Protein
6.7 g Carbohydrate
0.3 g Fat ★★★★
0.1 g Saturated Fat ★★★★
4.1 g Fibre ★★★★
No Added Sugar ★★★★
194 mg Salt ★

Pasta-Vegetable Soup

The vegetable stock used here is quick to make and excellent to use in any recipe that requires a full-flavour vegetable stock.

SERVES 4

15 ml (1 tbsp) chopped fresh mixed herbs

2 medium carrots, scrubbed and thinly sliced

2 celery sticks, trimmed and thinly sliced

75 g (3 oz) firm button mushrooms, thinly sliced

40 g (1½ oz) frozen peas

25 g (1 oz) small wholewheat pasta shapes

pepper, to taste

FOR THE VEGETABLE STOCK

1 small onion, skinned and thinly sliced

3 courgettes (zucchini), trimmed and finely chopped

2 leeks, washed and finely chopped

3 carrots, scrubbed and sliced

1 bouquet garni

2 bay leaves

5 ml (1 tsp) black peppercorns

1 For the stock, put all the ingredients into a saucepan with 900 ml (1½ pints) water. Bring to the boil and simmer for 10-12 minutes.
2 Set aside until cool, then strain the stock. Discard the vegetables.
3 Pour the stock into a clean pan and bring just to the boil. Add the herbs, remaining vegetables and pasta.
4 Return to the boil and simmer for 5-6 minutes until the vegetables and pasta are just tender. Season to taste.

NUTRITIONAL ANALYSIS
129 kcals/540 kJ
4.1 g Protein
26.7 g Carbohydrate
1.4 g Fat ★★★★
0.2 g Saturated Fat ★★★★
5.3 g Fibre ★★★★
No Added Sugar ★★★★
64 mg Salt ★★★★

Leek and Potato Soup

A member of the onion family, leeks have a more delicate flavour and a finer texture than the onion.

SERVES 4

5 ml (1 tsp) sunflower oil

2 medium leeks, washed and sliced into 1 cm (½ inch) pieces

450 g (1 lb) potatoes, peeled and diced

pepper, to taste

60 ml (4 tbsp) chopped fresh parsley, to garnish

1 Heat the oil in a large non-stick saucepan and cook the leeks and potatoes for 2-3 minutes, stirring, without browning.
2 Add 900 ml (1½ pints) water, cover and bring to the boil. Simmer for about 20 minutes until the vegetables are cooked.
3 Allow to cool slightly, then purée the soup in a blender or food processor. Season to taste. Return to the pan and reheat for serving. Garnish with parsley.

Ceviche (PAGE 43)

Cannellini Bean Soup

Cannellini beans are small, dried white beans, usually available from supermarkets and health food shops. Other beans, such as white haricot beans, can be used instead.

SERVES 4
15 ml (1 tbsp) sunflower oil
4 celery sticks, trimmed and chopped
1 medium onion, skinned and sliced
2 garlic cloves, skinned and crushed
100 g (4 oz) French beans, trimmed and cut into 1 cm (½ inch) pieces
30 ml (2 tbsp) chopped fresh parsley
225 g (8 oz) dried cannellini beans, soaked overnight
900 ml (1½ pints) vegetable stock
pepper, to taste

NUTRITIONAL ANALYSIS
204 kcals/854 kJ
13.5 g Protein
28.8 g Carbohydrate
4.7 g Fat ★★★
0.6 g Saturated Fat ★★★★
17.3 g Fibre ★★★★
No Added Sugar ★★★★
312 mg Salt ★★★

1 Heat the oil in a non-stick saucepan and gently cook the celery, onion, garlic, French beans and parsley for about 5 minutes until the onion is soft.
2 Drain the cannellini beans and rinse. Add to the pan and cook for a further 5 minutes, stirring continuously.
3 Add the vegetable stock, bring to the boil and simmer for 1½ hours until the cannellini beans are tender. Add a little water during the cooking time if the soup begins to dry out. Season to taste.

Tomato and Celery Soup

If, for convenience and to save time, you use a stock cube to make the chicken stock, use about a half less of the cube than recommended. Do not add extra salt to the soup as stock cubes tend to be salty.

SERVES 4
15 g (½ oz) polyunsaturated margarine
1 large onion, skinned and finely chopped
1 garlic clove, skinned and crushed (optional)
3 celery sticks, trimmed and sliced
900 g (2 lb) tomatoes, skinned and quartered
10 ml (2 tsp) chopped fresh thyme or 5 ml (1 tsp) dried
1.1 litres (2 pints) chicken stock
pepper, to taste
chopped fresh thyme or parsley, to garnish

NUTRITIONAL ANALYSIS
75 kcals/312 kJ
5.1 g Protein
7.3 g Carbohydrate
3.1 g Fat ★★
0.7 g Saturated Fat ★★★
8.7 g Fibre ★★★★
No Added Sugar ★★★★
334 mg Salt ★

1 Melt the margarine in a non-stick saucepan and cook the onion, garlic and celery over a low heat for 5 minutes. Stir in the tomatoes, thyme and stock. Bring to the boil and simmer for 20-25 minutes until cooked.
2 Allow to cool slightly, then purée the soup in a blender or food processor. Press through a sieve. Reheat the soup, season to taste and serve garnished with fresh thyme or parsley.

Fish and Prawn Terrine (PAGE 58)

NUTRITIONAL ANALYSIS
278 kcals/1164 kJ
15.4 g Protein
39.7 g Carbohydrate
7.4 g Fat ★★★
1.7 g Saturated Fat ★★★★
12.4 g Fibre ★★★★
No Added Sugar ★★★★
183 mg Salt ★★★★

Spicy Chick-Pea Soup

This filling soup is ideal to serve on a winter's day.

SERVES 4

225 g (8 oz) dried chick-peas, soaked overnight
1 fresh rosemary sprig or 2.5 ml (1/2 tsp) dried
1 bay leaf
15 ml (1 tbsp) sunflower oil
3 garlic cloves, skinned and crushed
1 small onion, skinned and chopped
2 small green chillies, seeded and finely chopped
45 ml (3 tbsp) chopped fresh parsley
15 ml (1 tbsp) Worcestershire sauce
45 ml (3 tbsp) tomato purée
50 g (2 oz) wholewheat pasta rings or small pasta shapes
pepper, to taste

1 Drain the chick-peas and rinse. Put the chick-peas in a saucepan with 600 ml (1 pint) water, the rosemary and bay leaf. Bring to the boil and simmer for 1½ hours. Drain the chick-peas, reserving the cooking liquid. Set aside.
2 Heat the oil in a non-stick saucepan and cook the garlic and onion for 3-5 minutes until soft. Stir in the chillies, 30 ml (2 tbsp) of the parsley, the Worcestershire sauce and tomato purée. Add the chick-peas.
3 Make up the reserved cooking liquid to 900 ml (1½ pints) with water and add to the pan. Bring to the boil, then add the pasta and simmer for 15-20 minutes or until the pasta is tender.
4 Season to taste and sprinkle with the remaining chopped parsley.

NUTRITIONAL ANALYSIS
61 kcals/254 kJ
2.7 g Protein
12.7 g Carbohydrate
0.2 g Fat ★★★★
0 g Saturated Fat ★★★★
4.9 g Fibre ★★★★
No Added Sugar ★★★★
259 mg Salt ★

Autumn Barley Soup

Pot barley is the whole of the grain with only the rough outer husk removed. Make double the quantity of this soup and freeze the remainder. Leave a 2.5 cm (1 inch) gap at the top of the container, as the soup will expand during freezing.

SERVES 4

25 g (1 oz) pot barley, washed and drained
1 litre (1¾ pints) vegetable stock
2 large carrots, scrubbed and diced
1 turnip, peeled and diced
2 leeks, washed and sliced
2 celery sticks, trimmed and diced
1 small onion, skinned and finely chopped
1 bouquet garni
pepper, to taste
30 ml (2 tbsp) chopped fresh parsley

1 Put the barley and stock in a saucepan. Simmer for 45 minutes until tender.
2 Add the vegetables to the pan with the bouquet garni and season to taste. Bring to the boil and simmer for about 20 minutes or until the vegetables are tender.
3 Discard the bouquet garni. Add the parsley, stir well and serve immediately.

Mussel Chowder

This tasty variation of Moules Marinières should be served with warm, crusty French bread.

SERVES 4
1.1 litres (2 pints) fresh mussels, scrubbed and cleaned
15 ml (1 tbsp) sunflower oil
1 small green pepper, cored, seeded and finely chopped
1 medium onion, skinned and finely chopped
3 celery sticks, trimmed and finely chopped
1 garlic clove, skinned and chopped
400 g (14 oz) can chopped tomatoes
1 bay leaf
15 ml (1 tbsp) chopped fresh thyme or 7.5 ml (1½ tsp) dried
pepper, to taste
chopped fresh parsley and pared rind of 1 lemon, to garnish

NUTRITIONAL ANALYSIS
129 kcals/538 kJ
16.3 g Protein
3.9 g Carbohydrate
5.5 g Fat ★★
0.9 g Saturated Fat ★★★★
2.6 g Fibre ★★★★
No Added Sugar ★★★★
679 mg Salt ★

1 Put the mussels in a large saucepan and add 300 ml (½ pint) water. Cover, bring to the boil, then cook gently for a few minutes until the mussel shells have opened.
2 Meanwhile, heat the oil in a non-stick saucepan and gently cook the green pepper, onion, celery and garlic for about 5 minutes until soft.
3 Drain the mussels, reserving the liquid and discard any unopened mussels. Shell, reserving 4 in shells for garnish.
4 Make the reserved cooking liquid up to 450 ml (¾ pint) with cold water if necessary. Add the tomatoes and their juice, the bay leaf, thyme and seasoning to the vegetables. Bring to the boil, cover and simmer for 25 minutes.
5 Add the shelled mussels to the soup and cook for a further 5 minutes. Remove the bay leaf. Ladle the soup into serving bowls, add a mussel in its shell to each bowl and garnish with parsley and lemon rind.

Parsnip and Orange Soup

The nutty sweet flavour of parsnip complements the orange in this quick and healthy soup.

SERVES 4
10 ml (2 tsp) sunflower oil
1 small onion, skinned and chopped
350 g (12 oz) parsnips, peeled and chopped
finely grated rind of ½ orange
juice of 1 orange
600 ml (1 pint) chicken stock
pepper, to taste

NUTRITIONAL ANALYSIS
72 kcals/300 kJ
1.7 g Protein
11.3 g Carbohydrate
2.6 g Fat ★★★
0.3 g Saturated Fat ★★★★
3.7 g Fibre ★★★★
No Added Sugar ★★★★
57 mg Salt ★★★★

1 Heat the oil in a large non-stick saucepan and cook the onion and parsnip for 5-8 minutes until the onion is soft. Add the orange rind, orange juice, stock and pepper. Cover and cook for about 10 minutes until the parsnips are tender.
2 Allow to cool slightly, then purée the soup in a blender or food processor. Return to the pan and reheat for serving.

Pumpkin Soup

You can serve this soup in the pumpkin shell, if liked. If you choose to do this, prepare the pumpkin carefully in step 1 and reserve the shell.

NUTRITIONAL ANALYSIS
132 kcals/551 kJ
4.5 g Protein
21.6 g Carbohydrate
3.9 g Fat ★★★
0.6 g Saturated Fat ★★★★
4.4 g Fibre ★★★★
No Added Sugar ★★★★
104 mg Salt ★★★★

SERVES 4

1 pumpkin, weighing about 2.5 kg (5½ lb)
15 ml (1 tbsp) sunflower oil
5 ml (1 tsp) grated fresh root ginger
5 ml (1 tsp) grated nutmeg
2.5 ml (½ tsp) freshly ground coriander
1 celery stick, trimmed and diced
350 g (12 oz) tomatoes, chopped
600 ml (1 pint) vegetable stock
30 ml (2 tbsp) low-fat natural yogurt, to garnish

1 Slice the top off the pumpkin, about one third of the way down, and discard the seeds and fibre. Using a spoon, scoop out the flesh into a bowl, leaving a thickness of about 1 cm (½ inch) of flesh in the shell. Set the shell aside.
2 Heat the oil in a large non-stick saucepan and cook the ginger, nutmeg and coriander over a low heat for 2 minutes. Add the celery, pumpkin flesh and tomatoes, stir thoroughly and cook for 1 minute.
3 Stir in the vegetable stock. Bring to the boil and simmer for 20-25 minutes or until the pumpkin is tender.
4 Allow to cool slightly, then purée the soup in a blender or food processor until smooth. Add extra stock if the soup is too thick. Reheat the soup, pour into the pumpkin shell and garnish with a swirl of yogurt.

Curried Chicken Soup

Garam masala is a combination of Indian spices, and is available at most supermarkets and specialist shops.

NUTRITIONAL ANALYSIS
183 kcals/765 kJ
21.3 g Protein
17 g Carbohydrate
3.9 g Fat ★★★
1.2 g Saturated Fat ★★★★
3.7 g Fibre ★★★★
No Added Sugar ★★★★
241 mg Salt ★★★

SERVES 4

1 medium onion, skinned and chopped
100 g (4 oz) split red lentils
5 ml (1 tsp) ground turmeric
5 ml (1 tsp) garam masala
2.5 ml (½ tsp) chilli powder or to taste
900 ml (1½ pints) chicken stock
225 g (8 oz) cooked chicken meat, skinned and roughly chopped
pepper, to taste
low-fat natural yogurt, paprika and parsley sprigs, to garnish

1 Put the onion, lentils, spices, stock and half the chicken into a saucepan. Bring to the boil, cover and simmer for 20 minutes.
2 Allow to cool slightly, then purée the soup in a blender or food processor until smooth.
3 Return to the pan and add the remaining chicken. Simmer for a further 10 minutes, then season to taste. Serve garnished with yogurt, paprika and parsley.

Courgette (Zucchini) and Spinach Soup

This versatile soup that can be served hot or cold uses vegetables which are available in abundant supplies during the summer months.

SERVES 4
5 ml (1 tsp) sunflower oil
225 g (8 oz) courgettes (zucchini), trimmed and chopped
350 g (12 oz) spinach, washed and roughly chopped
600 ml (1 pint) chicken stock
150 g (5 oz) potato, peeled and chopped
100 ml (4 fl oz) white wine or water
15 g (½ oz) fresh basil
pepper, to taste
grated nutmeg, to taste
4 extra basil leaves or lemon slices to garnish

NUTRITIONAL ANALYSIS
95 kcals/399 kJ
3.3 g Protein
13 g Carbohydrate
2 g Fat ★★★
0.2 g Saturated Fat ★★★★
2 g Fibre ★★★★
No Added Sugar ★★★★
160 mg Salt ★★★

1 Heat the oil in a large non-stick saucepan and cook the courgettes (zucchini) and spinach for 5 minutes, stirring, until slightly softened.
2 Stir in the stock and potato. Bring to the boil, cover and simmer for about 15 minutes until all the vegetables are soft. Add the wine, bring back to the boil. Remove from the heat and add the basil.
3 Allow to cool slightly, then purée the soup in a blender or food processor, press through a sieve. To serve hot, return the soup to the pan, season and reheat until boiling. To serve cold, season the soup with pepper and nutmeg and leave to cool. Refrigerate for at least 2 hours before serving. Garnish with basil.

Crab and Corn Soup

This is a variation of the classic Chinese soup. Fresh root ginger is a knobbly light brown underground stem and is available in supermarkets and specialist shops.

SERVES 4
600 ml (1 pint) chicken or vegetable stock
2.5 ml (½ tsp) grated fresh root ginger
15 ml (1 tbsp) cornflour
15 ml (1 tbsp) dry sherry
100 g (3½ oz) canned sweetcorn, drained
175 g (6 oz) can crab meat
1 egg white
1 spring onion, trimmed and finely chopped, to garnish

NUTRITIONAL ANALYSIS
69 kcals/287 kJ
9.6 g Protein
5.2 g Carbohydrate
0.7 g Fat ★★★★
0.1 g Saturated Fat ★★★★
3.1 g Fibre ★★★★
1.9 g Added Sugar ★★
841 mg Salt ★

1 Put the stock into a saucepan and add the ginger.
2 Mix the cornflour with the sherry until smooth. Add the sweetcorn, crab with its liquid and cornflour mixture to the stock. Bring to the boil and simmer for 2-3 minutes, stirring constantly. Turn off the heat and cover.
3 Whisk the egg white until light and foamy, then stir it into the soup. Serve garnished with spring onion.

NUTRITIONAL ANALYSIS
110 kcals/460 kJ
5.1 g Protein
16.4 g Carbohydrate
3.2 g Fat ★★★
0.6 g Saturated Fat ★★★★
2.6 g Fibre ★★★★
No Added Sugar ★★★★
232 mg Salt ★★

Buttermilk and Dill Soup

Buttermilk is the low-fat liquid left after fresh cream has been churned to make butter.

SERVES 4

15 g (½ oz) polyunsaturated margarine

6 spring onions, trimmed and sliced, or 1 medium onion, skinned and thinly sliced

225 g (8 oz) potatoes, peeled and thinly sliced

600 ml (1 pint) chicken stock

30 ml (2 tbsp) roughly chopped fresh dill or 10 ml (2 tsp) dried

1 blade of mace or 1.25 ml (¼ tsp) ground mace

300 ml (½ pint) buttermilk plus 60 ml (4 tbsp) buttermilk, to serve

pepper, to taste

4 fresh dill sprigs, to garnish

1 Melt the margarine in a non-stick saucepan and gently cook the onions for about 5 minutes, without browning. Add the potato slices and gently cook for 5 minutes.
2 Add the stock, chopped dill and mace. Bring to the boil, cover and gently simmer for 20-30 minutes or until the vegetables are tender.
3 Allow to cool slightly. Remove the blade of mace (if used). Purée the soup in a blender or food processor until smooth. Pour into a bowl. Add the buttermilk and stir well. Cover and chill for about 3 hours.
4 To serve, season to taste and pour the soup into individual bowls. Spoon 15 ml (1 tbsp) buttermilk into each bowl and garnish with dill.

NUTRITIONAL ANALYSIS
138 kcals/578 kJ
3 g Protein
18.9 g Carbohydrate
6.2 g Fat ★★
0.7 g Saturated Fat ★★★★
1.9 g Fibre ★★★★
No Added Sugar ★★★★
275 mg Salt ★★★

Cold Garlic and Grape Soup

This cold, deliciously pungent soup requires no cooking. When selecting a head of garlic, choose one that is heavy for its size. The less papery the skin, the more moist the cloves will be.

SERVES 4

75 g (3 oz) day-old bread

25 g (1 oz) ground almonds

2 garlic cloves, skinned and crushed

10 ml (2 tsp) sunflower oil

15 ml (1 tbsp) wine vinegar

225 g (8 oz) white grapes, seeded

paprika and pepper, to garnish

1 Soak the bread in water then squeeze out firmly.
2 Purée the bread, almonds, garlic, oil, vinegar and grapes in a blender or food processor. With the motor running, add 450 ml (¾ pint) cold water.
3 Pour the soup into a tureen. Chill for several hours. Serve sprinkled with paprika pepper.

3

Starters

Starters act as an appetizer to the main course. They should be light and tasty and should complement the dish you plan to serve next; the serving should be small enough to leave people wanting more. Because most starters are served when you're entertaining, it makes sense to choose those which can be made in advance. This takes the pressure off you and lets you spend more time with your guests. Many of the starters included here can also be served as a light meal if eaten with wholemeal bread and fresh fruit.

Curried Flageolet Salad

NUTRITIONAL ANALYSIS
166 kcals/694 kJ
6.4 g Protein
18.2 g Carbohydrate
8 g Fat ★★
1.1 g Saturated Fat ★★★★
8.4 g Fibre ★★★★
No Added Sugar ★★★★
52 mg Salt ★★★★

If preferred, the dried flageolet beans in this recipe can be replaced with a 397 g (14 oz) can of green flageolet beans. Accompany the salad with wholemeal bread.

SERVES 4

100 g (4 oz) dried flageolet beans, soaked overnight
1 green eating apple, cored and diced
225 g (8 oz) tomatoes, diced
1 medium onion, skinned and thinly sliced
fresh coriander sprigs, to garnish

FOR THE DRESSING

15 ml (1 tbsp) lemon juice
15 ml (1 tbsp) wine vinegar
30 ml (2 tbsp) olive oil
2.5-5 ml (½-1 tsp) curry powder
pepper, to taste

1 Rinse and drain the beans. Put in a saucepan and cover with plenty of water. Bring to the boil, cover and simmer for 1¼ hours or until tender.
2 Meanwhile for the dressing, whisk together the lemon juice, vinegar, oil and curry powder. Season to taste.
3 Drain the beans and put into a bowl. Stir in the dressing while still warm. Set aside to cool.
4 Fold the apple into the bean mixture. Stir in the tomatoes and onion. Transfer the salad to a serving dish, cover and chill for 2 hours. Serve garnished with coriander sprigs.

Mangetout (Snow Pea) and Carrot Salad

NUTRITIONAL ANALYSIS
40 kcals/169 kJ
1.6 g Protein
2.9 g Carbohydrate
2.6 g Fat ★
0.4 g Saturated Fat ★★★
1.8 g Fibre ★★★★
No Added Sugar ★★★★
20 mg Salt ★★★★

In French, mange tout *means 'eat all'. The whole pods are eaten very young when the peas are underdeveloped. Combined with ribbons of carrot and fresh sage, they are delicious served as a light starter.*

SERVES 6

50 g (2 oz) carrot, peeled
1 lemon
175 g (6 oz) mangetout (snow peas)
10 ml (2 tsp) chopped fresh sage
15 ml (1 tbsp) olive oil
pepper, to taste

1 Using a potato peeler, pare the carrot into thin ribbons. Cover with cold water and chill.
2 Pare the rind from the lemon and cut into thin shreds. Squeeze the lemon, reserving the juice.
3 Put the mangetout (snow peas) and lemon rind into a saucepan and add just enough cold water to cover. Bring to the boil for 1 minute. Drain and refresh under cold water.
4 Toss together the mangetout (snow peas), lemon rind, drained carrot, 30 ml (2 tbsp) of the lemon juice, the sage and oil. Season to taste. Serve immediately.

Cauliflower Mousses

For saving time on the day you want to serve these mousses, prepare the sauce in advance and chill.

SERVES 4
1 cauliflower, divided into florets
pepper, to taste
1.25 ml (1/4 tsp) grated nutmeg
45 ml (3 tbsp) low-fat natural yogurt
2 eggs, separated
15 ml (1 tbsp) snipped fresh chives
snipped fresh chives, to garnish

FOR THE FRESH TOMATO SAUCE
1 kg (2 1/4 lb) ripe tomatoes, skinned and roughly chopped
1 small onion, skinned and finely chopped
1 medium carrot, scrubbed and chopped
2 celery sticks, trimmed and finely chopped
1 garlic clove, skinned and crushed
30 ml (2 tbsp) chopped fresh parsley
pepper, to taste
15 ml (1 tbsp) chopped fresh basil or 7.5 ml (1/2 tbsp) dried

1 For the sauce, put all the ingredients in a saucepan, cover and simmer for about 40 minutes or until the vegetables are very soft. Allow to cool slightly, then purée the sauce in a blender or food processor. Chill until ready to serve.
2 For the mousses, put the cauliflower in a saucepan of boiling water and simmer for about 8-10 minutes until just tender. Drain thoroughly.
3 Mash the cauliflower to a purée. Season to taste, then beat in the nutmeg, yogurt, egg yolks and chives. Whisk the egg whites until stiff, then fold into the purée.
4 Spoon the cauliflower mixture into 4 individual 225 ml (8 fl oz) soufflé dishes. Cover with lightly greased circles of foil. Stand the dishes in a deep roasting tin and add sufficient hot water to come halfway up the sides of the dishes. Bake at 160°C (325°F) mark 3 for 30 minutes or until the mousses are just set.
5 To serve, unmould the mousses on to a warmed plate. Garnish with chives and accompany with the cold tomato sauce.

NUTRITIONAL ANALYSIS
114 kcals/477 kJ
11 g Protein
11.2 g Carbohydrate
3.2 g Fat ★★★
1.2 g Saturated Fat ★★★
7.9 g Fibre ★★★★
No Added Sugar ★★★★
497 mg Salt ★

Aubergine Pâté

When choosing aubergines, give a gentle press. They should have a firm skin and resilient feel if they are young and fresh.

SERVES 4
2 aubergines, each weighing about 225 g (8 oz)
1 small green pepper
1 small red pepper
2 large tomatoes, skinned, seeded and chopped
30 ml (2 tbsp) olive oil
2 garlic cloves, skinned
30 ml (2 tbsp) chopped fresh parsley
pepper, to taste
large pinch of paprika

1 Make a few slits in each aubergine and put in a baking dish. Bake at 200°C (400°F) mark 6 for 10 minutes.
2 Place the peppers alongside the aubergines and continue baking for a further 10 minutes or until the skins of the aubergines and peppers are charred.
3 Cool the vegetables slightly, then scrape off the charred skins. Scoop the aubergine flesh into a blender or food processor. Core and seed the peppers and add to the aubergines.
4 Add the tomatoes, oil, garlic, parsley, pepper and paprika. Purée until fairly smooth but still slightly textured. Spoon the pâté into a bowl. Cover and chill for 2-3 hours.

NUTRITIONAL ANALYSIS
129 kcals/540 kJ
2.4 g Protein
7.5 g Carbohydrate
10.3 g Fat ★
1.5 g Saturated Fat ★★★
5.4 g Fibre ★★★★
No Added Sugar ★★★★
24 mg Salt ★★★★

NUTRITIONAL ANALYSIS
148 kcals/620 kJ
3.5 g Protein
3.5 g Carbohydrate
13.5 g Fat ★
1.6 g Saturated Fat ★★★
2.1 g Fibre ★★★★
No Added Sugar ★★★★
27 mg Salt ★★★★

Guacamole

A spicy Mexican dip, Guacamole makes a satisfying lunch with wholemeal bread, as well as a delicious starter.

SERVES 4
1 ripe avocado
finely grated rind and juice of 1 lime
5 ml (1 tsp) chilli sauce
2 garlic cloves, skinned
15 ml (1 tbsp) chopped fresh coriander
1 small onion, skinned and chopped
30 ml (2 tbsp) low-fat natural yogurt
pepper, to taste
1 tomato, skinned, seeded and finely chopped
lime slices and fresh coriander leaves, to garnish
celery and carrot sticks, radishes, cauliflower florets and other vegetables of your choice, and wholemeal pitta bread for dipping

1 Halve and stone the avocado. Scoop the flesh into a blender or food processor. Add all the remaining ingredients, except the chopped tomato and garnishes, and work until smooth.
2 Turn the guacamole into a bowl and stir in the chopped tomato. Cover and chill for 30 minutes.
3 Garnish the dip with lime slices and fresh coriander. Serve with the raw vegetables and pitta bread for dipping.

NUTRITIONAL ANALYSIS
115 kcals/479 kJ
7.2 g Protein
12.4 g Carbohydrate
4.4 g Fat ★★★
2.4 g Saturated Fat ★★
2.1 g Fibre ★★★★
No Added Sugar ★★★★
691 mg Salt ★

Date and Apple Dip

You can make your own flavoured low-fat soft cheese by adding mixed herbs and crushed garlic to taste. Serve the dip immediately as the apple may discolour if kept. Alternatively, make the dip, but do not add the grated apple; store in the refrigerator and add the apple just before serving.

SERVES 4
200 g (7 oz) low-fat soft cheese with garlic and herbs
30 ml (2 tbsp) skimmed milk
50 g (2 oz) dried stoned dates, finely chopped
2 celery sticks, trimmed and finely chopped
1 red eating apple, cored and grated
pepper, to taste
raw vegetables, such as carrot or courgette sticks, cauliflower florets, button mushrooms and spring onions for dipping
celery leaves, to garnish

1 Put the cheese and milk into a bowl and beat together until smooth. Mix in the dates, celery and apple. Season to taste.
2 Turn the dip into a bowl to serve, surrounded with raw vegetables. Garnish with celery leaves.

Green Bean and Walnut Dip

Accompany with a selection of raw vegetables and pitta bread. This unusual dip also makes an excellent spread or topping for hunks of bread.

SERVES 4	75 g (3 oz) walnut pieces, finely chopped
2 eggs	finely grated rind of ½ lemon
350 g (12 oz) green beans, trimmed and chopped	2.5 ml (½ tsp) grated nutmeg, or to taste
2.5 ml (½ tsp) sunflower oil	pepper, to taste
1 small onion, skinned and finely chopped	section of mixed raw vegetables and wholemeal pitta bread for dipping
30 ml (2 tbsp) low-fat natural yogurt	

1 Bring a saucepan of water to the boil. Add the eggs, return to the boil and simmer for 10-12 minutes. Drain. Place the eggs under cold running water, then remove the shell. Roughly chop the eggs, then set aside.
2 Cook the green beans in a saucepan of boiling water for about 8 minutes or until tender. Drain, then place under cold running water. Leave to cool.
3 Heat the oil in a non-stick saucepan and cook the onion for about 5 minutes until soft but not coloured.
4 Remove the onion with a slotted spoon and place in a blender or food processor with the eggs, green beans, yogurt, 50 g (2 oz) of the walnuts, the lemon rind and nutmeg. Season to taste. Blend these ingredients until well mixed.
5 Spoon the dip into individual ramekin dishes, level the surfaces and sprinkle with the remaining walnuts. Cover and chill until ready to serve.

NUTRITIONAL ANALYSIS
163 kcals/682 kJ
6.8 g Protein
4.2 g Carbohydrate
13.4 g Fat ★
2.1 g Saturated Fat ★★★
4.2 g Fibre ★★★★
No Added Sugar ★★★★
128 mg Salt ★★★★

Ceviche

This is a Mexican dish in which the acidic lime juice pickles and tenderises the fish so that it does not need cooking.

SERVES 4	30 ml (2 tbsp) chopped fresh coriander
450 g (1 lb) firm-fleshed white fish fillets, skinned and cubed	10 ml (2 tsp) dried oregano
	30 ml (2 tbsp) sunflower oil
juice of 3 lemons	1 small garlic clove, skinned and finely chopped
4 tomatoes, skinned and chopped	tabasco sauce, to taste
1 green pepper, cored, seeded and cut into thin strips	pepper, to taste
	1 avocado
½ red onion, skinned and finely chopped	sprigs of fresh oregano, to garnish

1 Put the fish in a bowl. Pour over the lemon juice, mixing well. Cover and chill for 4 hours, turning the fish occasionally.
2 Drain the fish and reserve the marinade. Mix the fish with the tomatoes, green pepper, onion, coriander and oregano.
3 Mix 10 ml (2 tsp) of the marinade with the oil, garlic, tabasco and pepper. Pour over the fish mixture.
4 To serve, skin and stone the avocado, then cut into slices. Sprinkle with a little of the marinade and arrange around the edge of a serving dish. Pile the fish mixture in the centre. Garnish with fresh oregano.

NUTRITIONAL ANALYSIS
260 kcals/1088 kJ
23.3 g Protein
5.3 g Carbohydrate
16.4 g Fat ★
2.1 g Saturated Fat ★★★★
3.5 g Fibre ★★★★
No Added Sugar ★★★★
528 mg Salt ★★★

Soused Mackerel

Fromage frais is a soft unripened cheese available from supermarkets and delicatessens. Their fat content varies so read the label to know exactly what you are buying.

NUTRITIONAL ANALYSIS
337 kcals/1408 kJ
28.6 g Protein
0.6 g Carbohydrate
24.5 g Fat ★
5.4 g Saturated Fat ★★★
0.1 g Fibre ★
No Added Sugar ★★★★
496 mg Salt ★★★

SERVES 4-6

- *4 small mackerel, each weighing about 225 g (8 oz), cleaned and boned, with heads removed*
- *150 ml (1/4 pint) malt vinegar*
- *150 ml (1/4 pint) unsweetened apple juice*
- *15 ml (1 tbsp) pickling spice*
- *finely grated rind of 1 orange*
- *pepper, to taste*
- *1 medium onion, skinned and thinly sliced*
- *100 g (4 oz) button mushrooms, sliced*
- *orange segments, to garnish*
- *low-fat fromage frais, to serve*

1 Roll up each mackerel, starting at the head end, with the skin on the outside. Lay them in an ovenproof dish.
2 Spoon over the vinegar, apple juice, pickling spice, orange rind, pepper and onion.
3 Cover and cook at 150°C (300°F) mark 2 for 1 hour or until liquid is reduced by half.
4 Add the mushrooms, cover and continue cooking for a further 30 minutes.
5 Cool, then chill thoroughly in the cooking liquid at least 6 hours.
6 Place each mackerel on a small plate. Garnish with orange segments and serve accompanied by fromage frais.

Courgettes (Zucchini) Stuffed with Mushrooms and Dates

Dates provide natural sweetness to this unusual baked starter.

NUTRITIONAL ANALYSIS
92 kcals/386 kJ
2.2 g Protein
10.9 g Carbohydrate
4.7 g Fat ★★
0.6 g Saturated Fat ★★★★
2.5 g Fibre ★★★★
No Added Sugar ★★★★
17 mg Salt ★★★★

SERVES 4

- *2 large courgettes (zucchini)*
- *5 ml (1 tsp) sunflower oil*
- *1 small onion, skinned and finely chopped*
- *100 g (4 oz) mushrooms, finely chopped*
- *50 g (2 oz) dried stoned dates, chopped*
- *25 g (1 oz) walnuts, chopped*
- *5 ml (1 tsp) tomato purée*
- *pepper, to taste*

1 Steam the courgettes (zucchini) for 10-15 minutes until just soft. Discard the seeds and scoop out the flesh, to within 0.5 cm (1/4 inch) of the skin, leaving boat shapes. Chop the flesh.
2 Heat the oil in a non-stick saucepan and gently cook the onion for about 5 minutes until soft. Stir in the mushrooms, dates, walnuts, tomato purée and chopped courgette (zucchini). Cook over a medium heat for 2-3 minutes. Season well with pepper.
3 Lay the courgette (zucchini) halves in a lightly greased ovenproof dish and fill with the mixture.
4 Bake at 200°C (400°F) mark 6 for 15-20 minutes.

Melon and Grape Salad

A refreshing starter for a hot summer day. For a more delicate effect, cut the melon into balls using a melon baller. This useful little gadget will also cut root vegetables, apples and cheese.

SERVES 4
1 very small melon, peeled, seeded and cubed
100 g (4 oz) green grapes, halved and seeded
tarragon sprigs, to garnish
FOR THE DRESSING
150 ml (¼ pint) low-fat natural yogurt
15 ml (1 tbsp) olive oil
15 ml (1 tbsp) wine vinegar
15 ml (1 tbsp) chopped fresh tarragon
pepper, to taste

NUTRITIONAL ANALYSIS
85 kcals/355 kJ
2.7 g Protein
9.9 g Carbohydrate
4.1 g Fat ★★
0.7 g Saturated Fat ★★★
1.2 g Fibre ★★★★
No Added Sugar ★★★★
117 mg Salt ★★★

1 For the dressing, mix together the yogurt, oil, vinegar and tarragon. Season to taste.
2 Mix the melon and grapes and divide between 4 long-stemmed glasses. Pour over the dressing and garnish with a few tarragon sprigs.

Stuffed Mushrooms

This recipe may be prepared up to the grilling stage several hours ahead, then left covered with plastic wrap and refrigerated. The mushrooms may then be grilled immediately prior to serving.

SERVES 4
4 thick slices wholemeal bread
4 large open brown-gilled mushrooms, stalks removed and finely chopped
50 g (2 oz) low-fat Cheddar cheese, grated
2.5 ml (½ tsp) Dijon mustard
2.5 ml (½ tsp) curry powder
5 ml (1 tsp) minced onion
30 ml (2 tbsp) low-fat natural yogurt
30 ml (2 tbsp) chopped fresh parsley, to garnish

NUTRITIONAL ANALYSIS
157 kcals/656 kJ
10.4 g Protein
21.6 g Carbohydrate
3.8 g Fat ★★★
1.5 g Saturated Fat ★★★
6.9 g Fibre ★★★★
No Added Sugar ★★★★
1020 mg Salt ★

1 Using a round pastry cutter the same size as the mushrooms, cut 4 rounds from the bread.
2 Mix together the mushroom stalks, cheese, mustard, curry powder, onion and yogurt in a bowl. Spoon the mixture into the mushroom cups.
3 Cook the mushrooms under a hot grill until the cheese bubbles and browns. Just before they are cooked, grill the bread rounds on both sides.
4 Place the toast on 4 small warmed plates and top each with a mushroom. Garnish with chopped parsley and serve immediately.

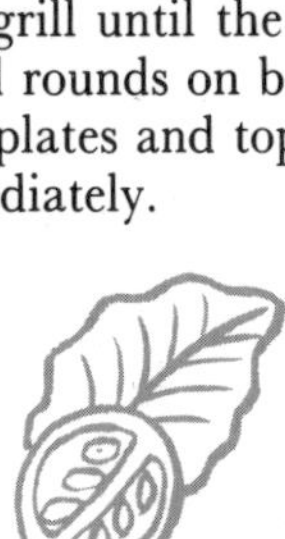

NUTRITIONAL ANALYSIS
153 kcals/638 kJ
12.2 g Protein
6.4 g Carbohydrate
8.9 g Fat ★★
1.7 g Saturated Fat ★★★
1.5 g Fibre ★★★
No Added Sugar ★★★★
303 mg Salt ★★★

Hot Chicken Liver Salad

The hot piquant chicken livers, spooned over the crisp curly endive, are quite mouthwatering. These 'hot and cold' salads must be served immediately.

SERVES 4	
½ curly endive, broken into sprigs	*225 g (8 oz) chicken livers, trimmed and cut into small pieces*
1 thick slice wholemeal bread	*large pinch of dried sage*
5 ml (1 tsp) sunflower oil	*30 ml (2 tbsp) wine vinegar*
1 shallot or small onion, skinned and finely chopped	*15 ml (1 tbsp) walnut oil*

1 Line 4 individual salad bowls with the curly endive. Toast the bread and cut into small cubes. Set aside.
2 Heat the oil in a non-stick frying pan and gently cook the shallot for about 5 minutes until soft. Add the chicken livers and sage and fry for about 5-8 minutes until just cooked through. Pour on the wine vinegar and heat.
3 Spoon the livers into the centre of the endive, garnish with the toasted croûtons and sprinkle with the walnut oil. Serve immediately.

NUTRITIONAL ANALYSIS
147 kcals/615 kJ
19.2 g Protein
8.3 g Carbohydrate
4.3 g Fat ★★★
1 g Saturated Fat ★★★★
3.4 g Fibre ★★★★
No Added Sugar ★★★★
356 mg Salt ★★

Chicken and Spinach Loaf with Carrot Orange Sauce

Serve this colourful layered chicken loaf with the carrot sauce either hot or cold. Fresh tarragon lifts the flavour of the dish.

SERVES 4	*FOR THE CARROT SAUCE*
350 g (12 oz) spinach, stalks removed and washed	*5 ml (1 tsp) sunflower oil* *225 g (8 oz) carrots, peeled and roughly chopped*
2 boned chicken breasts, skinned	*1 small onion, skinned and chopped*
30 ml (2 tbsp) chopped fresh tarragon	*juice of 1 orange*
45 ml (3 tbsp) chicken stock	*pinch of freshly grated nutmeg*
black pepper, to taste	*pepper, to taste*

1 Blanch the spinach leaves in boiling water for 10 seconds. Drain thoroughly and dry. Slice the chicken breasts horizontally.
2 Grease a non-stick 450 g (1 lb) loaf tin with polyunsaturated margarine. Line the base and sides of the tin with spinach. Reserve four leaves and roughly chop the remaining spinach.
3 Layer the chicken breasts, tarragon, pepper and chopped spinach, ending with a layer of the reserved spinach leaves. Pour over the chicken stock and cover with damp greaseproof paper. Place the loaf tin in a roasting tin half-filled with hot water. Bake at 180°C (350°F) mark 4 for 1 hour.
4 Drain off any excess liquid into a measuring jug, put weights on top of the loaf and allow to cool.
5 Pour off any liquid into the jug before turning out. Invert a serving dish over the loaf tin and then turn both the dish and the tin over together. Give both a sharp shake and remove the tin.
6 Heat the oil in a non-stick pan. Add the onion and cook for 5 minutes or until soft. Meanwhile make the liquid from the loaf up to 300 ml (½ pint) with water. Add the carrots, chicken juices, pepper and nutmeg to the pan. Bring to the boil, cover and then simmer for 30 minutes or until tender.
7 Allow to cool slightly, then purée in a blender or food processor. If the sauce seems too thick add more water. Sieve the sauce. The sauce can either be chilled and served cold or reheated and served hot.

4

Light Meals

The beauty of the light meals included here lies in their versatility. Whether you want a quick lunchtime snack, a late-night supper or even something suitable for a lunchbox, there is plenty to choose from. All of the recipes are easy to prepare and concentrate on the lightest of ingredients.

Curried Chicken Toasts

Lean chicken meat, low-fat yogurt and polyunsaturated margarine make this a healthy low-fat snack.

NUTRITIONAL ANALYSIS
290 kcals/1210 kJ
28 g Protein
21.5 g Carbohydrate
10.8 g Fat ★★★
2.5 g Saturated Fat ★★★
4.2 g Fibre ★★★★
No Added Sugar ★★★★
922 mg Salt ★

MAKES 4

60 ml (4 tbsp) low-fat natural yogurt
10 ml (2 tsp) curry paste
350 g (12 oz) cold cooked chicken meat, shredded
pepper, to taste
4 slices granary bread
15 g (1/2 oz) low-fat spread
4 large lettuce leaves
25 g (1 oz) flaked almonds, toasted
pinch of paprika
few cucumber slices

1 Mix together the yogurt, curry paste and chicken in a bowl. Season to taste.
2 Toast the bread, then spread with the low-fat spread. Top each slice with a lettuce leaf.
3 Spoon some of the chicken mixture over each slice of toast. Sprinkle with flaked almonds and paprika. Arrange a few cucumber slices on top.

Chicken and Chicory Sandwiches

Low-fat cottage cheese and yogurt and lean chicken lower the fat content of these tasty layered sandwiches. Wholemeal bread increases the fibre.

NUTRITIONAL ANALYSIS
423 kcals/1767 kJ
32 g Protein
52.7 g Carbohydrate
10.8 g Fat ★★★
2.9 g Saturated Fat ★★★★
11.3 g Fibre ★★★★
No Added Sugar ★★★★
2477 mg Salt ★

MAKES 4

12 slices wholemeal bread
40 g (1 1/2 oz) low-fat spread
60 ml (4 tbsp) low-fat natural yogurt
30 ml (2 tbsp) chopped fresh parsley
pepper, to taste
225 g (8 oz) cooked chicken, shredded
1 head chicory, finely shredded
175 g (6 oz) low-fat cottage cheese
1 small red pepper, cored, seeded and diced
15 ml (1 tbsp) snipped fresh chives
lettuce leaves

1 Spread each slice of bread on one side only with low-fat spread. Mix together the yogurt and parsley in a bowl. Season to taste, then mix in the chicken and chicory. Mix the cottage cheese with the red pepper and chives.
2 Spread 4 of the slices of bread with the chicken and chicory mixture. Line 4 slices with a lettuce leaf, then spread with the cottage cheese mixture.
3 Stack in pairs, sitting a cottage cheese topped slice on top of a chicken one. Place the remaining slices of bread on top, low-fat spread side down. Cut in quarters and serve.

Moules à la Marinière (PAGE 59)

Pizza Chilli

Italian pizzas are traditionally made with white flour but they are equally delicious and more nutritious made with wholemeal flour.

SERVES 4	1 small onion, skinned and finely chopped
FOR THE BASE	1 garlic clove, skinned and very finely chopped (optional)
225 g (8 oz) wholemeal or plain flour	200 g (7 oz) can tomatoes with their juice, chopped
pinch of salt	15 ml (1 tbsp) tomato purée
5 ml (1 tsp) easy mix dried yeast	2.5 ml (½ tsp) dried or fresh basil
50 ml (2 fl oz) boiling water	pepper, to taste
150 ml (¼ pint) cold water	chilli flakes, to taste
FOR THE TOPPING	3 black olives, stoned and chopped
5 ml (1 tsp) sunflower oil	100 g (4 oz) Mozzarella cheese, very thinly sliced

NUTRITIONAL ANALYSIS
277 kcals/1156 kJ
13.7 g Protein
40.2 g Carbohydrate
7.8 g Fat ★★★
3.8 g Saturated Fat ★★★
6.4 g Fibre ★★★★
No Added Sugar ★★★★
537 mg Salt ★★★

1 For the base, combine the flour, salt and yeast in a bowl. Mix the hot and cold water together and stir sufficient into the flour mixture to make a soft dry dough.
2 Turn the dough on to a lightly floured work surface and knead for 5 minutes. Place in a lightly oiled bowl, cover with polythene and leave to rise in a warm place until doubled in size.
3 Meanwhile for the filling, heat the oil in a non-stick saucepan and gently cook the onion for about 5 minutes until soft. Add the garlic, if using, tomatoes and tomato purée and simmer gently for about 10 minutes or until thick. Cool.
4 When the dough has risen, lightly grease 2 baking sheets. Knead the dough until smooth and divide in half. Roll out each piece into a 23 cm (9 inch) round and transfer to a baking sheet. Cover again with polythene and leave in a warm place to prove for 20-30 minutes until the bases are well risen and puffy.
5 Spread the tomato sauce over the pizza bases, leaving a 1 cm (½ inch) border around the edges. Sprinkle with basil, pepper, chilli flakes, black olives and Mozzarella.
6 Bake at 230°C (450°F) mark 8 for 10-15 minutes or until the top is bubbling and the base looks cooked. Serve piping hot.

Grilled Herring Roe on Toast

The most common soft roe comes from the herring but soft cod's roe is also available and could be used in this recipe. Soft roes can be bought separately but if you buy a large fish with a thick roe attached, it is better to remove the roe and cook it separately.

SERVES 4	pepper, to taste
350 g (12 oz) soft herring roe	25 g (1 oz) polyunsaturated margarine or low-fat spread, melted
finely grated rind and juice of ½ lemon	4 thin slices wholemeal bread
30 ml (2 tbsp) chopped fresh parsley	lemon wedges, to garnish

NUTRITIONAL ANALYSIS
151 kcals/631 kJ
14.3 g Protein
11 g Carbohydrate
5.9 g Fat ★★
0.8 g Saturated Fat ★★★★
3.3 g Fibre ★★★★
No Added Sugar ★★★★
460 mg Salt ★★★

1 Put the herring roe into a shallow flameproof dish and sprinkle over the lemon rind and juice and 15 ml (1 tbsp) of the parsley. Season to taste. Cover and chill for 30 minutes, turning gently once or twice.
2 Brush the roe with the margarine. Grill under a moderate heat for 4-5 minutes, carefully turning once.
3 Toast the bread on both sides. Place on warmed serving plates and spoon the hot roe and cooking juices on top. Serve garnished with lemon wedges and the remaining chopped parsley.

Piquant Chicken (PAGE 68)

NUTRITIONAL ANALYSIS
211 kcals/882 kJ
12 g Protein
18.7 g Carbohydrate
10.3 g Fat ★★
2.1 g Saturated Fat ★★★
3.1 g Fibre ★★★★
No Added Sugar ★★★★
886 mg Salt ★

Carrot Quiches

Low-fat quark is used here to add a creamy cheese taste to these quiches.

SERVES 4	15 ml (1 tbsp) dried oregano
100 g (4 oz) carrots, scrubbed and finely diced, with a few thin slices reserved	*pepper, to taste*
200 g (7 oz) low-fat quark	FOR THE WHOLEMEAL PASTRY
1 egg, beaten	*100 g (4 oz) wholemeal flour*
5 ml (1 tsp) ground mace	*40 g (1½ oz) polyunsaturated margarine*

1 For the pastry, put the flour and salt into a bowl. Rub in the margarine until the mixture resembles fine breadcrumbs. Gradually add 25 ml (1½ tbsp) cold water and mixed to form a smooth dough.

2. Divided the dough into 4 equal pieces. Roll out each on a lightly floured work surface and use to line 4 individual quiche moulds or Yorkshire pudding tins. Cover and chill for 25 minutes.

3. Cook the carrot in a saucepan of boiling water for 5 minutes or until just tender. Drain well. Reserve the carrot slices for garnish.

4. Put the diced carrots, quark, egg, mace, 10 ml (2 tsp) of the oregano in a bowl and mix well. Season to taste. Divide the mixture between the pastry-lined tins and lightly sprinkle with the remaining dried oregano.

5. Bake at 200°C (400°F) mark 6 for 10-15 minutes or until risen and set. Serve hot, garnished with the reserved carrot slices.

NUTRITIONAL ANALYSIS
246 kcals/1026 kJ
8.5 g Protein
37.3 g Carbohydrate
8 g Fat ★★★
2.3 g Saturated Fat ★★★
4.2 g Fibre ★★★★
No Added Sugar ★★★★
603 mg Salt ★★

Onion Tart

This low-fat, yeasted pastry can be made with all wholemeal flour, white flour or, as below, a mixture of the two.

SERVES 4	*50 ml (3-4 tbsp) skimmed milk, warmed*
FOR THE PASTRY	FOR THE FILLING
50 g (2 oz) plain unbleached flour	*700 g (1½ lb) onions, skinned and finely sliced*
50 g (2 oz) wholemeal flour	*60 ml (4 tbsp) skimmed milk*
5 ml (1 tsp) easy mix dried yeast	*large pinch of dried thyme*
pinch of salt	*pepper, to taste*
25 g (1 oz) polyunsaturated margarine	*25 g (1 oz) very strong Cheddar cheese, grated*

1 For the pastry, mix the flour, yeast and salt in a bowl. Rub in the margarine until the mixture resembles fine breadcrumbs. Gradually add enough milk to make a soft dry dough. Knead until smooth.

2 Grease a 25.5 cm (10 inch) flan tin. Roll out the dough on an unfloured work surface and use to line the flan tin. Cover with greased polythene and leave in a warm place while preparing the filling.

3 For the filling, put the onions into a saucepan and add 150 ml (¼ pint) water. Bring to the boil, cover and simmer gently for 25-35 minutes or until the onions are soft. Drain. Mix in the milk and thyme. Season to taste.

4 Remove the polythene and cover the base of the flan with crumpled greaseproof paper, weighed down with dried beans. Bake at 200°C (400°F) mark 6 for 10 minutes. Remove the paper and beans and bake for a further 5 minutes.

5 Fill the flan with the onion mixture and sprinkle over the cheese. Bake for 15-20 minutes or until browned. Serve hot or warm.

Summer Vegetable Flan

The usual quantity of fat used in pastry-making is halved in this crisp, light, yeasted pastry. The secret is to roll out the dough very thinly as the yeast will raise and thicken it.

SERVES 4-6

FOR THE PASTRY

50 g (2 oz) plain unbleached flour

50 g (2 oz) wholemeal flour

5 ml (1 tsp) easy mix dried yeast

pinch of salt

25 g (1 oz) polyunsaturated margarine

45-60 ml (3-4 tbsp) skimmed milk, warmed

FOR THE FILLING

15 g (1/2 oz) polyunsaturated margarine

25 g (1 oz) wholemeal flour

300 ml (1/2 pint) skimmed milk

pepper, to taste

10 ml (2 tsp) sunflower oil

1 large onion, skinned and thinly sliced

225 g (8 oz) courgettes (zucchini), trimmed and thinly sliced

100 g (4 oz) button mushrooms

225 g (8 oz) runner beans, trimmed and thinly sliced

1.25 ml (1/4 tsp) dried rosemary, oregano or mixed herbs

4 tomatoes, skinned and quartered

50 g (2 oz) walnuts, chopped

NUTRITIONAL ANALYSIS
340 kcals/1419 kJ
11.6 g Protein
34.8 g Carbohydrate
18.1 g Fat ★★
2.6 g Saturated Fat ★★★★
7.3 g Fibre ★★★★
No Added Sugar ★★★★
598 mg Salt ★★★

1 For the pastry, mix the flour, yeast and salt in a bowl. Rub in the margarine until the mixture resembles fine breadcrumbs. Gradually add enough milk to make a soft dry dough. Knead until smooth.

2 Grease a 25.5 cm (10 inch) flan ring. Roll out the dough on an unfloured work surface and use to line the flan ring. Cover with greased polythene and leave in a warm place while preparing the filling.

3 For the filling, put margarine, flour and milk into a saucepan. Heat, whisking continuously, until the sauce thickens, boils and is smooth. Simmer for 1-2 minutes. Season to taste, leave to cool.

4 Heat the oil in a non-stick saucepan and cook the onion and courgettes (zucchini) for about 8 minutes or until just cooked. Remove with a slotted spoon. Leave to cool. Cook the mushrooms in the remaining liquid for 3-4 minutes. Put the beans in a pan containing the minimum of boiling water and cook for about 5 minutes, then drain.

5 Remove the polythene and cover the base of the flan with crumpled greaseproof paper, weighed down with dried beans. Bake blind at 200°C (400°F) mark 6 for 10 minutes. Remove the paper and beans and bake for a further 5 minutes.

6 Arrange the onion, beans and courgettes (zucchini) over the base of the flan, sprinkle with the herbs and spoon over the sauce. Arrange the tomatoes, cut side down, in a circle around the flan. Fill the centre with the whole mushrooms.

7 Bake for 20 minutes. Sprinkle with the chopped nuts and bake for a further 5 minutes. Serve hot.

NUTRITIONAL ANALYSIS
193 kcals/806 kJ
14.3 g Protein
16.5 g Carbohydrate
8.2 g Fat ★★
2.4 g Saturated Fat ★★★
4.7 g Fibre ★★★★
No Added Sugar ★★★★
568 mg Salt ★★

Vegetable Lasagne

Prepare this quick and easy dish in advance and then cook either later that day or the next day.

SERVES 4

15 ml (1 tbsp) sunflower oil
1 small onion, skinned and chopped
1 carrot, scrubbed and chopped
1 small green pepper, cored, seeded and chopped
1 garlic clove, skinned and chopped
350 g (12 oz) mushrooms, chopped
400 g (14 oz) can tomatoes
30 ml (2 tbsp) tomato purée
5 ml (1 tsp) chopped fresh basil or 2.5 ml (½ tsp) dried
5 ml (1 tsp) chopped fresh oregano or 2.5 ml (½ tsp) dried
pepper, to taste
225 g (8 oz) courgettes, trimmed and thinly sliced diagonally
175 g (6 oz) fresh spinach (or wholemeal) lasagne
1 egg
300 ml (½ pint) natural low-fat yogurt
15 ml (1 tbsp) freshly grated Parmesan cheese

1 Heat the oil in a saucepan. Add the onion, carrot, green pepper and garlic. Gently fry for 5 minutes. Add the mushrooms and cook for a further 5 minutes. Add the tomatoes and their juice, tomato purée, herbs and seasoning. Bring to the boil, then gently simmer for about 20 minutes, until the sauce has thickened, stirring occasionally.
2 Cook the courgettes for about 3 minutes in a little boiling water. Drain well to remove excess moisture.
3 Cook the lasagne sheets in boiling water for 3-4 minutes or until just tender. Drain and set aside on a clean cloth in a single layer.
4 Pour half the tomato sauce into the base of an ovenproof dish. Top with half the courgettes, then arrange half the lasagne on top. Repeat the layers.
5 Beat together the egg, yogurt and cheese and spoon over the lasagne. Cook at 190°C (375°F) mark 5 for 30-40 minutes, until golden. Serve hot.

NUTRITIONAL ANALYSIS
385 kcals/1611 kJ
27.1 g Protein
53.5 g Carbohydrate
7.5 g Fat ★★★
1.3 g Saturated Fat ★★★★
9.1 g Fibre ★★★★
0.1 g Added Sugar ★★★★
1411 mg Salt ★

Singapore Noodles

Root ginger provides a piquancy to this high fibre dish from the East. If you are unable to find root ginger substitute 5 ml (1 tsp) lemon juice instead.

SERVES 4

275 g (10 oz) wholemeal spaghetti
10 ml (2 tsp) sunflower oil
1 large onion, skinned and chopped
2.5 cm (1 inch) piece of root ginger, peeled and finely chopped
2 large garlic cloves, skinned and crushed
15 ml (1 tbsp) curry powder
45 ml (3 tbsp) chicken stock
30 ml (2 tbsp) dry sherry
15 ml (1 tbsp) tomato purée
15 ml (1 tbsp) soy sauce
125 g (4 oz) mushrooms
125 g (4 oz) beansprouts
125 g (4 oz) prawns
125 g (4 oz) cooked chicken, cut into 2.5 cm (1 inch) pieces
3 spring onions, trimmed and finely chopped

1 Cook the spaghetti in boiling water for 10 minutes. Drain and rinse with cold water.
2 Heat the oil in a wok, add the onion and ginger and stir-fry for 2 minutes. Add the garlic and curry powder and stir-fry for a further minute.
3 Add the chicken stock, dry sherry, tomato purée, soy sauce, mushrooms and beansprouts and cook for 4 minutes, stirring frequently.
4 Add the spaghetti, chicken and prawns and cook for 5 minutes. Garnish with spring onions.

Pasta with Feta and Cauliflower Salad

Greek feta cheese is traditionally made from sheep or goat's milk. It is curdled naturally without the addition of rennet.

SERVES 4
½ medium cauliflower, broken into florets
handful of fresh mint
100 g (4 oz) wholemeal pasta twists or shells
50 g (2 oz) feta cheese
FOR THE DRESSING
30 ml (2 tbsp) lemon juice
10 ml (2 tsp) olive oil
pepper, to taste

1 Steam the cauliflower with a couple of sprigs of mint for about 8 minutes or until tender. Drain and put into a bowl.
2 Put the pasta into a saucepan of boiling water and cook for 12 minutes or until tender. Drain and add to the cauliflower. Crumble the feta over the cauliflower and pasta. Chop a few sprigs of fresh mint and add to the salad.
3 For the dressing, mix together the lemon juice, oil and a generous amount of pepper and pour over the salad.

NUTRITIONAL ANALYSIS
170 kcals/709 kJ
8 g Protein
22.6 g Carbohydrate
5.9 g Fat ★★★
3.2 g Saturated Fat ★★
5.1 g Fibre ★★★★
No Added Sugar ★★★★
424 mg Salt ★★

Neapolitan Tortelloni

For best results, use the fresh pasta available at most large supermarkets with your own home-made sauce. Tortelloni are half-moon shaped pasta with fluted edges; in this recipe they are filled with spinach.

SERVES 4
10 ml (2 tsp) sunflower oil
2 garlic cloves, skinned and finely chopped
225 ml (8 fl oz) passata or other sieved tomatoes
2.5 ml (½ tsp) dried or fresh oregano
pepper, to taste
500 g (18 oz) fresh spinach tortelloni
15 g (½ oz) Parmesan cheese, freshly grated

1 Heat the oil in a large non-stick saucepan and gently cook the garlic until beginning to change colour. Add the tomatoes and oregano. Season to taste. Bring to the boil, turn off the heat and cover. Keep warm while cooking the pasta.
2 Cook the tortelloni according to packet directions. Drain well.
3 Divide the tortelloni between 4 soup plates, pour over the sauce and sprinkle with the Parmesan cheese.

NUTRITIONAL ANALYSIS
222 kcals/927 kJ
9.6 g Protein
27.8 g Carbohydrate
8.8 g Fat ★★
1.3 g Saturated Fat ★★★★
8 g Fibre ★★★★
No Added Sugar ★★★★
400 mg Salt ★★★

NUTRITIONAL ANALYSIS
305 kcals/1276 kJ
15.7 g Protein
37.2 g Carbohydrate
11.4 g Fat ★★★
2.2 g Saturated Fat ★★★★
2.9 g Fibre ★★★
No Added Sugar ★★★★
1974 mg Salt ★

Kedgeree

Before refrigeration and fast transport, fish was heavily smoked to preserve it. Today, fish is usually only lightly smoked to create flavour rather than to improve its keeping qualities.

SERVES 4	100 g (4 oz) smoked fish
25 g (1 oz) polyunsaturated margarine	*100 g (4 oz) firm-fleshed white fish*
1 small onion, skinned and finely chopped	*1 egg, hard-boiled and chopped*
7.5 ml (1½ tsp) medium curry powder	*30 ml (2 tbsp) chopped fresh parsley*
175 g (6 oz) brown rice	*pepper, to taste*
600 ml (1 pint) fish stock or water	*finely grated rind of ½ lemon*

1 Melt 15 g (½ oz) of the margarine in a large non-stick saucepan and cook the onion for 3 minutes. Add the curry powder and cook for 1 minute.
2 Add the rice with the stock. Cover and simmer gently for about 30 minutes or until the rice is just tender and the liquid absorbed.
3 Meanwhile, place the fish in a large frying pan with just enough water to cover. Simmer for 10-15 minutes or until tender. Drain, flake and discard all the bones.
4 When the rice is cooked, add the fish, egg, remaining margarine and 15 ml (1 tbsp) of the parsley. Season to taste. Stir gently until heated through.
5 Spoon into a warmed serving dish and sprinkle with the remaining chopped parsley and the grated lemon rind. Serve immediately.

NUTRITIONAL ANALYSIS
484 kcals/2022 kJ
28.8 g Protein
50.8 g Carbohydrate
19.8 g Fat ★★
4 g Saturated Fat ★★★★
6 g Fibre ★★★★
No Added Sugar ★★★★
308 mg Salt ★★★★

Chicken Liver Risotto

This is a rich and nutritious dish that needs only a simple green salad as an accompaniment.

SERVES 4	225 g (8 oz) brown rice
15 ml (1 tbsp) sunflower oil	*2.5 ml (½ tsp) ground turmeric*
450 g (1 lb) chicken livers, trimmed and roughly chopped	*5 ml (1 tsp) fresh oregano or marjoram or 2.5 ml (½ tsp) dried oregano*
1 medium onion, skinned and chopped	*pepper, to taste*
1 small green pepper, cored, seeded and diced	*900 ml (1½ pints) chicken stock*
1 garlic clove, skinned and crushed	*225 g (8 oz) broccoli, cut into florets*
100 g (4 oz) mushrooms, sliced	*25 g (1 oz) walnut halves, roughly chopped*

1 Heat 10 ml (2 tsp) of the oil in a non-stick saucepan and cook the livers over a moderate heat for about 5 minutes or until lightly brown. Remove from the pan with a slotted spoon.
2 Add the remaining oil to the pan, then add the onion, green pepper and garlic and cook for about 3 minutes. Add the mushrooms and cook for a further 2 minutes or until the onion is soft. Add the rice and stir until it glistens, then add the tumeric and oregano. Season to taste.
3 Gradually add the stock, about 150 ml (¼ pint) at a time. Continue cooking, adding more stock as it is absorbed. Cook gently, uncovered, for 30-35 minutes, stirring frequently. Stir in the chicken livers and cook for a further 10 minutes or until the rice is tender.
4 Meanwhile, put the broccoli in a pan containing a little boiling water and cook for 10 minutes until just tender. Drain. Lightly stir the broccoli and walnuts into the risotto and serve hot.

Aubergine and Cheese Pilaf

Cracked wheat consists of wholewheat grains broken or ground into coarse pieces. Since the cracked wheat does not need precooking, this is a quick dish to prepare.

SERVES 4	
700 g (1½ lb) aubergines, cubed	*225 g (8 oz) cracked wheat, washed and drained thoroughly*
salt	*pepper, to taste*
5 ml (1 tsp) sunflower oil	*100 g (4 oz) Mozzarella cheese, cut into tiny cubes*
1 medium onion, skinned and finely chopped	*small bunch of spring onions, trimmed and finely chopped*
2.5 ml (½ tsp) ground cumin	*60 ml (4 tbsp) chopped fresh parsley*
5 ml (1 tsp) ground coriander	*2.5 ml (½ tsp) paprika*

1 Put the aubergine cubes into a colander, sprinkle with salt and allow to drain for 30 minutes. Rinse off the salt and dry with absorbent kitchen paper.
2 Heat the oil in a non-stick frying pan and gently cook the onion, covered, for 5-10 minutes, until beginning to brown.
3 Add the aubergines to the pan, cover and cook gently for 5 minutes. Stir in the cumin, coriander and cracked wheat and cook for 1-2 minutes, turning from time to time.
4 Add 400 ml (14 fl oz) water, bring to the boil, cover and simmer very slowly for 7-10 minutes or until all the water is absorbed. Stir in the cheese, spring onions and parsley. Season to taste then sprinkle with paprika. Serve immediately.

NUTRITIONAL ANALYSIS
316 kcals/1322 kJ
13.2 g Protein
52.2 g Carbohydrate
7.6 g Fat ★★★
3.8 g Saturated Fat ★★★
7.3 g Fibre ★★★★
0.1 g Added Sugar ★★★★
308 mg Salt ★★★★

Refried Beans in Taco Shells

The shells needed for this classic Mexican dish may be found on the delicatessen shelves at most supermarkets. Serve with bought taco sauce or chutney, if liked.

SERVES 6
50 g (2 oz) lean bacon, diced
5 ml (1 tsp) sunflower oil
1 large onion, skinned and chopped
1 garlic clove, skinned and crushed
two 400 g (14 oz) cans red chilli beans
6 taco shells
few lettuce leaves
few cucumber slices

1 Fry the bacon in a non-stick frying pan until crisp. Drain on absorbent kitchen paper.
2 Add the oil to the pan and gently cook the onion and garlic, covered, for 5-8 minutes until beginning to brown.
3 Purée all but 30 ml (2 tbsp) of the beans in a food processor or blender, or mash them with a potato masher.
4 Add the puréed and whole beans to the pan with the bacon and cook over a medium heat for 5-10 minutes or until a very thick paste.
5 Divide the bean mixture between the taco shells and top with lettuce and cucumber.

NUTRITIONAL ANALYSIS
149 kcals/622 kJ
9.7 g Protein
20.7 g Carbohydrate
3.5 g Fat ★★★
0.7 g Saturated Fat ★★★★
10.7 g Fibre ★★★★
4.5 g Added Sugar ★★
2067 mg Salt ★

NUTRITIONAL ANALYSIS
303 kcals/1266 kJ
19.6 g Protein
50.1 g Carbohydrate
4.1 g Fat ★★★★
0.7 g Saturated Fat ★★★★
22.6 g Fibre ★★★★
No Added Sugar ★★★★
416 mg Salt ★★★

Pot of Butter Beans

This Greek-style dish is excellent served with wholemeal bread.

SERVES 4	*5 ml (1 tsp) dried oregano*
350 g (12 oz) dried butter beans, soaked overnight	*5 ml (1 tsp) savory*
	1 bay leaf
1 large carrot, scrubbed and finely chopped	*15 ml (1 tbsp) tomato purée*
1 large onion, skinned and finely chopped	*1 garlic clove, skinned and crushed*
1 celery stick, trimmed and finely chopped	*60 ml (4 tbsp) chopped fresh parsley*
	15 ml (1 tbsp) polyunsaturated margarine
400 g (14 oz) can tomatoes, chopped	*pepper, to taste*

1 Drain the beans and rinse. Put into a saucepan with the carrot, onion, celery, tomatoes with their juice, oregano, savory and bay leaf. Add just enough fresh water to cover the beans. Bring to the boil, cover and simmer for 1½-2 hours or until the beans are almost soft.
2 Stir in the tomato purée, garlic, 30 ml (2 tbsp) of the parsley and the margarine. Season to taste. Cover and continue to simmer for 10-20 minutes or until the beans are tender but not beginning to disintegrate.
3 Increase the heat, uncover and boil fast to thicken the sauce. There should be sufficient thick sauce to coat the beans liberally. Sprinkle with the remaining parsley. Serve with a green salad and granary bread.

NUTRITIONAL ANALYSIS
131 kcals/548 kJ
6.9 g Protein
11.8 g Carbohydrate
6.7 g Fat ★★
1 g Saturated Fat ★★★★
5.2 g Fibre ★★★★
No Added Sugar ★★★★
239 mg Salt ★★★

Curried Tofu and Vegetables

Tofu is an excellent source of low-fat protein. In a dish, it provides an interesting texture, but as it has a slightly bland taste it has to be prepared with a tasty sauce.

SERVES 4	*juice of 1 lemon*
15 ml (1 tbsp) sunflower oil	*2 carrots, scrubbed and diced*
1 large onion, skinned and chopped	*100 g (4 oz) cauliflower, divided into florets*
2 garlic cloves, skinned and crushed	*2 courgettes (zucchini), trimmed and diced*
10 ml (2 tsp) freshly ground coriander	*4 tomatoes, chopped*
10 ml (2 tsp) fresh ground cumin	*100 g (4 oz) French beans, trimmed and cut into 2.5 cm (1 inch) pieces*
5 ml (1 tsp) ground turmeric	
5 ml (1 tsp) ground ginger	*175 g (6 oz) firm tofu, cut into 1 cm (½ inch) cubes*
5-10 ml (1-2 tsp) chilli powder	
5 ml (1 tsp) freshly ground fenugreek	*30 ml (2 tbsp) low-fat natural yogurt*
300 ml (½ pint) vegetable stock	*chopped fresh coriander, to garnish*

1 Heat the oil in a large non-stick saucepan and cook the onion and garlic for 3 minutes until soft. Add the spices and continue to cook for a further 5 minutes, stirring occasionally.
2 Stir in the stock and lemon juice with the carrots, cauliflower and courgettes (zucchini). Bring to the boil, cover and simmer for 10 minutes. Add the tomatoes and beans and cook for a further 5 minutes.
3 Add the tofu and continue cooking for 5 minutes. Stir in the yogurt and heat through, without boiling. Garnish with coriander and serve hot.

Piperade

Besides being a nutritious, egg-based snack, this traditional Basque dish is colourful and easy to prepare. The basil provides a warm, pungent fragrance.

SERVES 4	
15 ml (1 tbsp) sunflower oil	pepper, to taste
1 medium onion, skinned and finely chopped	5 ml (1 tsp) chopped fresh basil or 2.5 ml (½ tsp) dried
1 garlic clove, skinned and crushed	4 eggs, beaten
1 small green pepper, cored, seeded and cut into thin strips	175 g (6 oz) tomatoes, cut into wedges
1 small red pepper, cored, seeded and cut into thin strips	basil leaves, to garnish

1 Heat the oil in a non-stick frying pan and cook the onion, garlic and green and red peppers for 5 minutes.
2 Add the pepper, basil and 15 ml (1 tbsp) water to the eggs and pour into the pan. Stir lightly, then leave to cook for 3 minutes.
3 Add the tomatoes, stir again and gently shake the pan from side to side, allowing the uncooked mixture to flow underneath the cooked egg mixture. Cook for 3-5 minutes or until the eggs are set. Cut into quarters, garnish with basil leaves and serve immediately.

NUTRITIONAL ANALYSIS
138 kcals/575 kJ
7.9 g Protein
4.3 g Carbohydrate
10 g Fat ★
2.5 g Saturated Fat ★★
1.5 g Fibre ★★★
No Added Sugar ★★★★
210 mg Salt ★★★

Savoury Nut Pancakes

The nuts, wholemeal flour and vegetables make these pancakes relatively high in fibre.

SERVES 8	FOR THE NUT FILLING
50 g (2 oz) wholemeal flour	100 g (4 oz) low-fat cottage cheese
50 g (2 oz) plain flour	50 g (2 oz) unsalted cashew nuts, chopped
1 egg, beaten	50 g (2 oz) unsalted Brazil nuts, chopped
300 ml (½ pint) skimmed milk	1 small red pepper, cored, seeded and finely chopped
15-30 ml (1-2 tbsp) sunflower oil	1 bunch spring onions, cut into 2.5 cm (1 inch) pieces
snipped fresh chives, to garnish	15 ml (1 tbsp) snipped fresh chives
	30 ml (2 tbsp) low-fat natural yogurt

1 Put the flours into a bowl and make a well in the centre. Add the egg and 150 ml (¼ pint) of the milk and gradually mix in the flour from the sides of the bowl, whisking until smooth. Slowly whisk in the remaining milk.
2 Heat 5 ml (1 tsp) of the oil in a 20 cm (8 inch) non-stick frying pan and pour in 45 ml (3 tbsp) of the batter. Tilt the pan so that the batter flows evenly over the base. Cook over a medium heat for 2 minutes or until golden brown. Toss or turn the pancake and cook for a further 2 minutes. Place on a plate, cover with foil and put in the oven at 170°C (325°F) mark 3 to keep hot while cooking the remaining pancakes.
3 For the filling, put all the ingredients into a small saucepan and heat through gently, stirring occasionally, until piping hot.
4 To serve, place 15-30 ml (1-2 tbsp) of the filling on each pancake, roll up and serve at once, garnished with chives.

NUTRITIONAL ANALYSIS
175 kcals/730 kJ
7.6 g Protein
14.6 g Carbohydrate
9.9 g Fat ★★
1.9 g Saturated Fat ★★★
2.2 g Fibre ★★★★
0.2 g Added Sugar ★★★★
235 mg Salt ★★★

NUTRITIONAL ANALYSIS
174 kcals/729 kJ
30.4 g Protein
4.1 g Carbohydrate
3.3 g Fat ★★★★
1 g Saturated Fat ★★★★
1.1 g Fibre ★★
No Added Sugar ★★★★
1492 mg Salt ★

Fish and Prawn Terrine

This dish can be made in advance and stored, covered, in the refrigerator.

SERVES 4	
450 g (1 lb) firm-fleshed white fillet, skinned	*100 g (4 oz) peeled cooked prawns, thawed if frozen, chopped*
60 ml (4 tbsp) chopped fresh dill or 30 ml (2 tbsp) dried	*1 small bunch watercress, finely chopped*
50 ml (2 fl oz) dry white wine	*4 tomatoes, skinned, seeded and finely chopped*
1 egg white, size 2	*1 garlic clove, skinned and crushed*
pepper, to taste	*150 ml (¼ pint) low-fat natural yogurt*
	unpeeled cooked prawns, to garnish

1 Purée the fish, dill, wine, egg white and seasoning in a blender or food processor until smooth. Mix the prawns and watercress together in a bowl.
2 Spread half the fish purée in the base of a lightly oiled 450 g (1 lb) loaf tin. Sprinkle over the prawns and watercress, then spread the remaining purée over the top. Smooth with a knife, then cover with foil.
3 Put the loaf tin in a roasting tin with enough boiling water to come half way up the side. Cook at 200°C (400°F) mark 6 for 45 minutes or until firm. Drain off any liquid, then leave to cool for 1 hour.
4 Meanwhile, make the tomato sauce. Put the tomatoes and garlic in a small saucepan and simmer for 10 minutes, stirring occasionally. Mix in the yogurt and season to taste. Leave the sauce to cool.
5 Turn out the terrine on to a serving dish and garnish with the unpeeled cooked prawns. Cut the terrine into slices and serve with the tomato sauce.

NUTRITIONAL ANALYSIS
288 kcals/1204 kJ
23.4 g Protein
36.6 g Carbohydrate
6.5 g Fat ★★★
2.1 g Saturated Fat ★★★★
3.8 g Fibre ★★
No Added Sugar ★★★★
1276 mg Salt ★

Seafood Gratin

This versatile dish may be served with piped potatoes in individual gratin dishes or as a starter in ramekins.

SERVES 4	*15 g (½ oz) polyunsaturated margarine*
450 g (1 lb) potatoes, peeled	*35 g (1¼ oz) plain flour*
45 ml (3 tbsp) skimmed milk	*pepper, to taste*
300 ml (½ pint) skimmed milk	*225 g (8 oz) firm-fleshed white fish, skinned*
1 slice onion	*juice of ½ lemon*
1 slice carrot	*75 g (3 oz) peeled prawns*
6 peppercorns	*50 g (2 oz) button mushrooms, finely sliced*
1.25 ml (¼ tsp) ground mace	*30 ml (2 tbsp) freshly grated Parmesan cheese*

1 For the gratin, put the potatoes in a saucepan of water and cook for about 20 minutes. Drain and mash them very thoroughly with the 45 ml (3 tbsp) milk. Lightly grease 4 individual gratin dishes and pipe or spoon the potato around the edge. Set aside.
2 For the ramekins, lightly grease six 100 ml (4 fl oz) ramekins.
3 Put the 300 ml (½ pint) milk, the onion, carrot, peppercorns and mace in a saucepan and heat through until almost boiling. Allow the milk to cool, then strain into a pan. Add the margarine and flour. Heat, whisking continuously, until the sauce thickens, boils and is smooth. Simmer for 1-2 minutes. Season liberally with pepper and add a little salt if required.
4 Cut the fish into thin strips, divide between the dishes and pour over the lemon juice. Arrange the prawns and mushrooms over the fish. Pour over the sauce and sprinkle with Parmesan cheese.
5 Bake at 180°C (350°F) mark 4 for 20-25 minutes or until golden.

Salmon Ring with Cucumber and Dill Sauce

With a flavour similar to caraway, dill has pretty feathery green leaves. These leaves dry well and are known as dill weed.

SERVES 4	50 g (2 oz) fresh wholemeal breadcrumbs
220 g (7¾ oz) can salmon, skinned and boned, liquid reserved	pepper, to taste
	sliced cucumber and dill leaves, to garnish
150 ml (¼ pint) low-fat natural yogurt	FOR THE SAUCE
15 ml (1 tbsp) tomato purée	½ medium cucumber
5 ml (1 tsp) Dijon mustard	2.5 ml (½ tsp) salt
10 ml (2 tsp) lemon juice	150 ml (¼ pint) low-fat natural yogurt
1 egg	30 ml (2 tbsp) chopped fresh dill

1 Flake the salmon. Beat the yogurt, tomato purée, mustard, lemon juice, reserved salmon liquid and egg together. Stir in the flaked salmon and breadcrumbs. Season to taste. Firmly pack the mixture into a lightly greased 600 ml (1 pint) ovenproof ring mould. Cover with foil.
2 Place the mould into a baking tin and pour in warm water to come halfway up the mould. Bake at 180°C (350°F) mark 4 for 45 minutes – 1 hour or until the mixture feels firm when pressed lightly with a finger. Leave to cool then chill.
3 For the sauce, work the cucumber in a food processor until finely chopped. Put into a sieve, sprinkle with the salt and allow to drain for 30 minutes.
4 Rinse the cucumber well under running cold water and squeeze out all the excess liquid. Transfer to a bowl and stir in the yogurt, dill and pepper to taste. Chill.
5 Unmould the salmon ring on to a serving plate, spoon the sauce into the centre and garnish with sliced cucumber and dill leaves.

NUTRITIONAL ANALYSIS
184 kcals/767 kJ
18.7 g Protein
11.5 g Carbohydrate
7.3 g Fat ★★
2.2 g Saturated Fat ★★★
1.7 g Fibre ★★★
No Added Sugar ★★★★
1182 mg Salt ★

Moules à la Marinière

Mussels are at their best during those seasons when the weather is cold. Always eat mussels on the day they are bought.

SERVES 4	60 ml (4 tbsp) chopped fresh parsley
1.6 kg (3½ lb) mussels	1 bouquet garni
2 shallots or 1 onion, skinned and very finely chopped	pepper, to taste
	200 ml (7 fl oz) dry white wine or cider

1 Check that all the mussels are firmly closed. If not sharply tap any which look doubtful on a hard surface. Any which do not close are dead and must be discarded. Scrape the shells to remove the barnacles. Pull out the beards. Wash thoroughly.
2 Place all the ingredients into a large saucepan, bring to the boil, cover and cook over a medium heat for 7-8 minutes, shaking the pan from time to time so that they cook evenly. As soon as the mussels are open they are cooked: discard any that remain closed.
3 Transfer the mussels with a slotted spoon into a warmed serving bowl and keep warm.
4 Strain the cooking liquid through a sieve lined with muslin into a saucepan. Reheat and pour over the mussels. Serve immediately in soup bowls with chunks of wholemeal bread.

NUTRITIONAL ANALYSIS
132 kcals/550 kJ
19.6 g Protein
0.6 g Carbohydrate
2.3 g Fat ★★★★
0.4 g Saturated Fat ★★★★
0 g Fibre ★
No Added Sugar ★★★★
605 mg Salt ★

NUTRITIONAL ANALYSIS
294 kcals/1227 kJ
12.6 g Protein
30.7 g Carbohydrate
14.3 g Fat ★★
3 g Saturated Fat ★★★
7.7 g Fibre ★★★★
No Added Sugar ★★★★
748 mg Salt ★★

Spinach Gnocchi

Gnocchi are light dumplings served like pasta with a sauce. These spinach-flavoured gnocchi are accompanied with a fresh tomato sauce.

SERVES 4	FOR THE TOMATO SAUCE
450 g (1 lb) fresh spinach, washed, or 225 g (8 oz) packet frozen spinach	1 kg (2¼ lb) ripe tomatoes, skinned and roughly chopped
50 g (2 oz) polyunsaturated margarine	1 small onion, skinned and finely chopped
150 ml (¼ pint) skimmed milk	1 carrot, scrubbed and chopped
40 g (1½ oz) wholemeal flour	2 celery sticks, trimmed and finely chopped
45 g (1¾ oz) plain flour	
2 eggs, beaten	1 garlic clove, skinned and crushed
10 ml (2 tsp) chopped fresh basil or 5 ml (1 tsp) dried	30 ml (2 tbsp) chopped fresh parsley
2.5 ml (½ tsp) grated nutmeg	15 ml (1 tbsp) chopped fresh basil or 7.5 ml (1½ tsp) dried
pepper, to taste	

1 For the sauce, put all ingredients into a saucepan. Cover and simmer for about 45 minutes or until the vegetables are soft. Purée the sauce in a blender or food processor, then set aside.
2 Meanwhile to cook the spinach, put in a saucepan with only the water clinging to the leaves and cook for 5-10 minutes until tender, or 7-8 minutes if using frozen spinach. Drain well, pressing out excess water, then set aside.
3 Put the margarine and milk in a saucepan and bring to the boil. Remove from the heat and add the flours. Beat until smooth and the mixture forms a ball in the centre of the pan. Cool slightly then gradually add the eggs, beating well after each addition.
4 Purée the spinach in a blender or food processor. Mix in the basil, nutmeg and pepper. Work the spinach mixture thoroughly into the dough using a wooden spoon.
5 Drop tablespoonfuls of the gnocchi mixture into a large saucepan of gently boiling water and poach for 10-12 minutes or until they rise to the surface.
6 Drain the gnocchi well, then place a single layer in a lightly greased shallow ovenproof dish. Cover with gently warmed sauce. Bake at 200°C (400°F) mark 6 for 10 minutes or until the gnocchi and tomato sauce are hot. Serve immediately.

NUTRITIONAL ANALYSIS
227 kcals/949 kJ
17.9 g Protein
21.2 g Carbohydrate
8.5 g Fat ★★★
3.5 g Saturated Fat ★★★
5.8 g Fibre ★★★★
No Added Sugar ★★★★
1532 mg Salt ★

Mixed Vegetable Bake

Accompany this easy to make vegetable dish with wholemeal rolls. Use lean bacon to keep the fat content of the dish as low as possible.

SERVES 4	100 g (4 oz) fresh wholemeal breadcrumbs
50 g (2 oz) lean bacon, trimmed of all fat	450 g (1 lb) mixed fresh root vegetables, peeled, finely cubed and lightly steamed
3 eggs	30 ml (2 tbsp) chopped fresh parsley
450 ml (¾ pint) skimmed milk	pepper, to taste
2.5 ml (½ tsp) cayenne	30 ml (2 tbsp) fresh Parmesan cheese

1 Cook the bacon in a frying pan until crisp. Drain on kitchen paper and chop.
2 Beat together the eggs and milk in a bowl. Mix in the cayenne, breadcrumbs, bacon, vegetables and parsley. Season to taste.
3 Pour the mixture into a lightly greased 900 ml (1½ pint) shallow ovenproof dish. Sprinkle with the Parmesan cheese. Stand the dish in a roasting tin half-filled with hot water. Bake at 180°C (350°F) mark 4 for 1-1¼ hours.

Tuna and Haricot Bake

The cooking times for dried beans depends on how long they have been in stock for. The older the beans, the longer the cooking time.

SERVES 4
175 g (6 oz) dried haricot beans, soaked overnight
200 g (7 oz) can tuna in brine, drained and flaked
60 ml (4 tbsp) chopped fresh parsley
30 ml (2 tbsp) chopped fresh chives
pepper, to taste
15 g (½ oz) dried wholemeal breadcrumbs
15 g (½ oz) Parmesan cheese, freshly grated
2 tomatoes, sliced, to garnish

NUTRITIONAL ANALYSIS
279 kcals/1168 kJ
29.1 g Protein
37 g Carbohydrate
2.8 g Fat ★★★★
0.9 g Saturated Fat ★★★★
17.3 g Fibre ★★★★
0.1 g Added Sugar ★★★★
761 mg Salt ★★

1 Drain the beans and rinse. Put into a saucepan and cover with plenty of fresh water. Bring to the boil and boil for 10 minutes, then simmer for about 50 minutes or until tender.
2 Drain the beans, reserving the cooking liquid. Purée half the beans with just enough of the cooking liquid to make a smooth, thick mixture. Spread over the base of a lightly greased 600 ml (1 pint) shallow ovenproof dish.
3 Mix the remaining beans with the tuna, parsley and chives. Season to taste. Spread over the puréed mixture.
4 Mix the breadcrumbs with the Parmesan and sprinkle over the top. Garnish with the sliced tomatoes. Bake at 200°C (400°F) mark 6 for 20-30 minutes until crisp on the top.

Vegetable Fritters

The vegetables provide plenty of fibre, especially as they are not peeled.

SERVES 4
350 g (12 oz) potatoes, scrubbed
1 medium onion, skinned and coarsely grated
1 large courgette (zucchini), trimmed and coarsely grated
1 large carrot, scrubbed and coarsely grated
100 g (4 oz) fennel bulb, trimmed and coarsely grated
pepper, to taste
30 ml (2 tbsp) chopped fresh basil or parsley
15 ml (1 tbsp) sunflower oil

NUTRITIONAL ANALYSIS
129 kcals/541 kJ
3.1 g Protein
21.9 g Carbohydrate
3.9 g Fat ★★★
0.5 g Saturated Fat ★★★★
4 g Fibre ★★★★
No Added Sugar ★★★★
165 mg Salt ★★★

1 Put the potatoes in a saucepan of water and parboil for 8 minutes. Drain and cool, then coarsely grate into a large bowl.
2 Mix the remaining ingredients except the oil into the potato. Carefully form into 8 flat fritters, pressing together with the hands.
3 Heat the oil in a non-stick frying pan and cook the fritters for about 5 minutes on each side or until golden brown. Use a wide spatula to carefully turn the fritters, trying not to break them. Press the fritters with the spatula to keep them together. Serve immediately.

NUTRITIONAL ANALYSIS
302 kcals/1262 kJ
11 g Protein
42.4 g Carbohydrate
11.4 g Fat ★★★
0.9 g Saturated Fat ★★★★
2.7 g Fibre ★★★
0.5 g Added Sugar ★★★★
1025 mg Salt ★

Spinach Pie

Warm the oil very slightly before brushing between the leaves of wafer thin filo pastry; this will enable the oil to be used more economically. For a small family make the full quantity and freeze half.

SERVES 6-8	*50 g (2 oz) pine kernels*
175 g (6 oz) brown rice	*50 g (2 oz) currants*
450 g (1 lb) spinach, washed	*225 g (8 oz) low-fat cottage cheese*
150 g (5 oz) filo pastry	*a little freshly grated nutmeg*
25 ml (1 fl oz) sunflower oil, warmed	*pepper, to taste*

1 Put the rice into a saucepan of boiling water and cook for about 40 minutes until just cooked. Drain and cool. Put the spinach into a pan with only the water clinging to the leaves and cook for 5-10 minutes until just tender. Drain very well and cool.
2 Grease a 25.5×18 cm (10×7 inch) shallow ovenproof dish and cover the base and sides with sheets of filo pastry. Brush with the warmed oil. Continue layering until two thirds of the pastry has been used.
3 Mix together the rice, spinach, pine kernels, currants, cottage cheese and nutmeg in a bowl. Season to taste. Spread over the base of the lined dish.
4 Cover with the remaining filo and oil. Score through the top layers with a sharp knife, making a diamond pattern.
5 Bake at 200°C (400°F) mark 6 for 30-40 minutes or until golden brown.

NUTRITIONAL ANALYSIS
99 kcals/413 kJ
11 g Protein
4 g Carbohydrate
4.4 g Fat ★★
1.4 g Saturated Fat ★★★
1.3 g Fibre ★★★★
No Added Sugar ★★★★
827 mg Salt ★

Watercress Roulade with Piquant Pimento Sauce

Watercress, an excellent source of vitamins and minerals, provides the colour in this impressive dish. Accompany with a rice salad and wholemeal bread.

SERVES 6	FOR THE SAUCE
FOR THE ROULADE	*400 g (14 oz) can red pimentos, drained, liquid reserved*
2 bunches watercress	*5 ml (1 tsp) Worcestershire sauce*
4 eggs, separated	*45 ml (3 tbsp) sugarless tomato ketchup*
	FOR THE FILLING
pepper, to taste	*225 g (8 oz) low-fat fromage frais*

1 For the roulade, line a 33×23 cm (13×9 inch) Swiss roll tin with non-stick baking parchment.
2 Put the watercress into a saucepan of boiling water, return to the boil and boil for 2 minutes. Drain the watercress and plunge into cold water. Drain again.
3 Work the watercress and egg yolks in a food processor or blender for 3-4 minutes until the mixture is light and fluffy. Whisk the egg whites until stiff but not dry and fold into the watercress mixture. Season to taste.
4 Very gently spread the mixture over the prepared tin. Bake at 190°C (375°F) mark 5 for 15-20 minutes or until the centre is firm to the touch. Cover with a damp cloth and allow to cool in the tin.
5 Cut one pimento into strips and set aside. For the sauce, purée the remaining pimentos, Worcestershire sauce and tomato ketchup in a food processor or blender. Chill.
6 Just before serving, turn out the roulade on to a damp cloth, remove the parchment and spread with the fromage frais. Distribute the reserved pimento strips over the top, reserving a few for garnish. Roll up the roulade.
7 Pour the sauce over a flat oval serving dish, lay the roulade on top and garnish with the reserved pimento strips.

Cornish Pasties

A healthy low-fat version of a favourite snack.

SERVES 4	60-75 ml (4-5 tbsp) skimmed milk, warmed
FOR THE PASTRY	FOR THE FILLING
75 g (3 oz) plain unbleached flour	1 small onion, skinned and finely chopped
75 g (3 oz) wholemeal flour	150 g (5 oz) potato, peeled and diced
5 ml (1 tsp) easy mix dried yeast	50 g (2 oz) swede, peeled and diced
pinch of salt	100 g (4 oz) lean stewing steak, diced very small
40 g (1½ oz) polyunsaturated margarine	pepper, to taste
	10 ml (2 tsp) wholemeal flour

1 For the pastry, mix together the flours, yeast and salt in a bowl. Rub in the margarine until the mixture resembles fine breadcrumbs. Mix in enough milk to make a soft dry dough. Knead until smooth.
2 Roll out the dough very thinly on an unfloured work surface and cut into four 18 cm (7 inch) rounds, re-rolling the dough as necessary. Cover with greased polythene and leave in a warm place until risen a little.
3 For the filling, mix together the onion, potato, swede and meat in a bowl. Place the filling in mounds in the centre of each dough round. Season to taste and add 5 ml (1 tsp) water to each. Sprinkle with the flour. Dampen the edges of the pastry and bring the opposite sides up and over the filling, pressing firmly to seal the pastry. Cut a small hole in the top of each to allow the steam to escape.
4 Place the pasties on a lightly greased baking sheet. Bake at 200°C (400°F) mark 6 for 10 minutes, then reduce the oven temperature to 170°C (325°F) mark 3 and bake for a further 1 hour. Check towards the end of the cooking time and, if the pasties are becoming too brown, cover with foil.

NUTRITIONAL ANALYSIS
282 kcals/1177 kJ
11.5 g Protein
38.8 g Carbohydrate
10 g Fat ★★★
1.9 g Saturated Fat ★★★★
3.9 g Fibre ★★★★
No Added Sugar ★★★★
536 mg Salt ★★★

Spiced Bean Sausages

Cumin and coriander give these unusual sausages made from haricot beans a delicious spicy flavour.

MAKES 12	5 ml (1 tsp) fresh ground coriander
225 g (8 oz) dried haricot beans, soaked overnight	15 ml (1 tbsp) chopped fresh coriander
	pepper, to taste
1 small onion, skinned and grated	1 egg, beaten
15 ml (1 tbsp) lemon juice	50 g (2 oz) fresh wholemeal breadcrumbs
5 ml (1 tsp) freshly ground cumin	15 ml (1 tbsp) sunflower oil

1 Drain the beans and rinse. Put in a saucepan with plenty of fresh water and cook for 1¼ hours or until tender. Drain well, then press the beans through a sieve or purée in a food processor.
2 Add the onion, lemon juice, spices and fresh coriander. Season to taste and mix well. If the mixture is a little soft, chill for 15 minutes.
3 Divide the bean mixture into 12 and roll each piece into a sausage shape about 5 cm (2 inches) long, dusting your hands with a little flour if necessary. Coat the sausages in the egg and breadcrumbs.
4 Heat the oil in a non-stick frying pan and cook the sausages on all sides for about 5-10 minutes until evenly browned and crisp. Drain on absorbent kitchen paper and serve hot.

NUTRITIONAL ANALYSIS
83 kcals/347 kJ
5.2 g Protein
11.1 g Carbohydrate
2.3 g Fat ★★★
0.4 g Saturated Fat ★★★★
5.4 g Fibre ★★★★
No Added Sugar ★★★★
107 mg Salt ★★★

NUTRITIONAL ANALYSIS
241 kcals/1007 kJ
19.6 g Protein
22.3 g Carbohydrate
8.8 g Fat ★★★
2.2 g Saturated Fat ★★★
2.6 g Fibre ★★★
No Added Sugar ★★★★
363 mg Salt ★★★

Baked Beef and Vegetable Crumble

Leaving the skins on the jacket baked potatoes increases the fibre content of this substantial dish.

SERVES 4

225 g (8 oz) cold cooked lean beef or other meat, cut into strips

175 g (6 oz) cold baked or boiled potatoes, cut into 1 cm (½ inch) cubes

3 spring onions, trimmed and finely chopped

175 g (6 oz) cold cooked courgettes (zucchini) or other green vegetable, thinly sliced

10 ml (2 tsp) grated fresh or bottled horseradish

pepper, to taste

300 ml (½ pint) beef stock

25 g (1 oz) polyunsaturated margarine

40 g (1½ oz) fresh wholemeal breadcrumbs

40 g (1½ oz) rolled oats

5 ml (1 tsp) paprika

10 ml (2 tsp) chopped fresh parsley

1 Put the meat, potatoes, spring onions and courgettes into a bowl. Add the horseradish, pepper and 150 ml (¼ pint) of the stock. Put the mixture into a 1.1 litre (2 pint) ovenproof serving dish.
2 Rub the margarine into the breadcrumbs in a bowl, then stir in the oats, paprika and parsley. Sprinkle over the meat mixture.
3 Bake at 190°C (375°F) mark 5 for 40-45 minutes or until the top is crisp. Warm the remaining stock and serve with the crumble.

NUTRITIONAL ANALYSIS
170 kcals/709 kJ
17.8 g Protein
1.9 g Carbohydrate
10.2 g Fat ★
1.9 g Saturated Fat ★★★
0.5 g Fibre ★
No Added Sugar ★★★★
735 mg Salt ★

Devilled Kidneys

Kidneys are an excellent source of B vitamins and iron. Serve these quickly prepared, piquant kidneys with hot wholemeal toast.

SERVES 4

15 ml (1 tbsp) Worcestershire sauce

15 ml (1 tbsp) tomato purée

10 ml (2 tsp) mustard powder

1.25 ml (¼ tsp) cayenne

15 g (½ oz) polyunsaturated margarine

15 ml (1 tbsp) sunflower oil

8 lambs' kidneys, skinned, halved and cored

chopped fresh parsley, to garnish

1 Whisk together the Worcestershire sauce, tomato purée, mustard powder, cayenne pepper and margarine in a bowl.
2 Heat the oil in a large non-stick frying pan and cook the kidneys over a low heat for 3-4 minutes on each side or until they change colour.
3 Add the sauce mixture and cook for 2-3 minutes, stirring, until heated through. Garnish with chopped parsley and serve at once.

Lamb Fillet with Leek Sauce (PAGE 85)

Main Meals

The aim of all the dishes in this book is to be low in fats (especially saturated fats), added sugars and salt, but high in fibre. However, it is important to remember that you should view the meal as a whole – if you combine a recipe which is high in fats with one that has hardly any fat, the meal will be healthier. It is the overall balance which counts.

Before cooking always trim off any fat from meat, and remove the skin from poultry as the fat is concentrated in and under the skin. If you have to brown meat, use a non-stick pan as this will cut down on the amount of polyunsaturated fat or oil you need to use.

Chillied Baked Potatoes (PAGE 92) and *Natural Courgettes (Zucchini) and Carrots* (PAGE 99)

NUTRITIONAL ANALYSIS
297 kcals/1242 kJ
48.2 g Protein
11.1 g Carbohydrate
8 g Fat ★★★
2.8 g Saturated Fat ★★★
2.2 g Fibre ★★
No Added Sugar ★★★★
560 mg Salt ★★★

Chicken in Yogurt

Marinating the chicken breasts beforehand flavours and helps keep them moist without adding any fat during the cooking. The spicy coating is equally delicious with turkey breasts.

SERVES 4

300 ml (½ pint) low-fat natural yogurt

15 ml (1 tbsp) freshly ground coriander

15 ml (1 tbsp) freshly ground cumin

1 cm (½ inch) piece of fresh root ginger, peeled and finely chopped, or 10 ml (2 tsp) ground

5 ml (1 tsp) chilli powder

1 garlic clove, skinned and crushed

4 chicken breasts on the bone, each weighing about 275 g (10 oz), skinned

fresh coriander sprigs, to garnish

1 Mix together the yogurt, coriander, cumin, ginger, chilli and garlic in a bowl.
2 Prick the chicken pieces all over with a fork and spread with half of the yogurt mixture. Cover and marinate for at least 3-4 hours or overnight in the refrigerator, turning occasionally.
3 Transfer the chicken to a roasting pan. Bake at 200°C (400°F) mark 6 for 45 minutes. Remove from the pan and keep warm.
4 Put the roasting pan over a gentle heat, stir in the reserved yogurt mixture and heat through, but do not boil, scraping up any sediment and juices from the base of the pan.
5 Pour the sauce over the chicken and serve hot, garnished with coriander sprigs.

NUTRITIONAL ANALYSIS
285 kcals/1192 kJ
41 g Protein
9.3 g Carbohydrate
9.7 g Fat ★★★
2.4 g Saturated Fat ★★★
1.4 g Fibre ★★
No Added Sugar ★★★★
351 mg Salt ★★★

Jerusalem Chicken

This chicken dish has a nutty flavour provided by the Jerusalem artichokes. Use them as soon as possible after buying as they quickly lose their lovely creamy colour.

SERVES 4

15 ml (1 tbsp) wholemeal flour

pepper, to taste

4 chicken breast fillets, each weighing 175-225 g (6-8 oz), skinned

15 ml (1 tbsp) sunflower oil

2 medium onions, skinned and chopped

300 ml (½ pint) chicken or vegetable stock plus 15-30 ml (1-2 tbsp) extra, if necessary

grated rind and juice of ½ lemon

4 fresh thyme sprigs or 2.5 ml (½ tsp) dried

450 g (1 lb) Jerusalem artichokes

1 small red pepper, cored, seeded and thinly sliced

chopped fresh parsley, to garnish

1 Mix the flour with the seasoning and use to lightly coat the chicken breasts. Heat the oil in a large non-stick frying pan and cook the chicken breasts for 3 minutes on each side or until golden brown. Remove and drain well on absorbent kitchen paper.
2 Pour the hot oil into a large non-stick saucepan and gently cook the onions for 3-5 minutes until soft but not brown. Pour in the stock with the lemon rind and juice and thyme.
3 Peel the artichokes and cut into slices or dice. Place in the pan at once and add the red pepper.
4 Bring to the boil, then add the chicken. Cover and simmer gently for 30-40 minutes or until the chicken is tender and the artichokes are soft.
5 Remove the chicken to a warmed serving dish and keep hot. Reserve some of the pepper slices for garnish and discard the thyme sprigs. Purée the remaining vegetables and stock in a blender or food processor until smooth.
6 Reheat the sauce and season to taste, adding a little stock to thin if necessary. Pour the sauce over the chicken breasts. Garnish with the reserved pepper and chopped parsley.

Chicken in a Pot

The liquid left in the pot can be skimmed and served as chicken soup, or used as chicken stock in another dish. It will keep in the refrigerator for 2-3 days, or in the freezer for several months.

NUTRITIONAL ANALYSIS
216 kcals/905 kJ
33.6 g Protein
5.7 g Carbohydrate
6.7 g Fat ★★★
2.2 g Saturated Fat ★★★
5.8 g Fibre ★★★★
No Added Sugar ★★★★
596 mg Salt ★★

SERVES 4
1.4 kg (3 lb) oven-ready chicken, skinned
225 g (8 oz) celeriac, peeled, trimmed and cut into large chunks
225 g (8 oz) carrots, scrubbed and cut into large chunks
3 celery sticks, trimmed and cut into large chunks
1 small onion, skinned and sliced
30 ml (2 tbsp) chopped fresh thyme or 15 ml (1 tbsp) dried
2 garlic cloves, skinned and crushed
15 ml (1 tbsp) lemon juice
pepper, to taste
chopped fresh parsley, to garnish

1 Put all the ingredients, except the parsley, in a large flameproof pot and add 600 ml (1 pint) water. Cover and simmer for 1 hour or until the chicken is cooked and the juices run clear when a skewer is inserted into the thickest part of the leg.
2 Remove the chicken and vegetables with a slotted spoon and arrange on a platter. Sprinkle with chopped parsley and serve immediately.

Middle-Eastern Stuffed Chicken

Dried fruits are full of concentrated goodness. They are an excellent source of dietary fibre and minerals. Serve the chicken with saffron rice.

NUTRITIONAL ANALYSIS
328 kcals/1370 kJ
33.4 g Protein
18.7 g Carbohydrate
13.9 g Fat ★★
3 g Saturated Fat ★★★
4.8 g Fibre ★★★★
No Added Sugar ★★★★
348 mg Salt ★★★

SERVES 4
15 ml (1 tbsp) sunflower oil
1 small onion, skinned and finely chopped
50 g (2 oz) raisins
50 g (2 oz) no-soak dried stoned prunes, chopped
25 g (1 oz) blanched almonds, chopped
1 eating apple, peeled, cored and finely chopped
2.5 ml (½ tsp) ground allspice
2.5 ml (½ tsp) ground cinnamon
30 ml (2 tbsp) lemon juice
pepper, to taste
1.4 kg (3 lb) oven-ready chicken

1 Heat the oil in a small non-stick saucepan and cook the onion for about 5 minutes until lightly browned.
2 Mix together the raisins, prunes, almonds, apple and spices in a bowl. Add the onion and 15 ml (1 tbsp) of the lemon juice. Season to taste and mix well.
3 Stuff the neck end of the chicken with the fruit mixture. Place the chicken in a roasting tin, season and sprinkle with the remaining lemon juice.
4 Roast at 190°C (375°F) mark 5 for 1¼ hours or until browned and the juices run clear when a skewer is inserted into the thickest part of the leg.

NUTRITIONAL ANALYSIS
213 kcals/891 kJ
33.5 g Protein
2.9 g Carbohydrate
7.5 g Fat ★★★
2.3 g Saturated Fat ★★★
0.2 g Fibre ★
No Added Sugar ★★★★
384 mg Salt ★★★

Chicken with Mustard Sauce

Whole grain mustard is a hot, pungent mustard made from whole mustard seeds, allspice, black pepper and white wine. The liquid, in this case the white wine, brings out the flavour of the mustard.

SERVES 4

4 chicken portions, each weighing about 175 g (6 oz), skinned

20 ml (4 tsp) whole grain mustard

juice of 1 small lemon

150 ml (1/4 pint) low-fat natural yogurt

fresh coriander leaves, to garnish

1 Put the chicken in a roasting tin and spread the mustard equally on each portion. Sprinkle over the lemon juice.
2 Roast at 200°C (400°F) mark 6 for about 40 minutes, turning once, until cooked through and tender.
3 Remove the chicken with a slotted spoon and arrange on warmed serving plates. Keep warm. Add the yogurt to the roasting tin and stir to mix with any juices and excess mustard from the base of the tin. Heat the sauce without boiling, stirring, then pour over the chicken. Garnish with fresh coriander.

NUTRITIONAL ANALYSIS
222 kcals/926 kJ
24.8 g Protein
9 g Carbohydrate
8.1 g Fat ★★★
1.7 g Saturated Fat ★★★★
2.5 g Fibre ★★★★
0.1 g Added Sugar ★★★★
231 mg Salt ★★★★

Piquant Chicken

Using skinned chicken helps to reduce the fat content of this dish. Serve the chicken with brown rice and a green salad.

SERVES 4

15 ml (1 tbsp) sunflower oil

4 chicken breasts, each weighing about 100 g (4 oz), skinned

1 large onion, skinned and finely chopped

10 ml (2 tsp) ground ginger

15 ml (1 tbsp) Dijon mustard

25 g (1 oz) wholemeal flour

450 ml (3/4 pint) vegetable or chicken stock

60 ml (4 tbsp) dry sherry

175 g (6 oz) button mushrooms, roughly chopped

pepper, to taste

watercress sprigs, to garnish

1 Heat the oil in a large non-stick saucepan and cook the chicken breasts until evenly browned. Remove with a slotted spoon and place in a large casserole. Keep warm.
2 Add the onion to the pan and cook for 5 minutes until soft. Add the ginger and mustard, stir well then add the flour. Cook for a few minutes, then remove from the heat and stir in the stock and sherry. Return to the heat and bring to the boil, stirring. Add the mushrooms and season to taste.
3 Pour the sauce over the chicken breasts. Cook at 180°C (350°F) mark 4 for 50 minutes or until tender.
4 Place the chicken breasts on a serving dish and keep warm. Quickly reduce the sauce a little by boiling. Pour over the chicken and serve.

Spiced Chicken

Light, aromatic cumin and cinnamon are used to spice the chicken. Accompany the dish with brown rice and green beans.

SERVES 4	
4 chicken breasts on the bone, skinned	*15 ml (1 tbsp) paprika*
5 ml (1 tsp) ground cinnamon	*5 ml (1 tsp) cumin seeds*
300 ml (½ pint) low-fat natural yogurt	*1 small red pepper, cored, seeded and finely chopped*
10 ml (2 tsp) sunflower oil	*45 ml (3 tbsp) tomato juice*
2 large onions, skinned and finely chopped	*pinch of finely grated lemon rind*
1 garlic clove, skinned and crushed	*pepper, to taste*
1 fresh green chilli, seeded and chopped	*15 ml (1 tbsp) cornflour*

1 Rub the chicken breasts with the cinnamon. Put into a dish, pour over the yogurt, reserving 30 ml (2 tbsp), and marinate for at least 30 minutes.
2 Heat 5 ml (1 tsp) of the oil in a non-stick frying pan and gently cook the onions for 5-8 minutes until lightly browned. Remove and transfer to a casserole. Add the garlic and chilli to the pan and gently cook for 2 minutes. Stir in the paprika and cumin seeds and cook for a further 2 minutes. Transfer to the casserole.
3 Remove the chicken from the marinade, reserving the marinade. Heat the remaining oil in the pan and brown the chicken on all sides.
4 Place the chicken, marinade, red pepper, tomato juice, lemon rind and pepper in the casserole. Cover and cook at 180°C (350°F) mark 4 for about 1 hour.
5 Mix the cornflour and reserved yogurt together. Blend in some of the hot liquid from the casserole, then mix with the rest of the casserole juices. Cook until the juices have thickened.

NUTRITIONAL ANALYSIS
291 kcals/1217 kJ
38.1 g Protein
16.1 g Carbohydrate
8.8 g Fat ★★★
2.5 g Saturated Fat ★★★
2.2 g Fibre ★★★
0.4 g Added Sugar ★★★★
524 mg Salt ★★★

Chicken in a Brick with Tarragon

Use a chicken brick in combination with a gravy jug with a spout set right at the bottom. With this, you can pour off the delicious juices without the fat for healthier cooking.

SERVES 4	
1.25 kg (2¾ lb) oven-ready chicken	*15 ml (1 tbsp) dried tarragon*
4 thin lemon slices	*2.5 ml (½ tsp) sunflower oil*
	5 ml (1 tsp) cornflour (optional)

1 Soak the chicken brick in cold water for 10 minutes while preparing the chicken.
2 Remove the fatty deposits from just inside the main cavity of the chicken and discard them. Slide your fingers gently under the skin on the breast to make pockets.
3 Dip the lemon slices in the tarragon. Slide 2 slices under the skin. Place the 2 remaining slices with the rest of the tarragon in the base of the chicken brick and place the chicken on top. Rub the skin all over with the oil.
4 Put the brick into a cold oven and bake at 240°C (475°F) mark 9 for 1½ hours.
5 Pour the juices into a fat-saver gravy jug and allow to stand for a few minutes, keeping warm.
6 Carve the chicken and pour the thin fat-free gravy over, taking care not to use the fat at the top of the jug. This should be discarded. If you prefer a thick gravy, blend the cornflour with a little cold water then mix with the fat free juices. Bring to the boil, stirring.

NUTRITIONAL ANALYSIS
280 kcals/1170 kJ
33 g Protein
1.4 g Carbohydrate
15 g Fat ★★★
5.6 g Saturated Fat ★★★
0.4 g Fibre ★
No Added Sugar ★★★★
330 mg Salt ★★★

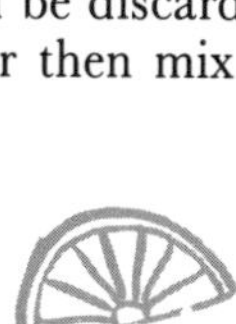

Baked Gingered Chicken

Where possible, remove the skin of chicken, as most of the fat is in, or just under, the skin.

NUTRITIONAL ANALYSIS
174 kcals/729 kJ
24.9 g Protein
5.2 g Carbohydrate
5.2 g Fat ★★★
1.7 g Saturated Fat ★★★
0.2 g Fibre ★★★★
0.1 g Added Sugar ★★★★
254 mg Salt ★★★

SERVES 4

4 small chicken portions, skinned

10 ml (2 tsp) soy sauce

30 ml (2 tbsp) dry sherry

60 ml (4 tbsp) unsweetened apple juice

2 lemon slices, finely chopped

1 garlic clove, skinned and crushed

10 ml (2 tsp) grated fresh root ginger

1 Arrange the chicken in a baking dish just large enough to take the pieces in one layer, fleshy side down.
2 Mix the rest of the ingredients together and pour over the chicken. Cover and leave to marinate for several hours.
3 Bake at 200°C (400°F) mark 6 for 30-40 minutes or until the juices run clear when a skewer is inserted into the thickest part of the leg. Turn the chicken half way through cooking and baste frequently.

Fruited Turkey Braise

Here, the turkey legs are braised in a spicy stock. Fresh fruits are added half way through the cooking time.

NUTRITIONAL ANALYSIS
262 kcals/1095 kJ
31.8 g Protein
13.3 g Carbohydrate
9.5 g Fat ★★★
2.4 g Saturated Fat ★★★
3.2 g Fibre ★★★★
No Added Sugar ★★★★
285 mg Salt ★★★

SERVES 4

2 large turkey legs, total weight about 700-800 g (1½-1¾ lb), skinned

10 ml (2 tsp) wholemeal flour

15 ml (1 tbsp) sunflower oil

1 medium onion, skinned and chopped

10 ml (2 tsp) finely chopped fresh root ginger

450 ml (¾ pint) chicken stock

2.5 ml (½ tsp) ground allspice

2.5 ml (½ tsp) ground cinnamon

1 cooking apple, peeled, cored and chopped

1 firm ripe pear, peeled, cored and chopped

1 red pepper, cored, seeded and chopped

pepper, to taste

1 Dust the turkey legs with the flour. Heat the oil in a flameproof casserole and cook the turkey on all sides for about 8-10 minutes until lightly browned. Remove from the casserole and set aside.
2 Add the onion and ginger to the casserole and fry for 5 minutes until soft. Stir in the stock, allspice and cinnamon and bring to the boil. Return the turkey legs to the casserole, cover tightly and cook gently for 45 minutes.
3 Add the apple, pear and red pepper and season to taste. Cook for a further 45 minutes or until the turkey is tender.
4 Remove the turkey legs from the casserole and slice the meat from the bone. Skim off any fat from the surface of the sauce, then return the pieces of meat to warm through. Serve hot.

Turkey Fillets with Mushrooms

Here, turkey fillets are filled with herby mushrooms, rolled and then braised.

SERVES 4
4 turkey fillets, each weighing about 150 g (5 oz)
15 ml (1 tbsp) sunflower oil
1 medium onion, skinned and finely chopped
175 g (6 oz) mushrooms, chopped
1 garlic clove, skinned and crushed
5 ml (1 tsp) finely grated lemon rind
10 ml (2 tsp) chopped fresh thyme or 5 ml (1 tsp) dried
15 ml (1 tbsp) capers, well drained and chopped
pepper, to taste
300 ml (½ pint) hot chicken stock
30 ml (2 tbsp) lemon juice
15 ml (1 tbsp) chopped fresh parsley
lemon slices and parsley sprigs, to garnish

NUTRITIONAL ANALYSIS
206 kcals/863 kJ
36.4 g Protein
2.3 g Carbohydrate
5.8 g Fat ★★★
1.1 g Saturated Fat ★★★★
2.4 g Fibre ★★★★
No Added Sugar ★★★★
194 mg Salt ★★★★

1 Cut each turkey fillet in half crossways and place each half between sheets of greaseproof paper. Beat until fillets measure about 10×15 cm (4×6 inches).
2 Heat 5 ml (1 tsp) of the oil in a non-stick frying pan and cook the onion and mushrooms for 5-10 minutes over a gentle heat until excess moisture has evaporated. Remove from the heat and add the garlic, lemon rind, thyme and capers. Season to taste and mix well.
3 Divide the mushroom mixture into 8 and spread over the fillets. Roll up and secure at both ends with string.
4 Heat the remaining oil in a non-stick frying pan just large enough to hold the 8 rolls. Cook the rolls, 4 at a time, for about 5 minutes each batch, turning until pale golden on all sides.
5 Return all the rolls to the pan with the stock and lemon juice. Cover and simmer gently for 20 minutes.
6 Transfer the rolls to a serving plate, remove the string and keep warm. Boil the pan juices until reduced, then stir in the parsley and pour over the turkey rolls. Serve garnished with lemon slices and parsley sprigs.

Turkey Meatballs in Egg and Lemon Sauce

Traditionally these little meatballs are made with minced veal. They are lower in fat and equally delicious made with boneless turkey, which is now readily available from supermarkets.

SERVES 4
FOR THE MEATBALLS
2 thick slices wholemeal bread, crusts removed
45 ml (3 tbsp) dry white wine
pepper, to taste
15 ml (1 tbsp) chopped fresh tarragon
1 egg
225 g (8 oz) skinless boneless turkey, minced
750 ml (1¼ pints) chicken stock
FOR THE SAUCE
15 g (½ oz) cornflour
juice of 1 lemon
1 egg

NUTRITIONAL ANALYSIS
174 kcals/728 kJ
18.9 g Protein
14.1 g Carbohydrate
4.3 g Fat ★★★
1.3 g Saturated Fat ★★★★
2.6 g Fibre ★★★★
No Added Sugar ★★★★
528 mg Salt ★★

1 For the meatballs, put the bread, 45 ml (3 tbsp) water and the wine in a bowl and beat well with a fork until smooth. Beat in the pepper, tarragon, egg and turkey. Chill the mixture in the refrigerator for several hours until firm.
2 Divide the mixture into 20 pieces and form into neat firm meatballs with wet hands.
3 Bring the stock to the boil in a saucepan. Add the meatballs to the stock in 2 batches, simmering gently, covered, for 7 minutes. Remove the meatballs on to a warmed serving dish with a slotted spoon. Keep warm, retaining the stock.
4 For the sauce, mix together the cornflour and lemon juice in a bowl until smooth. Beat in the egg and add the reserved stock. Transfer to a small saucepan and heat gently, whisking rapidly all the time. Simmer for 1-2 minutes, then strain the sauce over the meatballs.

Roast Pheasant with Blackberry Sauce

Tell your poulterer that you require roasting pheasants or you may get older ones that are fit only for the pot.

NUTRITIONAL ANALYSIS
289 kcals/1207 kJ
31 g Protein
7.5 g Carbohydrate
12.5 g Fat ★★
3.4 g Saturated Fat ★★★
4.5 g Fibre ★★★★
No Added Sugar ★★★★
263 mg Salt ★★★★

SERVES 4

2 small hen pheasants
15 ml (1 tbsp) sunflower oil
pepper, to taste
15 ml (1 tbsp) fine wholemeal flour
150 ml (¼ pint) red wine

FOR THE SAUCE

225 g (8 oz) blackberries
5 ml (1 tsp) arrowroot
5 ml (1 tsp) sugar (optional)
5 ml (1 tsp) lemon juice

1 Rub the pheasants all over with the oil. Season the flour and sprinkle over the birds.
2 Put the pheasants in a roasting tin and cover with lightly greased greaseproof paper. Roast at 200°C (400°F) mark 6 for 30 minutes. Remove the paper and pour over the wine. Continue roasting for 15-20 minutes or until tender and the legs move freely when moved from side to side.
3 Meanwhile for the sauce, put the blackberries and 100 ml (4 fl oz) water in a saucepan and simmer for about 5 minutes until soft. Purée in a food processor or blender. Return the blackberry purée to the pan. Blend the arrowroot with a little cold water and stir into the purée with the sugar, if used. Return to the boil, then remove from the heat and add the lemon juice. Serve the pheasants with the sauce.

Rabbit with Prunes

A good source of fibre, prunes make an interesting addition to a casserole. The type of plum grown for drying is usually late-ripening and black skinned.

NUTRITIONAL ANALYSIS
199 kcals/831 kJ
18.4 g Protein
14.4 g Carbohydrate
7.9 g Fat ★★
1.9 g Saturated Fat ★★★
5.1 g Fibre ★★★★
No Added Sugar ★★★★
277 mg Salt ★★★

SERVES 4

6-8 back fillets of rabbit, about 450-550 g (1-1¼ lb)
10 ml (2 tsp) wholegrain mustard
30 ml (2 tbsp) plain wholemeal flour
15 ml (1 tbsp) chopped mixed fresh herbs, such as basil and parsley
pepper, to taste
15 ml (1 tbsp) sunflower oil
15 g (½ oz) polyunsaturated margarine
12 shallots or pickling onions, skinned
3 medium carrots, scrubbed and sliced
450 ml (¾ pint) chicken stock
5 ml (1 tsp) tomato purée
12 no-cook dried stoned prunes
fresh herb sprig, to garnish

1 Brush the rabbit fillets lightly with mustard. Mix together the flour and herbs and season to taste. Use to coat the rabbit fillets, reserving the excess flour mixture.
2 Heat the oil and margarine in a flameproof casserole and cook the shallots, carrots and rabbit fillets for about 5 minutes, turning frequently, until the rabbit is sealed. Remove the rabbit and set aside.
3 Stir the reserved flour mixture into the casserole and cook for 1 minute. Gradually add the stock and tomato purée and bring to the boil, stirring. Remove from the heat. Return the rabbit to the casserole and cover.
4 Cook at 190°C (375°F) mark 5 for 50 minutes. Gently stir in the prunes. Cover again and cook for a further 30 minutes or until the rabbit is tender and cooked through. Garnish with a fresh herb sprig.

Hare Casserole

First marinated in red wine, the hare is then cooked with brown lentils.

SERVES 4	
150 ml (¼ pint) red wine vinegar	*pepper, to taste*
150 ml (¼ pint) red wine	*1 hare, skinned, jointed and trimmed of tough membrane*
1 medium onion, skinned and chopped	*15 ml (1 tbsp) sunflower oil*
2 medium carrots, scrubbed and sliced	*750 ml (1¼ pints) beef stock*
1 garlic clove, skinned and crushed	*175 g (6 oz) brown lentils*
1.25 ml (¼ tsp) dried thyme	*225 g (8 oz) button mushrooms, sliced*
1 bay leaf	*10 ml (2 tsp) Dijon mustard*

1 Mix together the vinegar, wine, onion, carrots, garlic, thyme, bay leaf and seasoning in a large bowl. Add the hare, coating well. Cover and marinate for at least 12 hours or overnight.
2 Drain the hare, reserving the marinade and vegetables. Pat the joints dry with absorbent kitchen paper. Strain the marinade and set the vegetables and liquid aside.
3 Heat the oil in a large flameproof casserole and brown the hare all over. Remove from the casserole; set aside. Add the vegetables to the casserole and cook, stirring, until just brown. Place the hare on top of the vegetables. Pour over the marinade liquid and stock and stir in the lentils. Bring to the boil.
4 Cover and cook at 170°C (325°F) mark 3 for 1½ hours. Stir in the mushrooms, cover again and cook for a further 30 minutes.
5 To serve, remove the hare from the casserole and transfer to a serving dish. Stir the mustard into the sauce and pour over the hare.

NUTRITIONAL ANALYSIS
563 kcals/2353 kJ
66.2 g Protein
27.6 g Carbohydrate
19 g Fat ★★
6.3 g Saturated Fat ★★★
7.9 g Fibre ★★★★
No Added Sugar ★★★★
368 mg Salt ★★★★

Baked Monkfish with Garlic

This is a very low-fat dish as monkfish contains very little fat and no fat has been used in the cooking method.

SERVES 4	
700 g (1½ lb) monkfish, skinned, boned and cut into 2 thick fillets	*1 carrot, scrubbed and sliced*
2 garlic cloves, skinned and cut into slivers	*2 bay leaves*
grated rind and juice of 1 lemon	*150 ml (¼ pint) fish stock*
pepper, to taste	*10 ml (2 tsp) chopped fresh chervil or 5 ml (1 tsp) dried*
2 celery sticks, trimmed and chopped	*30 ml (2 tbsp) low-fat natural yogurt*
	lemon slices and fresh chervil sprigs, to garnish

1 Slice the monkfish fillets lengthways, without separating, open them up and lay flat. Insert the garlic slivers into the fish and sprinkle with the lemon rind and pepper. Roll up, starting from the tail end, and secure with wooden cocktail sticks.
2 Put the celery, carrot and bay leaves into a baking tin and place the fish on top. Add the lemon juice to the stock and pour over the fish.
3 Cover and cook at 190°C (375°F) mark 5 for 30 minutes or until the fish is cooked. Discard the cocktail sticks, place the fish on a serving dish and keep warm while preparing the sauce.
4 Strain the fish juices into a small saucepan, discarding the vegetables and bay leaves. Bring to the boil, then boil for 3 minutes or until slightly reduced. Lower the heat, stir in the chopped chervil and yogurt and heat through gently.
5 Garnish the fish with lemon slices and chervil sprigs and serve the sauce separately. Cut the fish into slices to serve.

NUTRITIONAL ANALYSIS
146 kcals/610 kJ
31.3 g Protein
2.4 g Carbohydrate
1.3 g Fat ★★★★
0.3 g Saturated Fat ★★★★
1 g Fibre ★★
No Added Sugar ★★★★
507 mg Salt ★

NUTRITIONAL ANALYSIS
398 kcals/1662 kJ
48.1 g Protein
6.6 g Carbohydrate
18.6 g Fat ★★
3.2 g Saturated Fat ★★★★
3.7 g Fibre ★★★
0.4 g Added Sugar ★★★★
685 mg Salt ★★★

Trout with Almond Topping

Buy whole trout, the freshwater members of the salmon family, and bone the fish yourself. Otherwise ask your fishmonger to do this for you.

SERVES 4

- *15 g (½ oz) polyunsaturated margarine*
- *30 ml (2 tbsp) chopped fresh parsley*
- *50 ml (2 fl oz) dry white vermouth*
- *4 trout, each weighing about 350 g (12 oz), cleaned and boned*
- *pepper, to taste*
- *50 g (2 oz) fresh wholemeal breadcrumbs*
- *50 g (2 oz) blanched almonds, chopped*
- *parsley sprig, to garnish*

1 Grease a large ovenproof dish with a little of the margarine. Scatter over the parsley and pour in the vermouth.
2 Open out the trout like a book and place, skin-side down, in a single layer in the dish. Season to taste.
3 Combine the breadcrumbs and almonds. Spread evenly over the fish. Dot with the remaining margarine.
4 Cook at 190°C (375°F) mark 5 for 20 minutes or until the topping is crisp and the fish flakes easily when tested with a fork. Garnish with parsley.

NUTRITIONAL ANALYSIS
317 kcals/1323 kJ
33.4 g Protein
27 g Carbohydrate
9.4 g Fat ★★★
0.6 g Saturated Fat ★★★★
3.4 g Fibre ★★★
No Added Sugar ★★★★
503 mg Salt ★★★

Whiting Roll-Ups with Almond Sauce

Filled with a high-fibre stuffing, these spicy whiting rolls are accompanied by a golden almond sauce.

SERVES 4

- *100 g (4 oz) brown rice*
- *25 g (1 oz) raisins, roughly chopped*
- *25 g (1 oz) pine nuts*
- *2.5 ml (½ tsp) ground cumin*
- *2.5 ml (½ tsp) freshly ground coriander*
- *pepper, to taste*
- *8 whiting fillets, each weighing about 100 g (4 oz), skinned*
- *15 ml (1 tbsp) lemon juice*
- *lemon twists and parsley sprigs, to garnish*

FOR THE ALMOND SAUCE

- *25 g (1 oz) ground almonds*
- *300 ml (½ pint) chicken stock*
- *1 garlic clove, skinned and crushed*
- *15 ml (1 tbsp) lemon juice*
- *1.25 ml (¼ tsp) ground turmeric*

1 Put the rice in a saucepan containing 450 ml (¾ pint) boiling water, cover and simmer for 30 minutes or until tender and the liquid has been absorbed. Mix the rice with the raisins, pine nuts and spices. Season to taste.
2 Place the whiting, skinned side up, on a board. Divide the stuffing between the fillets, piling it into the centre of each. Roll up the fillets, securing with wooden cocktail sticks.
3 Place the rolls in a lightly greased shallow ovenproof dish. Sprinkle over the lemon juice and cover with foil. Cook at 180°C (350°F) mark 4 for 15-20 minutes or until tender.
4 Meanwhile for the sauce, put the ground almonds, chicken stock, garlic, lemon juice and turmeric in a saucepan. Bring to the boil and simmer for 10 minutes, stirring occasionally, until slightly thickened.
5 To serve, spoon some of the sauce on a warmed serving dish and arrange the fish rolls on top. Garnish with lemon twists and parsley, then serve at once, with the remaining sauce handed separately.

Mackerel with Orange Sauce

Mackerel, like other oily fish, is a source of certain fatty acids which are increasingly believed to guard against heart disease. The piquant orange sauce counterbalances the richness of the fish.

SERVES 4	*juice of 2 oranges*
1 very large or 2 medium mackerel, about 900 g (2 lb), cleaned	*thinly pared rind of 1 orange*
	2 red or yellow peppers
2 small leeks, washed and cut into matchstick strips	*5 ml (1 tsp) green peppercorns, crushed*
2 celery sticks, trimmed and cut into matchstick strips	*pepper, to taste*

1 Rinse and dry the mackerel, leaving the head and tail on. Scatter the leeks and celery over the bottom of a roasting tin and place the fish on top. Pour the orange juice over the fish.
2 Cover the tin with foil and bake at 190°C (375°F) mark 5 for 25-40 minutes or until the fish flakes easily when tested with a fork.
3 Meanwhile, cut the pared orange rind into very thin strips. Blanch in a saucepan of boiling water for 4-5 minutes, then drain and set aside.
4 Put the peppers under a hot grill and char the skins quickly all over. Cool slightly, then peel. Discard the core and seeds and finely chop the pepper. Put the pepper and 200 ml (⅓ pint) water in a saucepan and cook until very tender and almost all the water has evaporated.
5 When the fish is cooked, strain the juices into the pan with the peppers, reserving the vegetables. Purée the sauce in a blender or food processor and return to the pan. Add the peppercorns and season, then cook for a further minute.
6 Serve the mackerel garnished with the vegetables and orange rind. Serve the sauce separately.

NUTRITIONAL ANALYSIS
342 kcals/1430 kJ
27.8 g Protein
6.9 g Carbohydrate
22.8 g Fat ★
5 g Saturated Fat ★★★
2.1 g Fibre ★★
No Added Sugar ★★★★
573 mg Salt ★★★

Fish Steaks in Lime

This piquant dish is very simple to make, and remarkably quick to prepare. Serve with a mixed leaf salad.

SERVES 4	*30 ml (2 tbsp) chopped fresh basil or 15 ml (1 tbsp) dried*
4 firm-fleshed white fish steaks, each weighing about 175 g (6 oz)	*75 ml (3 fl oz) dry white wine*
lime slices and fresh basil leaves, to garnish	*2 garlic cloves, skinned and crushed*
	5 ml (1 tsp) paprika
FOR THE MARINADE	*15 ml (1 tbsp) sunflower oil*
grated rind and juice of 4 limes	*pepper, to taste*

1 For the marinade, mix all the ingredients together in a large bowl. Add the fish steaks and spoon over the marinade. Leave to marinate for 2 hours, carefully turning the fish at least once.
2 Remove the steaks from the marinade. Cook under the grill for 8 minutes on each side, basting with the marinade, until cooked through and the flesh flakes easily. Discard any remaining marinade. Serve immediately, garnished with the lime slices and basil leaves.

NUTRITIONAL ANALYSIS
144 kcals/604 kJ
27.4 g Protein
0.6 g Carbohydrate
2.9 g Fat ★★★
0.5 g Saturated Fat ★★★★
0 g Fibre ★
No Added Sugar ★★★★
304 mg Salt ★★

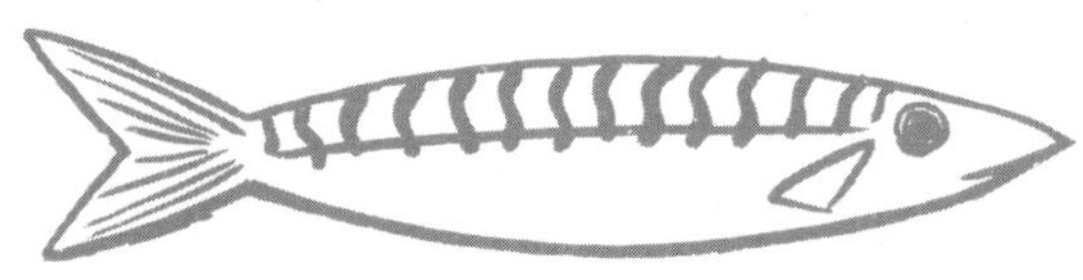

NUTRITIONAL ANALYSIS
253 kcals/1058 kJ
18.9 g Protein
22.3 g Carbohydrate
10.5 g Fat ★★
1.9 g Saturated Fat ★★★★
5.5 g Fibre ★★★★
No Added Sugar ★★★★
468 mg Salt ★★★

Stuffed Fish Rolls

Served with a tomato sauce, these healthy rolls are filled with burghul wheat and vegetables.

SERVES 4

75 g (3 oz) burghul wheat

4 white fish fillets, each weighing 75 g (3 oz), skinned and halved lengthways

pepper, to taste

FOR THE SAUCE

40 g (1½ oz) polyunsaturated margarine

30 ml (2 tbsp) finely chopped onion

1 garlic clove, skinned and crushed

1.25 ml (¼ tsp) dried thyme

900 g (2 lb) ripe tomatoes, roughly chopped

FOR THE FILLING

½ small green pepper, cored, seeded and finely diced

½ small red pepper, cored, seeded and finely diced

225 g (8 oz) button mushrooms, finely chopped

10 ml (2 tsp) lemon juice

1 Put the burghul wheat in a large bowl and cover with cold water. Soak for 1 hour.
2 Meanwhile, place the fish fillets between 2 sheets of greaseproof paper and flatten with a meat hammer. Lightly grease four 100 ml (4 fl oz) ramekin dishes. Season the inner side of each fillet and then use 2 to line each ramekin, skinned sides inwards. Cover and chill.
3 For the sauce, melt 15 g (½ oz) of the margarine in a non-stick saucepan and cook 15 ml (1 tbsp) of the onion for 3 minutes until soft. Add the garlic, thyme and tomatoes and cook over a high heat, stirring, until the liquid has evaporated and the sauce has thickened. Set aside.
4 For the filling, melt 15 g (½ oz) of the margarine in a non-stick frying pan and cook the peppers quickly for 2 minutes until soft. In another pan, melt the remaining margarine and cook the remaining onion for 3 minutes until very soft. Increase the heat and add the mushrooms and lemon juice, stirring occasionally. Cook until only 15 ml (1 tbsp) juice remains. Mix in drained wheat and peppers.
5 Spoon the hot mixture into the ramekins, pressing it down slightly. Cover each ramekin tightly with greased foil and place in a roasting tin. Pour in boiling water to come halfway up sides of ramekins, cover and simmer for 15 minutes.
6 To serve, reheat the tomato sauce, then unmould the ramekins on to warmed plates and spoon the sauce over.

NUTRITIONAL ANALYSIS
279 kcals/1167 kJ
31.8 g Protein
30.4 g Carbohydrate
1.7 g Fat ★★★★
0.4 g Saturated Fat ★★★★
5.3 g Fibre ★★★★
No Added Sugar ★★★★
262 mg Salt ★★★★

Italian Fish Chowder

Both the major ingredients of this dish are low in fat and, as no extra fat is added, the overall fat content of the dish is low.

SERVES 4

1 red pepper

700 g (1½ lb) tomatoes, skinned, seeded and roughly chopped

450 g (1 lb) potatoes, peeled and roughly chopped

150 ml (¼ pint) white wine

15 ml (1 tbsp) tomato purée

2 garlic cloves, skinned and crushed

5 ml (1 tsp) dried oregano

5 ml (1 tsp) dried marjoram

450 g (1 lb) firm-fleshed white fish fillet, skinned and roughly chopped

225 g (8 oz) prepared squid, cut into rings

pepper, to taste

1 Cook the red pepper under the grill until the skin is charred on all sides. Allow to cool, then peel off the skin. Remove the core and seeds, then roughly chop the pepper.
2 Put the pepper, tomatoes, potatoes, wine, tomato purée, garlic and herbs in a large saucepan. Add 750 ml (1¼ pints) water. Cover and simmer gently for 25-30 minutes or until the potatoes are tender and the soup is thickening.
3 Add the cod and simmer for 10 minutes, then add the squid and cook for a further 5 minutes. Season to taste and serve immediately.

Baked Fish with Aubergine

Keep this a low-fat dish by resisting the temptation to add extra oil when cooking the aubergine – it absorbs oil quickly.

SERVES 4

15 ml (1 tbsp) sunflower oil

225 g (8 oz) aubergine, thinly sliced

1 medium onion, skinned and finely chopped

3 tomatoes, chopped

pepper, to taste

4 white fish steaks, each weighing about 175 g (6 oz)

45 ml (3 tbsp) low-fat natural yogurt

15 ml (1 tbsp) capers, well drained

lemon slices and parsley sprigs, to garnish

1 Heat the oil in a non-stick saucepan and cook the aubergine and onion for 5 minutes until the onion is soft. Add the tomatoes and pepper, then cover and cook for a further 10 minutes.

2 Place the aubergine mixture in a shallow ovenproof dish and put the cod on top. Mix the yogurt with the capers and spoon over the cod.

3 Cover and cook at 180°C (350°F) mark 4 for about 25 minutes or until the fish is cooked and flakes easily when tested with a fork. Garnish with lemon slices and parsley sprigs.

NUTRITIONAL ANALYSIS
180 kcals/753 kJ
28.8 g Protein
5.6 g Carbohydrate
4.9 g Fat ★★★
0.8 g Saturated Fat ★★★★
3.6 g Fibre ★★★★
No Added Sugar ★★★★
321 mg Salt ★★★★

White Fish Portugaise

The fish and sauce can be prepared in advance, then cooked later in the day.

SERVES 4

700 g (1½ lb) firm-fleshed white fish, skinned

10 ml (2 tsp) sunflower oil

1 medium onion, skinned and finely chopped

1 green pepper, cored, seeded and chopped

397 g (14 oz) can chopped tomatoes

pinch of dried mixed herbs

pepper, to taste

1 Cut the fish into serving-sized pieces and place in a lightly greased ovenproof dish.

2 Heat the oil in a non-stick frying pan and cook the onion and pepper for about 5 minutes until soft. Add the tomatoes, herbs and pepper and cook for 10 minutes, stirring occasionally.

3 Pour the sauce over the fish and cover the dish. Cook at 180°C (350°F) mark 4 for 30-40 minutes or until the fish is cooked.

NUTRITIONAL ANALYSIS
182 kcals/759 kJ
32.2 g Protein
4.6 g Carbohydrate
4 g Fat ★★★
0.7 g Saturated Fat ★★★★
1.6 g Fibre ★★★
No Added Sugar ★★★★
425 mg Salt ★★

NUTRITIONAL ANALYSIS
415 kcals/1735 kJ
23 g Protein
64.7 g Carbohydrate
7.8 g Fat ★★★★
1.2 g Saturated Fat ★★★★
11.2 g Fibre ★★★★
No Added Sugar ★★★★
662 mg Salt ★★★

Spaghetti with Clam Sauce

This Mediterranean-style dish is made with canned clams but, if liked, fresh or frozen clams could be used instead. Alternatively, try substituting mussels.

SERVES 4

350 g (12 oz) wholewheat spaghetti
15 ml (1 tbsp) sunflower oil
1 medium onion, skinned and chopped
1 garlic clove, skinned and crushed
1.25 ml (1/4 tsp) chilli powder
15 ml (1 tbsp) wholemeal flour
400 g (14 oz) can chopped tomatoes
275 g (10 oz) can clams, drained, with juice reserved
60 ml (4 tbsp) dry white wine (optional)
30 ml (2 tbsp) chopped fresh parsley
pepper, to taste

1 Put the spaghetti in a large saucepan of boiling water and cook for about 10 minutes or until just tender.
2 Meanwhile, heat the oil in a non-stick saucepan and gently cook the onion for 5 minutes until soft. Add the garlic and chilli powder and cook for 1 minute, then stir in the flour. Add the tomatoes with their juice to the pan and bring to the boil, stirring until slightly thickened.
3 Add the clams and 60 ml (4 tbsp) of the clam liquid or the dry white wine. Return to the boil, stirring, then simmer for 2-3 minutes to heat the clams. Stir in the parsley and seasoning.
4 Drain the spaghetti and serve on warmed individual plates with the clam sauce.

NUTRITIONAL ANALYSIS
338 kcals/1411 kJ
44.5 g Protein
1.9 g Carbohydrate
15.6 g Fat ★★
3 g Saturated Fat ★★★
0.6 g Fibre ★
0.1 g Added Sugar ★★★★
493 mg Salt ★★★

Grey Mullet Steamed Chinese Style

The Chinese use their woks for steaming fish. If you do not have one, use a baking tin covered with foil and a wire rack.

SERVES 4

900 g (2 lb) grey mullet or other fish, cleaned with head left on
30 ml (2 tbsp) soya sauce
10 ml (2 tsp) finely chopped fresh root ginger
15 ml (1 tbsp) wine vinegar
1 small carrot, scrubbed and cut into matchsticks
6 spring onions, trimmed and finely shredded

1 Score the mullet skin in diagonal cuts about 5 cm (2 inches) apart. Lay the fish in a heatproof dish, which will fit inside the wok or baking tin.
2 Mix together the soya sauce, ginger and vinegar. Pour over the fish, then set aside for 1 hour.
3 Sprinkle the carrot and onions over the fish. Put the dish on a rack in a wok or baking tin and add sufficient water to come up to the rack. Cover, bring to the boil and cook over a high heat for 10-12 minutes or until the fish flakes easily near the bone with a fork.
4 Pour off most of the liquid, reserving about 60 ml (4 tbsp). Serve the fish with 15 ml (1 tbsp) of the reserved liquid spooned over each portion.

Vegetable Couscous

The ingredient couscous is made by cracking wholewheat berries with rollers. Steamed over a vegetable stew with chick-peas, it makes a nutritious North African dish of the same name.

SERVES 4	
100 g (4 oz) chick-peas, soaked overnight	1.25 ml (¼ tsp) chilli powder
225 g (8 oz) couscous	2 leeks, washed and sliced
15 ml (1 tbsp) sunflower oil	2 carrots, scrubbed and sliced
2 medium onions, skinned and chopped	600 ml (1 pint) vegetable stock
1 garlic clove, skinned and crushed	3 courgettes (zucchini), trimmed and sliced
5 ml (1 tsp) freshly ground cumin	1 large tomato, roughly chopped
5 ml (1 tsp) freshly ground coriander	50 g (2 oz) raisins

1 Drain the chick-peas and rinse. Put into a saucepan with plenty of fresh water and boil for 10-15 minutes. Lower the heat and simmer for 40-50 minutes. Drain.
2 Meanwhile, put the couscous in a bowl and add 450 ml (¾ pint) cold water. Leave to soak for 10-15 minutes until the water is absorbed.
3 Heat the oil in a large non-stick saucepan and cook the onion for 5 minutes. Add the garlic and spices and cook, stirring, for 1 minute. Add the leeks, carrots and stock. Bring to the boil.
4 Line a large sieve with muslin or all-purpose kitchen cloth and put over the vegetable stew. Put the couscous in the sieve. Cover the whole pan with foil to enclose the steam. Simmer for 20 minutes.
5 Add the chick-peas, courgettes, tomato and raisins to the stew. Replace the sieve and fluff up the couscous with a fork. Cover and simmer for 10 minutes. Spread the couscous on a large warmed serving dish and spoon the vegetable stew over.

NUTRITIONAL ANALYSIS
326 kcals/1363 kJ
11 g Protein
61.1 g Carbohydrate
6.2 g Fat ★★★★
1.3 g Saturated Fat ★★★★
8.9 g Fibre ★★★★
No Added Sugar ★★★★
178 mg Salt ★★★★

Curried Sweet Potato Pot

Sweet potatoes, despite their name, are not related to potatoes. They are a tuber vegetable, usually an elongated shape though there are some round varieties. The flesh is usually white, sweet and slightly perfumed. The outer skin may be white or purplish red.

SERVES 4	
225 g (8 oz) chick-peas, soaked overnight	1 corn on the cob, thawed if frozen, cut crossways into 4 pieces
15 ml (1 tbsp) sunflower oil	225 g (8 oz) tomatoes, quartered
1 medium onion, skinned and chopped	225 g (8 oz) green beans, trimmed and halved
15 ml (1 tbsp) curry powder or to taste	pepper, to taste
225 g (8 oz) red lentils	15 ml (1 tbsp) chopped fresh parsley
1.1 litres (2 pints) vegetable stock	150 ml (¼ pint) low-fat natural yogurt
225 g (8 oz) sweet potatoes, skinned and cut into chunks	5 ml (1 tsp) garam masala

1 Drain the chick-peas and rinse. Put into a saucepan with plenty of fresh water and boil for 10-15 minutes. Drain well and set aside.
2 Heat the oil in a flameproof casserole and cook the onion for 3-5 minutes until transparent. Add the curry powder and cook, stirring, for 1 minute.
3 Add the boiled chick-peas, lentils and stock to the casserole. Bring to the boil, cover and simmer gently for about 40 minutes or until the chick-peas are cooked but still slightly crunchy.
4 Add the sweet potatoes and corn on the cob and simmer for 10 minutes. Stir in the tomatoes, beans, seasoning and parsley and cook for 15 minutes.
5 To serve, top with the yogurt and sprinkle with garam masala.

NUTRITIONAL ANALYSIS
552 kcals/2308 kJ
32.1 g Protein
89.3 g Carbohydrate
9.9 g Fat ★★★★
1.2 g Saturated Fat ★★★★
22 g Fibre ★★★★
No Added Sugar ★★★★
298 mg Salt ★★★★

NUTRITIONAL ANALYSIS
340 kcals/1422 kJ
17.7 g Protein
59.2 g Carbohydrate
5.3 g Fat ★★★★
0.8 g Saturated Fat ★★★★
12.3 g Fibre ★★★★
No Added Sugar ★★★★
298 mg Salt ★★★★

Lentil Casserole

This lentil casserole, containing vegetables and brown rice, is high in fibre.

SERVES 4

225 g (8 oz) continental brown lentils
15 ml (1 tbsp) sunflower oil
2 medium onions, skinned and sliced
3 celery sticks, trimmed and sliced
1 aubergine, trimmed and diced
1 garlic clove, skinned and crushed
1 red pepper, cored, seeded and diced
100 g (4 oz) brown rice
1.25-2.5 ml (¼-½ tsp) mixed dried herbs
pepper, to taste
225 g (8 oz) can tomatoes
750 ml (1¼ pints) vegetable stock
red pepper rings and celery leaves, to garnish

1 Soak the lentils in enough boiling water to cover for 30 minutes, then drain well.
2 Heat the oil in a large flameproof casserole and gently cook the onions, celery, aubergine, garlic and red pepper for 4 minutes, stirring.
3 Stir in the lentils, rice, herbs, pepper, tomatoes with their juice and the stock.
4 Cover and cook at 190°C (375°F) mark 5 for 1¼ hours or until all the liquid has been absorbed and the rice and lentils are tender. Garnish and serve.

NUTRITIONAL ANALYSIS
267 kcals/1118 kJ
15.7 g Protein
38.5 g Carbohydrate
6.7 g Fat ★★★
0.4 g Saturated Fat ★★★★
11.4 g Fibre ★★★★
No Added Sugar ★★★★
95 mg Salt ★★★★

Chick-Pea Curry

Canned chick-peas are used for speed but dried ones, soaked and precooked, can be substituted. Use the cooking liquid in place of can juices.

SERVES 4

10 ml (2 tsp) sunflower oil
1 large onion, skinned and sliced
two 400 g (14 oz) cans chick-peas
1-2 green chillies, seeded if preferred
4 garlic cloves, skinned
2.5 cm (1 inch) fresh root ginger, roughly chopped
5 ml (1 tsp) garam masala
5 ml (1 tsp) tomato purée
1.25 ml (¼ tsp) freshly ground coriander
1.25 ml (¼ tsp) freshly ground cumin

1 Heat the oil in a non-stick saucepan and gently brown the onion for 5-8 minutes.
2 Drain the chick-peas, reserving the liquid from the cans. Purée the chillies, garlic, ginger and half of the chick-pea liquid in a food processor or blender until smooth. Add to the onion and cook for 2-3 minutes, stirring occasionally.
3 Add the garam masala, tomato purée, coriander, cumin, chick-peas and remaining liquid. Simmer gently for 15 minutes.

Stir-Fried Vegetables (PAGE 99)

Stuffed Peppers

The tiny, brown heart-shaped buckwheat seeds are used in the filling for these peppers. Serve with a mixed leaf salad.

SERVES 4	*300-350 ml (10-12 fl oz) vegetable stock*
15 ml (1 tbsp) sunflower oil	*10 ml (2 tsp) dried oregano*
1 medium onion, skinned and finely chopped	*10 ml (2 tsp) chopped fresh parsley*
75 g (3 oz) celery, trimmed and chopped	*pepper, to taste*
2 garlic cloves, skinned and crushed	*2 tomatoes, chopped*
75 g (3 oz) buckwheat	*4 peppers, each weighing about 175 g (6 oz)*
50 g (2 oz) mushrooms, finely chopped	*400 g (14 oz) can tomatoes, drained*

1 Heat the oil in a large non-stick frying pan and cook the onion, celery, 1 garlic clove and buckwheat for 2 minutes. Add the mushrooms and cook for 2 minutes.
2 Add the stock, 7.5 ml (1½ tsp) of the oregano and the chopped parsley. Season, cover and cook for 15 minutes or until the buckwheat is soft. Mix in the chopped tomatoes.
3 Cut the tops off the peppers and reserve as lids, then cut a thin slice from the base so the peppers stand upright. Core and seed, then blanch with the lids in a saucepan of boiling water for 5 minutes. Drain well.
4 Fill the peppers with the buckwheat mixture and top with the lids. Stand the peppers in an ovenproof dish and add a little water. Cover and cook at 180°C (350°F) mark 4 for 30-40 minutes or until cooked through.
5 Purée the canned tomatoes, remaining garlic and oregano in a blender or food processor. Heat gently and serve with the peppers.

NUTRITIONAL ANALYSIS
155 kcals/649 kJ
5.9 g Protein
23.8 g Carbohydrate
4.8 g Fat ★★★
0.8 g Saturated Fat ★★★★
4.6 g Fibre ★★★★
No Added Sugar ★★★★
174 mg Salt ★★★

Mixed Bean Chilli

This colourful dish is speeded up by the use of canned beans, thus omitting the overnight soaking and simmering necessary when using dried beans.

SERVES 4	*425 g (15 oz) can chick-peas, drained*
10 ml (2 tsp) sunflower oil	*425 g (15 oz) can borlotti beans, drained*
1 medium onion, skinned and sliced	*225 g (8 oz) can red kidney beans, drained*
1 garlic clove, skinned and crushed	*15 ml (1 tbsp) tomato purée*
1 small green pepper, cored, seeded and cut into rings	*pepper, to taste*
	10 ml (2 tsp) mild chilli powder
450 g (1 lb) tomatoes, skinned and roughly chopped	*parsley sprigs and tomato wedges, to garnish*

1 Heat the oil in a large non-stick saucepan and cook the onion, garlic and green pepper for 5 minutes until soft.
2 Add the tomatoes, chick-peas, borlotti beans and red kidney beans, stirring well. Add the tomato purée, seasoning, chilli powder and 300 ml (½ pint) water. Stir well, bring to the boil and simmer for 30 minutes. Garnish with parsley sprigs and tomato wedges.

NUTRITIONAL ANALYSIS
338 kcals/1413 kJ
22.2 g Protein
57 g Carbohydrate
4.2 g Fat ★★★★
0.8 g Saturated Fat ★★★★
21.2 g Fibre ★★★★
No Added Sugar ★★★★
184 mg Salt ★★★★

Pepper Salad (PAGE 108)

NUTRITIONAL ANALYSIS
520 kcals/2173 kJ
60 g Protein
31.9 g Carbohydrate
16.8 g Fat ★★★
5.7 g Saturated Fat ★★★
5.3 g Fibre ★★★
No Added Sugar ★★★★
674 mg Salt ★★★

Country Beef Braise

In braising, which is similar to pot roasting, the piece of meat is placed on a bed of vegetables and cooked gently in the steam from the cooking liquid.

SERVES 4-6

20 ml (4 tsp) wholemeal flour
2.5 ml (1/2 tsp) dried mixed herbs
pepper, to taste
1.1-1.4 kg (2 1/2-3 lb) lean topside of beef, well trimmed
15 ml (1 tbsp) sunflower oil
2 medium onions, skinned and quartered
3 medium potatoes, scrubbed and quartered
2 medium carrots, scrubbed and cut into large pieces
2 celery sticks, trimmed and cut into large pieces
1 turnip, peeled and cut into bite-sized pieces
1.25 ml (1/4 tsp) grated nutmeg
1 bay leaf
150 ml (1/4 pint) red wine

1 Mix together the flour, herbs and seasoning and use to coat the beef. Heat the oil in a flameproof casserole and cook the beef over a fairly high heat for about 5 minutes until browned all over. Remove from the casserole and set aside.
2 Add the vegetables to the casserole and cook for 3-4 minutes, stirring frequently. Stir any remaining seasoned flour into the casserole, then place the beef on top of the vegetables. Add the nutmeg, bay leaf and wine.
3 Cover tightly and cook at 180°C (350°F) mark 4, allowing 45 minutes per 450 g (1 lb) of meat.
4 To serve, lift the meat and vegetables on to a warmed serving dish. Discard the bay leaf and skim the fat from the cooking liquid. Pour a little of the liquid over the meat and vegetables, then serve the remainder separately.

NUTRITIONAL ANALYSIS
479 kcals/2001 kJ
43.6 g Protein
41.6 g Carbohydrate
12.5 g Fat ★★★
4 g Saturated Fat ★★★★
3.5 g Fibre ★★
No Added Sugar ★★★★
1134 mg Salt ★★

Beef in Beer

French mustards are smooth or grainy; the most famous are Dijon, Bordeaux and Meaux. Both Dijon and Bordeaux are smooth, sharp mustards; Meaux is a robust whole grain mustard, blended with herbs and spices.

SERVES 4

10 ml (2 tsp) sunflower oil
3 medium onions, skinned and chopped
2 large garlic cloves, skinned and chopped
700 g (1 1/2 lb) lean stewing steak, cut into 2.5 cm (1 inch) pieces
30 ml (2 tbsp) wholemeal flour
400 ml (14 fl oz) light ale
1 bay leaf
5 ml (1 tsp) juniper berries
pepper, to taste
5 ml (1 tsp) vinegar
1 small French stick, cut into slices
French mustard

1 Heat the oil in a non-stick frying pan and gently cook the onions for about 15 minutes until golden brown, stirring occasionally. Add the garlic and cook for a further 2 minutes. Remove the onions and garlic and place in a casserole. Add the meat to the pan and brown on all sides.
2 Stir the flour into the pan, then add 200 ml (7 fl oz) of the ale and bring to the boil, stirring well. Add the meat mixture to the casserole. Pour in the remaining ale, bay leaf, juniper berries and season to taste. Cover and cook at 170°C (325°F) mark 3 for 2 1/2 hours.
3 About 45 minutes before the end of the cooking time, stir in the vinegar. Spread the French bread with the mustard. Put as many slices as possible, mustard-side up, into the casserole. Push the bread down with a wooden spoon into the gravy – the pieces will rise to the surface again.
4 Replace the casserole in the oven without the lid; this allows the bread to become crisp and golden. Complete the cooking time and serve.

Orange Pork Chops with Apple

Invest in a zester for quick, attractive citrus rind shreds for garnishing.

SERVES 4	
4 loin pork chops, about 175 g (6 oz) each, trimmed of all fat	*1 spring onion, trimmed and finely chopped*
finely grated rind and juice of 2 oranges	*pepper, to taste*
7.5 ml (½ tbsp) sunflower oil	*4 large eating apples, peeled, cored and cut into slices*
1 large bay leaf, broken in half	*7.5 cm (3 inch) cinnamon stick, broken in half*
	4 cloves
	orange shreds and parsley sprigs, to garnish

1 Arrange the pork chops in a dish large enough to hold them in a single layer. Mix together the orange rind and juice, oil, bay leaf, spring onion and pepper, then pour over the chops.
2 Cover and marinate for at least 4 hours, turning the chops at least once and occasionally basting with the marinade.
3 Drain the chops, reserving the marinade. Cook under a medium grill for about 10 minutes on each side until cooked through, brushing with the marinade during cooking.
4 Meanwhile, put the apple slices and spices in a heavy-based saucepan with 50 ml (2 fl oz) water. Cover tightly and cook over a low heat for about 5 minutes until the apples are soft but still hold their shape. Discard the spices.
5 Put the marinade in a small saucepan and boil until reduced to about 60 ml (4 tbsp).
6 Serve the chops on warmed individual plates with the apple slices. Spoon over the reduced marinade and garnish with orange shreds and parsley sprigs.

NUTRITIONAL ANALYSIS
249 kcals/1039 kJ
31.4 g Protein
2.6 g Carbohydrate
12.5 g Fat ★★
4.3 g Saturated Fat ★★
0.3 g Fibre ★
No Added Sugar ★★★★
293 mg Salt ★★★

Veal and Tomato Casserole

Herbs, garlic and onions, flavour this dish. Serve with brown rice accompanied by a crisp green salad.

SERVES 4	
15 ml (1 tbsp) sunflower oil	*1 garlic clove, skinned and crushed*
1 large onion, skinned and chopped	*175 g (6 oz) button mushrooms*
450 g (1 lb) lean veal, cubed	*15 ml (1 tbsp) tomato purée*
2.5 ml (½ tsp) dried oregano	*400 g (14 oz) can tomatoes*
5 ml (1 tsp) finely chopped fresh basil or 2.5 ml (½ tsp) dried	*pepper, to taste*
	chopped fresh parsley, to garnish

1 Heat the oil in a non-stick saucepan and gently cook the onion, covered, for 6-8 minutes until soft.
2 Increase the heat slightly and add the veal, stirring until all the pieces are lightly browned. Mix in the herbs, garlic and mushrooms, then stir in the tomato purée and tomatoes with the juices.
3 Bring to the boil, then cover and simmer for 40 minutes. Uncover and continue cooking for about 10 minutes to reduce the sauce slightly. Season to taste then serve garnished with chopped parsley.

NUTRITIONAL ANALYSIS
191 kcals/799 kJ
26.5 g Protein
5.4 g Carbohydrate
7.2 g Fat ★★★
1.9 g Saturated Fat ★★★
2.9 g Fibre ★★★★
No Added Sugar ★★★★
415 mg Salt ★★

NUTRITIONAL ANALYSIS
264 kcals/1103 kJ
29.3 g Protein
25.3 g Carbohydrate
5.8 g Fat ★★★
1.9 g Saturated Fat ★★★★
6.3 g Fibre ★★★★
No Added Sugar ★★★★
1139 mg Salt ★

Lemon Veal

Unlike many veal escalope recipes, this one is healthier because the veal is grilled rather than fried.

SERVES 4
grated rind and juice of 2 lemons
60 ml (4 tbsp) chopped fresh parsley
15 ml (1 tbsp) dried oregano
5 ml (1 tsp) paprika
pepper, to taste
4 veal escalopes, each weighing about 100 g (4 oz), beaten
1 egg, beaten
60 ml (4 tbsp) skimmed milk
225 g (8 oz) fresh wholemeal breadcrumbs
watercress sprigs and lemon wedges, to garnish

1 Mix together the lemon rind and juice, parsley, oregano, paprika and seasoning in a dish. Lay the veal escalopes in the mixture, turning once or twice to ensure that they are evenly coated. Leave to stand in a cool place for 1 hour.
2 Mix together the egg and milk in a shallow dish. Place the breadcrumbs on a flat dish. One by one, dip the escalopes into the milk mixture and then into the breadcrumbs, patting the crumbs on gently.
3 Cook under a grill for about 7½ minutes each side or until golden brown and cooked through. Garnish with watercress sprigs and lemon wedges and serve.

NUTRITIONAL ANALYSIS
159 kcals/666 kJ
19.5 g Protein
4.6 g Carbohydrate
7.1 g Fat ★★
3.4 g Saturated Fat ★★
2 g Fibre ★★★★
No Added Sugar ★★★★
269 mg Salt ★★★

Escalopes of Veal with Herbs

The best quality veal is milk fed. The flesh is a paler pink and more delicate in texture and flavour than grain-fed veal.

SERVES 4
4 veal escalopes, each weighing about 75 g (3 oz)
15 g (½ oz) fine wholemeal flour
60 ml (4 tbsp) chopped fresh parsley
15 ml (1 tbsp) snipped fresh chives
30 ml (2 tbsp) chopped fresh tarragon
½ punnet cress, snipped
150 ml (¼ pint) Greek strained yogurt
5 ml (1 tsp) sunflower oil
pepper, to taste

1 Beat out the veal escalopes between 2 sheets of greaseproof paper until very thin. Coat them lightly with the flour.
2 Mix the parsley, chives, tarragon and cress with the yogurt.
3 Heat the oil in a non-stick frying pan and gently cook the veal for about 5 minutes on each side until golden. Arrange on an ovenproof serving dish.
4 Add the herb mixture to the pan and heat gently, scraping the bottom of the pan to mix in the meat juices, but do not boil. If the sauce is too thick, add a little water. Season to taste and pour over the veal.
5 Cook at 180°C (350°F) mark 4 for 10 minutes.

Moussaka

Traditional moussaka is very high in fat because the aubergines are fried in plenty of olive oil and soak up a considerable amount of it. In this method, the oil is reduced as the aubergines are steamed.

SERVES 4	pepper, to taste
5 ml (1 tsp) salt	5 ml (1 tsp) tomato purée
450 g (1 lb) aubergines, thinly sliced	2.5 ml (½ tsp) ground cumin
15 ml (1 tbsp) sunflower oil	2.5 ml (½ tsp) dried oregano
1 medium onion, skinned and chopped	25 g (1 oz) fresh wholemeal breadcrumbs
1 garlic clove, skinned and finely chopped	FOR THE TOPPING
225 g (8 oz) lean minced lamb	25 g (1 oz) fine wholemeal flour
400 g (14 oz) can tomatoes, chopped	150 ml (¼ pint) low-fat natural yogurt
30 ml (2 tbsp) chopped fresh parsley	1 egg

NUTRITIONAL ANALYSIS
242 kcals/1011 kJ
19.5 g Protein
17.5 g Carbohydrate
11 g Fat ★★
3.7 g Saturated Fat ★★★
6.4 g Fibre ★★★★
No Added Sugar ★★★★
440 mg Salt ★★★

1 Sprinkle the salt over the aubergine slices and leave for 30 minutes. Rinse off all the salt and drain well.
2 Heat the oil in a non-stick saucepan and gently cook the onion and garlic for 5 minutes until soft. Add the lamb and fry for about 5 minutes until browned. If there is any fat in the saucepan, drain it off.
3 Add the tomatoes with their juice, the parsley, seasoning, tomato purée, cumin and oregano. Cover and simmer for 10 minutes. Stir in the breadcrumbs.
4 Steam the aubergine slices for 5-10 minutes until just soft. Drain well.
5 Lightly grease a 1 litre (1¾ pint) shallow ovenproof dish and line the base with half the aubergine slices. Cover with the minced lamb mixture and arrange the remaining aubergine slices over the top.
6 For the topping, beat the flour and yogurt into the egg and pour the mixture over the aubergines.
7 Bake at 180°C (350°F) mark 4 for 45 minutes – 1 hour or until browned on top.

Lamb Fillet with Leek Sauce

This recipe uses lean lamb fillet and low-fat yogurt which means its total fat content is low.

SERVES 4	2 rosemary sprigs
2 lamb fillets, total weight about 550 g (1¼ lb), well trimmed	450 g (1 lb) leeks, washed and sliced 150 ml (¼ pint) low-fat natural yogurt
1 garlic clove, skinned and crushed	grated nutmeg, to taste
pepper, to taste	rosemary sprigs, to garnish

NUTRITIONAL ANALYSIS
278 kcals/1162 kJ
32.6 g Protein
9.3 g Carbohydrate
12.5 g Fat ★★
5.9 g Saturated Fat ★★
3.5 g Fibre ★★★★
No Added Sugar ★★★★
406 mg Salt ★★★

1 Put the lamb fillets in a roasting tin and spread the garlic on top. Season and add the rosemary sprigs. Roast at 180°C (350°F) mark 4 for 30 minutes or until tender and cooked.
2 Meanwhile, put the leeks in a saucepan of boiling water and cook for 10 minutes or until tender. Drain well. Blend in a food processor or blender until smooth. Return to the saucepan and stir in the yogurt. Add nutmeg and season to taste.
3 Add any cooking juices from the cooked lamb to the leek sauce. Slice the lamb and arrange on warmed serving plates. Stirring the sauce, reheat without boiling. Spoon a little sauce over the lamb and serve the rest separately. Garnish with rosemary.

NUTRITIONAL ANALYSIS
325 kcals/1358 kJ
33.2 g Protein
9.9 g Carbohydrate
17.3 g Fat ★★
6.5 g Saturated Fat ★★
3.2 g Fibre ★★★
No Added Sugar ★★★★
492 mg Salt ★★★

Lamb Curry

This rich lamb curry needs a plain accompaniment. For an authentic Indian meal, serve with boiled rice, a yogurt and cucumber raita and shredded lettuce.

SERVES 4

15 ml (1 tbsp) sunflower oil
550 g (1¼ lb) boned lean leg of lamb, cut into 1 cm (½ inch) cubes
2 large onions, skinned and chopped
2 garlic cloves, skinned and crushed
2.5 cm (1 inch) piece fresh root ginger, peeled and chopped
5 ml (1 tsp) freshly ground cumin
2.5 ml (½ tsp) ground cardamom
5 ml (1 tsp) freshly ground coriander
5 ml (1 tsp) ground turmeric
5 ml (1 tsp) ground cinnamon
1.25 ml (¼ tsp) chilli powder
150 ml (¼ pint) low-fat natural yogurt
300 ml (½ pint) chicken stock
15 ml (1 tbsp) tomato purée
15 ml (1 tbsp) lemon juice
pepper, to taste
1 bay leaf
175 g (6 oz) mushrooms, quartered
5 ml (1 tsp) garam masala
15 ml (1 tbsp) chopped fresh coriander, to garnish

1 Heat the oil in a non-stick saucepan and cook the lamb, a few cubes at a time, for about 5 minutes until browned on all sides. Remove from the pan.
2 Purée the onion, garlic, ginger, cumin, cardamom, coriander, turmeric, cinnamon and chilli powder in a blender or food processor until the onion is very finely chopped and the mixture well blended. Add to the pan and cook gently for about 5 minutes, stirring occasionally.
3 Gradually stir in the yogurt. Add the stock, tomato purée, lemon juice, seasoning and bay leaf. Mix well. Stir in the lamb and mushrooms. Bring to the boil, cover and simmer for 45 minutes.
4 Remove the lid and simmer, stirring occasionally, for 30 minutes or until the meat is tender. Stir in the garam masala. Serve garnished with chopped coriander.

NUTRITIONAL ANALYSIS
282 kcals/1179 kJ
25.8 g Protein
12.7 g Carbohydrate
14.6 g Fat ★★
4 g Saturated Fat ★★★
2.7 g Fibre ★★★
No Added Sugar ★★★★
303 mg Salt ★★★

Liver Provençal

Lamb's liver has an excellent flavour and texture, being only slightly coarser and darker than calf's liver. Calf's liver is usually the most expensive and considered the finest. Serve this colourful liver and vegetable casserole with brown rice.

SERVES 4

450 g (1 lb) lamb's liver, trimmed and cut into thin slices
30 ml (2 tbsp) wholemeal flour
10 ml (2 tsp) sunflower oil
1 onion, skinned and sliced
2 garlic cloves, skinned and crushed
1 green pepper, cored, seeded and sliced
1 red pepper, cored, seeded and sliced
397 g (14 oz) can chopped tomatoes
pepper, to taste

1 Coat the liver with the wholemeal flour. Heat the oil in a non-stick pan and gently cook the onion and garlic for 5-8 minutes until browned.
2 Remove from the pan and put into a casserole with the green and red peppers, tomatoes and pepper. Put the liver in the pan and fry for 5 minutes until browned. Transfer to the casserole.
3 Cover and cook at 180°C (350°F) mark 4 for 1 hour.

6

Accompanying Vegetables

Probably the healthiest vegetables you could serve with any meal would be those you'd grown yourself, then lightly steamed. But as the recipes included here show, it is possible to have tasty and healthy vegetables which are slightly more elaborate in presentation. However, you should only serve one of these dishes per meal; any other vegetables served should be lightly boiled or steamed. Avoid adding butter or margarine to plain, cooked vegetables as this increases your fat intake.

NUTRITIONAL ANALYSIS
26 kcals/107 kJ
1.8 g Protein
4.5 g Carbohydrate
0.3 g Fat ★★★★
0.1 g Saturated Fat ★★★★
4.8 g Fibre ★★★★
No Added Sugar ★★★★
37 mg Salt ★★★

Parisienne Beans

Even in a simple dish such as this, it is good to use a well-flavoured stock so salt is not needed.

SERVES 4

300 ml (½ pint) chicken or vegetable stock
450 g (1 lb) fresh or frozen French beans
1 large onion, skinned and chopped
1 soft-leaved lettuce, roughly shredded
pepper, to taste
knob of polyunsaturated margarine, to serve (optional)

1 Put the stock in a saucepan and bring to the boil. Add the beans and onion, cover and simmer for about 10 minutes or until the beans are tender.
2 Stir in the lettuce and cook for 2 minutes. Drain and season to taste. Transfer to a warmed serving dish, place the margarine on top, if liked, and serve.

NUTRITIONAL ANALYSIS
319 kcals/1332 kJ
6 g Protein
57.5 g Carbohydrate
8.8 g Fat ★★★
1.1 g Saturated Fat ★★★★
10.3 g Fibre ★★★★
No Added Sugar ★★★★
110 mg Salt ★★★★

Spicy Pilau Rice

Turmeric is a vivid yellow powder, giving colour and flavour to rice and curry dishes. Serve this nutritious pilau with meat, poultry or fish main dishes.

SERVES 4

15 ml (1 tbsp) sunflower oil
1 medium onion, skinned and finely chopped
2.5 ml (½ tsp) cumin seeds, crushed
10 ml (2 tsp) ground turmeric
pepper, to taste
15 ml (1 tbsp) lemon juice
175 g (6 oz) brown rice
600 ml (1 pint) chicken stock
100 g (4 oz) no-soak dried apricots, roughly chopped
1 bay leaf
50 g (2 oz) raisins
25 g (1 oz) flaked almonds

1 Heat the oil over a low heat in a large non-stick saucepan and cook the onion for 3 minutes until soft. Add the spices and pepper, lemon juice and rice. Mix together well so the rice is coated with the spices.
2 Bring the stock to the boil in another saucepan, then add immediately to the rice and mix well. Stir in the apricots and bay leaf.
3 Cover and simmer for 30 minutes or until all the liquid has been absorbed, adding the raisins about 10 minutes before the end of cooking to allow them to soften slightly and warm through. Stir in the almonds just before serving.

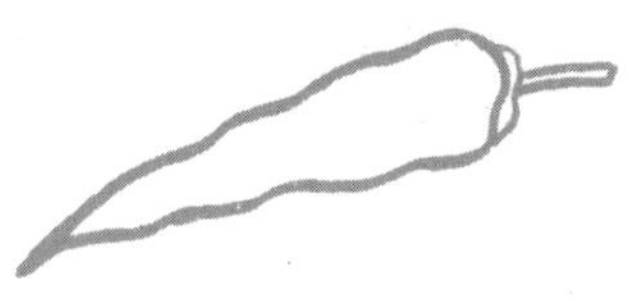

Layered Onions and Potatoes

This quick-to-prepare dish makes an economical accompaniment to oven baked meat, poultry or fish as it can be cooked at the same time.

SERVES 4

700 g (1½ lb) potatoes, peeled and sliced
1 medium onion, skinned and sliced
pinch of grated nutmeg
pepper, to taste
30 ml (2 tbsp) chopped fresh parsley
150 ml (¼ pint) vegetable stock

1 Lightly grease a shallow ovenproof dish and layer with the potato and onion slices, seasoning the layers with nutmeg, pepper and half the parsley. Finish with a neat layer of potatoes. Pour over the vegetable stock.
2 Cover with a piece of foil and bake at 190°C (375°F) mark 5 for 1½ hours or until a fork or fine skewer easily pierces the potatoes. Serve hot, garnished with the remaining parsley.

NUTRITIONAL ANALYSIS
162 kcals/679 kJ
4.4 g Protein
38.2 g Carbohydrate
0.3 g Fat ★★★★
0 g Saturated Fat ★★★★
4.8 g Fibre ★★★
No Added Sugar ★★★★
49 mg Salt ★★★★

Italian Lentils

Lentils are one of the quickest pulses to prepare because they do not require presoaking. Here they add nutritional goodness as well as making a hearty main dish.

SERVES 4

350 g (12 oz) whole green lentils
15 ml (1 tbsp) sunflower oil
1 large onion, skinned and chopped
175 g (6 oz) mushrooms, sliced
1 garlic clove, skinned and crushed
400 g (14 oz) can tomatoes
15 ml (1 tbsp) chopped fresh marjoram or basil or 5 ml (1 tsp) dried
pepper, to taste

1 Put the lentils in a saucepan and pour over 1.4 litres (2½ pints) water. Bring to the boil, cover and simmer for 30-40 minutes or until the lentils are tender. Drain.
2 Heat the oil in a non-stick saucepan and cook the onion for 3 minutes. Add the mushrooms and garlic and cook for a further 2 minutes until soft.
3 Add the tomatoes to the pan with their juice, the marjoram and seasoning. Add the lentils and bring to the boil, stirring. Cover and simmer gently for about 15 minutes or until most of the liquid is absorbed but the mixture is still moist. Serve hot.

NUTRITIONAL ANALYSIS
332 kcals/1386 kJ
23.2 g Protein
51.5 g Carbohydrate
5 g Fat ★★★★
0.7 g Saturated Fat ★★★★
12.9 g Fibre ★★★★
No Added Sugar ★★★★
177 mg Salt ★★★★

NUTRITIONAL ANALYSIS
40 kcals/168 kJ
4 g Protein
2.5 g Carbohydrate
1.7 g Fat ★★
0.1 g Saturated Fat ★★★★
4.3 g Fibre ★★★★
No Added Sugar ★★★★
177 mg Salt ★

Spring Greens and Mushrooms

Steaming the spring greens retains both their vitamins and their crunchiness. The mushrooms are cooked only briefly in lime juice, so the complete dish has a fairly crisp texture.

SERVES 4
225 g (8 oz) spring greens, trimmed and finely shredded
100 g (4 oz) mushrooms, sliced
juice of 1 lime or ½ lemon
pepper, to taste
15 ml (1 tbsp) sunflower seeds

1 Put the spring greens in the top of a steamer over a saucepan of gently boiling water and steam for 6-8 minutes or until amost cooked but still crunchy.
2 Meanwhile, put the mushrooms, lime juice and 30 ml (2 tbsp) water in a large saucepan and cook for 3 minutes.
3 Drain off all but 15 ml (1 tbsp) of the liquid, then add the spring greens to the pan. Season and cook over a high heat for 2 minutes. Place in a warmed serving dish and scatter over the sunflower seeds.

NUTRITIONAL ANALYSIS
70 kcals/294 kJ
3 g Protein
15.2 g Carbohydrate
0.2 g Fat ★★★★
0.1 g Saturated Fat ★★★★
6 g Fibre ★★★★
No Added Sugar ★★★★
176 mg Salt ★★

Vegetables in Parsnip Sauce

A creamy sauce made with parsnips and yogurt transforms this vegetable dish into an unusual accompaniment to meat or chicken dishes.

SERVES 4
175 g (6 oz) baby onions or shallots, skinned
175 g (6 oz) young carrots, scrubbed
350 g (12 oz) parsnips, peeled and cut into 4 cm (1½ inch) chunks
juice of 1 lemon
1 bay leaf
2 blades mace
2.5 ml (½ tsp) grated nutmeg
pepper, to taste
15 ml (1 tbsp) chopped fresh parsley
30 ml (2 tbsp) low-fat natural yogurt
chopped fresh parsley, to garnish

1 Put the onions, carrots and parsnips in a saucepan of boiling water, together with the lemon juice, bay leaf and mace. Cook for 6-7 minutes until tender, but still slightly crunchy. Drain, reserving 150 ml (¼ pint) of the vegetable water. Discard the bay leaf and mace. Set aside the onions, carrots and one third of the parsnips and keep warm.
2 For the parsnip sauce, put the remaining parsnips and reserved water in a pan. Cover and cook for a further 10 minutes or until tender. Purée with the water in a blender or food processor until smooth. Add the nutmeg and pepper. Stir in the parsley and yogurt.
3 Pour the sauce into a saucepan over a low heat. Add the vegetables and cook for 5 minutes or until heated through and well coated with the sauce. Serve at once, garnished with parsley.

Cabbage with Caraway

Tiny, crescent-shaped caraway seeds with their warm, bitter-sweet taste halfway between aniseed and fennel are used to flavour the cabbage.

NUTRITIONAL ANALYSIS
36 kcals/152 kJ
2.6 g Protein
5.7 g Carbohydrate
0.7 g Fat ★★★★
0.1 g Saturated Fat ★★★★
3.3 g Fibre ★★★★
No Added Sugar ★★★★
34 mg Salt ★★★★

SERVES 4

450 g (1 lb) red or white cabbage, finely shredded
1 garlic clove, skinned and halved
10 ml (2 tsp) caraway seeds, lightly crushed
150 ml (1/4 pint) vegetable or chicken stock
2 strips of lemon rind
10 ml (2 tsp) lemon juice
pepper, to taste
grated nutmeg
finely sliced orange rind, to garnish

1 Put the cabbage in a heatproof dish. Pour boiling water over to cover and leave to stand for 1 minute. Drain well.
2 Rub the inside of a large saucepan with the cut surfaces of the garlic clove, then add the caraway seeds. Discard the garlic. Heat the pan gently for 2-3 minutes, then add the stock and lemon rind and bring to the boil.
3 Add the cabbage and stir. Keep the heat high until the pan sizzles, then cover tightly and reduce the heat to very low. Cook for about 7 minutes for red and 5 minutes for white cabbage until just tender. When the cabbage is cooked, stir in the lemon juice, pepper and nutmeg. Garnish with orange rind and serve at once.

Spinach Catalan

Spinach is an excellent source of iron and calcium, and adds to the fibre content of this quick dish.

NUTRITIONAL ANALYSIS
124 kcals/516 kJ
5.2 g Protein
12.4 g Carbohydrate
6.3 g Fat ★★
0.6 g Saturated Fat ★★★★
2.7 g Fibre ★★★★
No Added Sugar ★★★★
348 mg Salt ★★

SERVES 4

900 g (2 lb) spinach, washed
25 g (1 oz) raisins
10 ml (2 tsp) sunflower oil
25 g (1 oz) hazelnuts, roughly chopped
1 garlic clove, skinned and crushed
pepper, to taste
15 ml (1 tbsp) lemon juice
lemon wedges, to garnish

1 Put the spinach in large saucepan with just the water that clings to the leaves. Heat rapidly until the spinach sizzles, then lower the heat, add the raisins and cook for 4 minutes, stirring occasionally.
2 Meanwhile, heat the oil in a non-stick frying pan and cook the nuts and garlic over a low heat until the nuts are lightly toasted.
3 Drain any water from the spinach and add to the frying pan. Cook, stirring, over a very low heat for 3-4 minutes. Stir in pepper and lemon juice and serve immediately, garnished with lemon wedges.

NUTRITIONAL ANALYSIS
46 kcals/193 kJ
1.2 g Protein
10.7 g Carbohydrate
0.1 g Fat ★★★★
0 g Saturated Fat ★★★★
1.9 g Fibre ★★★★
1 g Added Sugar ★★★
142 mg Salt ★★

Sweet and Sour Vegetables

In this sweet and sour dish the vegetables are cooked in fruit juices and honey; the thickened juices, rather than butter, are used as a glaze.

SERVES 4
225 g (8 oz) carrots, scrubbed and sliced diagonally
50 ml (2 fl oz) grapefruit juice
75 ml (3 fl oz) apple juice
5 ml (1 tsp) clear honey
pepper, to taste
225 g (8 oz) courgettes (zucchini), trimmed and sliced diagonally
5 ml (1 tsp) arrowroot

1 Put the carrots in a saucepan with the juices, honey and seasoning. Bring to the boil, cover and simmer for 5 minutes.
2 Add the courgettes (zucchini) and simmer for a further 6-8 minutes or until just tender.
3 Blend the arrowroot to a smooth paste with a little cold water. Stir into the cooking juices and simmer until the sauce is thickened and smooth.

NUTRITIONAL ANALYSIS
190 kcals/795 kJ
3.8 g Protein
35.6 g Carbohydrate
5 g Fat ★★★
0.8 g Saturated Fat ★★★★
5 g Fibre ★★★★
No Added Sugar ★★★★
324 mg Salt ★★★

Chillied Baked Potatoes

These new potatoes are ideal for livening up a simple main course of grilled meat or poultry. If a sauce is required, add 150 ml (1/4 pint) low-fat natural yogurt at the end of the cooking time and stir over a gentle heat, without boiling, until warmed through.

SERVES 4
15 ml (1 tbsp) mild chilli powder or to taste
15 ml (1 tbsp) ground cumin
7.5 ml (1/2 tbsp) dried oregano
pepper, to taste
15 ml (1 tbsp) sunflower oil
700 g (1 1/2 lb) new potatoes, scrubbed and pricked with a fork
2 spring onions, trimmed and finely chopped
1 garlic clove, skinned and very finely diced
coriander sprigs, to garnish

1 Mix together the chilli powder, cumin, oregano and seasoning until well blended.
2 Put the oil in a non-stick roasting tin and add the potatoes, spring onions and garlic. Add the spice mixture and gently stir until the potatoes are well coated with the spices.
3 Cook at 200°C (400°F) mark 6 for 25-30 minutes or until the potatoes are tender. Serve hot, garnished with coriander.

Carrot Curry

This deliciously fragrant curry can be served on its own with rice or served as part of a larger meal.

SERVES 4
25 g (1 oz) desiccated coconut
15 ml (1 tbsp) sunflower oil
2.5 ml (½ tsp) cumin seeds
2.5 ml (½ tsp) freshly ground coriander
2.5 ml (½ tsp) ground ginger
1.25 ml (¼ tsp) ground turmeric
1.25 ml (¼ tsp) ground cinnamon
1.25 ml (¼ tsp) mustard seeds
1.25 ml (¼ tsp) cayenne pepper
seeds of 4 cardamom pods
1 garlic clove, skinned and crushed
450 g (1 lb) carrots, scrubbed and coarsely shredded
15 ml (1 tbsp) poppy seeds
15 ml (1 tbsp) chopped fresh coriander
toasted flaked almonds, to garnish

NUTRITIONAL ANALYSIS
129 kcals/538 kJ
2.4 g Protein
8.6 g Carbohydrate
9.7 g Fat ★
4.1 g Saturated Fat ★
5.6 g Fibre ★★★★
No Added Sugar ★★★★
303 mg Salt ★★

1 First make the coconut milk. Put the coconut in a measuring jug and pour in 300 ml (½ pint) boiling water. Set aside.
2 Heat the oil in a large non-stick saucepan and cook the spices and garlic for a few minutes. Add the carrots and stir-fry with the spices for 1 minute. Add the coconut mixture. Cover and simmer for about 5 minutes until most of the liquid has been absorbed and the carrots are just tender.
3 Stir in the poppy seeds and chopped coriander. Turn into a warmed serving dish, sprinkle with toasted almonds and serve.

Flageolets

Popular in France and Italy, these attractive pale green beans have a subtle, delicate taste.

SERVES 4
225 g (8 oz) dried flageolet beans, soaked overnight
15 g (½ oz) polyunsaturated margarine
1 small onion, skinned and chopped
pepper, to taste

NUTRITIONAL ANALYSIS
198 kcals/826 kJ
12.7 g Protein
29.3 g Carbohydrate
4.1 g Fat ★★★
0.6 g Saturated Fat ★★★★
14.9 g Fibre ★★★★
No Added Sugar ★★★★
143 mg Salt ★★★★

1 Drain the beans and rinse. Put into a saucepan with plenty of fresh water and simmer, uncovered, for 1½-2 hours or until soft but not mushy, topping up with boiling water from time to time if necessary.
2 Meanwhile, melt the margarine in a non-stick pan and gently cook the onion for 5 minutes until soft.
3 Drain the beans, add to the onion, season and serve hot.

NUTRITIONAL ANALYSIS
176 kcals/736 kJ
6.9 g Protein
15.8 g Carbohydrate
9.9 g Fat ★★
1.7 g Saturated Fat ★★★
6.1 g Fibre ★★★★
1 g Added Sugar ★★★★
42 mg Salt ★★★★

Sweet and Sour Cabbage

If you like crispy cabbage, do not overcook this recipe by even 1 minute or the cabbage will become very limp. The less a vegetable is cooked, the more nutrients it retains.

SERVES 4

225 ml (8 fl oz) unsweetened orange juice
15 ml (1 tbsp) distilled white vinegar
5 ml (1 tsp) clear honey
7.5 ml (1/2 tbsp) arrowroot
15 ml (1 tbsp) sunflower oil
finely grated rind of 2 oranges
700 g (1 1/2 lb) white cabbage, cored and shredded
50 g (2 oz) skinned shelled peanuts, roughly chopped
15 ml (1 tbsp) chopped fresh parsley, to garnish

1 Mix together the orange juice, vinegar, honey and arrowroot in a bowl until the honey is blended into the liquid and the arrowroot dissolved. Set aside.
2 Heat the oil in a non-stick saucepan and add the orange rind and cabbage. Stir until the cabbage is well coated in the oil. Lower the heat, cover and cook for 1-2 minutes. Add the orange juice mixture and bring to the boil, stirring. Cook for 3-4 minutes until the sauce is clear and the cabbage is well coated and just starting to soften.
3 Add the peanuts and stir through. Serve at once, garnished with the parsley.

NUTRITIONAL ANALYSIS
52 kcals/216 kJ
1.7 g Protein
5.7 g Carbohydrate
2.6 g Fat ★★
0.4 g Saturated Fat ★★★
2.5 g Fibre ★★★★
No Added Sugar ★★★★
75 mg Salt ★★★

Baked Tomatoes with Herbs

Cook this warming dish when the weather does not tempt you to salads.

SERVES 4

15 ml (1 tbsp) chopped fresh parsley
15 ml (1 tbsp) snipped fresh chives
5 ml (1 tsp) dried oregano
1 garlic clove, skinned and finely chopped
450 g (1 lb) tomatoes, halved
10 ml (2 tsp) sunflower oil
pepper, to taste
25 g (1 oz) dried wholemeal breadcrumbs

1 Mix together the parsley, chives, oregano and garlic in a shallow dish.
2 Dip the cut sides of the tomatoes first in the oil, then into the herb mixture. Put the tomatoes, cut sides uppermost, in a lightly greased shallow ovenproof dish, large enough to take them in one layer. Season to taste and sprinkle over the breadcrumbs.
3 Bake at 180°C (350°F) mark 4 for 15-20 minutes.

Spinach and Black-Eyed Beans

Serve this spicy vegetable dish either with cold meat and brown rice or with dhal, brown rice, raita and salad

SERVES 4
125 g (4 oz) black-eyed beans, soaked overnight
450 g (1 lb) spinach, washed
10 ml (2 tsp) sunflower oil
1 large onion, skinned and chopped
2.5 cm (1 inch) piece root ginger, peeled and finely chopped
10 ml (2 tsp) cumin seeds
1 large garlic clove, skinned and crushed
2.5 ml (1/2 level tsp) ground cinnamon
60 ml (4 tbsp) white wine
15 ml (1 tbsp) vinegar
pepper, to taste
5 ml (1 tsp) garam masala

NUTRITIONAL ANALYSIS
175 kcals/733 kJ
10.3 g Protein
22.5 g Carbohydrate
4.7 g Fat ★★★
0.5 g Saturated Fat ★★★★
9.7 g Fibre ★★★★
No Added Sugar ★★★★
241 mg Salt ★★★

1 Drain the beans and rinse. Put into a saucepan with plenty of fresh water, bring to the boil and boil for 10 minutes. Reduce the heat and simmer for a further 40-50 minutes or until tender.
2 Meanwhile, put the spinach into a large saucepan with only the water that clings to the leaves. Cover and cook over a low heat for 7-10 minutes or until the spinach is tender. Drain the spinach, pressing it with the back of a wooden spoon to squeeze out all the excess liquid. Finely chop the spinach.
3 When the beans are cooked, heat the oil in a non-stick frying pan and cook the onion for 5 minutes until soft. Add the cumin, cinnamon and garlic and cook for a further 2 minutes. Add the drained beans, spinach, wine, vinegar and pepper. Cook over a low heat for 10 minutes, stirring frequently. Serve sprinkled with garam masala.

Braised Fennel

Fennel has a pronounced aniseed flavour and makes an excellent accompaniment to fish. When choosing, select pale green or white coloured fennel bulbs, avoiding any that are dark green.

SERVES 4
10 ml (2 tsp) sunflower oil
3 large fennel bulbs, cut into quarters, feathery green tops reserved and chopped
juice of 1/2 lemon
150 ml (1/4 pint) chicken stock
pepper, to taste

NUTRITIONAL ANALYSIS
32 kcals/136 kJ
1 g Protein
1.7 g Carbohydrate
2.5 g Fat ★
0.3 g Saturated Fat ★★★
2 g Fibre ★★★★
No Added Sugar ★★★★
404 mg Salt ★

1 Heat the oil in a non-stick frying pan and gently cook the fennel for about 8-10 minutes until lightly coloured on all sides. Sprinkle over the lemon juice and pour over the stock. Season to taste. Cover and simmer for 20-30 minutes or until tender.
2 Transfer the fennel with a slotted spoon to a warmed serving dish. Boil the liquid remaining in the pan until it reduces to 30-45 ml (2-3 tbsp), then pour over the fennel. Garnish with the chopped fennel tops.

NUTRITIONAL ANALYSIS
67 kcals/282 kJ
4.4 g Protein
9.9 g Carbohydrate
1.4 g Fat ★★★
0.2 g Saturated Fat ★★★★
6.1 g Fibre ★★★★
No Added Sugar ★★★★
46 mg Salt ★★★★

Broccoli with Apricot Sauce

When buying broccoli, look for heads or spears that are fresh and crisp, and with stalks that snap easily. Wilted, yellowing broccoli will have lost its valuable vitamin C.

SERVES 4

5 ml (1 tsp) sunflower oil

1 small onion, skinned and finely chopped

400 g (14 oz) can apricots in natural juice, drained, juice reserved

2.5 ml (½ tsp) freshly ground cumin

pepper, to taste

450 g (1 lb) broccoli

1 Heat the oil in a non-stick pan and gently cook the onion for 5 minutes until soft. Purée with the apricots and cumin in a blender or food processor until smooth. Add just enough of the reserved apricot juice to make a medium-thick sauce. Season to taste.
2 Put the broccoli in a saucepan of boiling water and cook for about 8 minutes until just tender. Arrange the broccoli cartwheel-style in a warmed round serving dish, stalks towards the centre.
3 Reheat the sauce and pour into the centre, covering the base of the stalks.

NUTRITIONAL ANALYSIS
126 kcals/527 kJ
3.5 g Protein
26.2 g Carbohydrate
1.6 g Fat ★★★★
0.2 g Saturated Fat ★★★★
2.8 g Fibre ★★★★
No Added Sugar ★★★★
70 mg Salt ★★★★

Potatoes Stuffed with Spinach

A high fibre dish, particularly if you eat the potato skins as well.

SERVES 4

2 potatoes, each weighing 225 g (8 oz), scrubbed

100 g (4 oz) fresh spinach, washed, or frozen spinach, thawed

pinch of freshly grated nutmeg

5 ml (1 tsp) sunflower oil

1 small onion, skinned and chopped

pepper, to taste

30 ml (2 tbsp) tomato purée

1 Put the potatoes in their skins in a saucepan of water and cook for about 15 minutes until just cooked. Cut each one in half lengthways. Scoop out the centres, mash and set aside. Reserve the potato shells.
2 Put the fresh spinach in a saucepan with just the water clinging to the leaves. Cover and cook for about 5-8 minutes. Drain well and chop the spinach.
3 Heat the oil in a non-stick saucepan and gently cook the onion for 5 minutes until soft. Add the spinach, nutmeg and season to taste. Mix in mashed potato and pile into the shells.
4 Arrange the stuffed potatoes in an ovenproof dish, just large enough to hold them in one layer.
5 Mix the tomato purée with 150 ml (¼ pint) water, season with pepper and bring to the boil. Pour over the potatoes.
6 Bake at 200°C (400°F) mark 6 for 20-30 minutes.

Chicken Véronique (PAGE 123)

Ratatouille

This mixed vegetable stew from the South of France is a colourful summer dish, to serve cold or warm, on its own with French bread or as an accompaniment to meat or fish.

SERVES 4
15 ml (1 tbsp) olive oil
225 g (8 oz) onions, skinned and thinly sliced
225 g (8 oz) peppers, cored, seeded and thinly sliced
225 g (8 oz) aubergines, cut into medium slices
225 g (8 oz) courgettes (zucchini), trimmed and cut into medium slices
400 g (14 oz) can tomatoes, chopped
5 ml (1 tsp) dried or fresh basil
5 ml (1 tsp) dried or fresh oregano
1 bay leaf
2 garlic cloves, skinned and chopped
pepper, to taste

NUTRITIONAL ANALYSIS
90 kcals/377 kJ
3 g Protein
10.9 g Carbohydrate
4.2 g Fat ★★
0.7 g Saturated Fat ★★★★
4.4 g Fibre ★★★★
No Added Sugar ★★★★
34 mg Salt ★★★★

1 Heat the oil in a medium non-stick saucepan and gently cook the onions, covered, for about 5 minutes until soft. Add the peppers, aubergines and courgettes (zucchini) and fry until beginning to soften.

2 Add the tomatoes with their juice, basil, oregano, bay leaf and garlic. Bring to the boil, cover and simmer for 40 minutes. Season to taste.

Onions Braised in Tomato Sauce

To skin pickling onions easily, place in a bowl, cover with boiling water and leave for 5 minutes; the skins will then slip off.

SERVES 4
5 ml (1 tsp) sunflower oil
700 g (1½ lb) pickling onions, skinned
225 g (8 oz) passata or other sieved tomatoes
2.5 ml (½ tsp) dried or fresh basil
2.5 ml (½ tsp) dried or fresh sage
pinch of sugar
15 ml (1 tbsp) wine vinegar
pepper, to taste

NUTRITIONAL ANALYSIS
62 kcals/261 kJ
2.2 g Protein
10.4 g Carbohydrate
1.6 g Fat ★★★
0.3 g Saturated Fat ★★★★
2.8 g Fibre ★★★★
No Added Sugar ★★★★
88 mg Salt ★★★

1 Heat the oil in a non-stick frying pan and gently cook the onions for about 8 minutes until browned all over.

2 Mix the rest of the ingredients together and pour over the onions. Bring to the boil, cover and simmer for 20-30 minutes or until the onions are tender.

Paella (PAGE 127)

NUTRITIONAL ANALYSIS
44 kcals/185 kJ
5.1 g Protein
5.5 g Carbohydrate
0.4 g Fat ★★★★
0.2 g Saturated Fat ★★★★
11 g Fibre ★★★★
No Added Sugar ★★★★
14 mg Salt ★★★★

French Peas

Older, larger fresh peas are also delicious cooked in this way. Button onions could be used instead of the quartered onion.

SERVES 4

outside leaves of a flat-leaved lettuce
1 medium onion, skinned and quartered
1 bouquet garni
350 g (12 oz) frozen peas
pepper, to taste

1 Place all the ingredients with 30 ml (2 tbsp) water into a saucepan with a tight-fitting lid. Simmer gently for 1 hour.
2 Alternatively, put the ingredients in a casserole and cook at 150°C (300°F) mark 2 for 1 hour.
3 Remove the bouquet garni before serving.

NUTRITIONAL ANALYSIS
121 kcals/507 kJ
2.7 g Protein
19.3 g Carbohydrate
3.2 g Fat ★★★
0.5 g Saturated Fat ★★★★
6 g Fibre ★★★★
No Added Sugar ★★★★
193 mg Salt ★★★

Red Cabbage with Apples

This tangy hot vegetable dish combines the cabbage with apples, cider and ginger.

SERVES 4

15 g (1/2 oz) polyunsaturated margarine
1 large onion, skinned and finely sliced
5 ml (1 tsp) chopped fresh root ginger
3 cloves
150 ml (1/4 pint) cider
450 g (1 lb) red cabbage, finely shredded
225 g (8 oz) cooking apples, peeled and sliced
10 ml (2 tsp) redcurrant jelly (optional)
pepper, to taste

1 Melt the margarine in a non-stick saucepan and gently cook the onion for 5 minutes until soft. Stir in the ginger, cloves and cider, then add the cabbage and apples.
2 Bring to the boil, cover and simmer for 30-45 minutes or until the cabbage is very soft.
3 Uncover, increase the heat and cook until most of the liquid has evaporated. Stir in the redcurrant jelly if using and season to taste.

Natural Courgettes (Zucchini) and Carrots

Serve these attractive, delicate vegetables with a pale subtly flavoured main dish such as turkey meatballs in egg and lemon sauce.

SERVES 4
350 g (12 oz) courgettes (zucchini)
225 g (8 oz) carrots, scrubbed
pepper, to taste

NUTRITIONAL ANALYSIS
28 kcals/116 kJ
1.4 g Protein
5.6 g Carbohydrate
0.1 g Fat ★★★★
0 g Saturated Fat ★★★★
2 g Fibre ★★★★
No Added Sugar ★★★★
142 mg Salt ★

1 Using a very sharp vegetable peeler, cut the courgettes (zucchini) and carrots lengthways in one sweep, making long wafer-thin strips the width of the vegetables.
2 Put the courgettes (zucchini) into a saucepan of boiling water. Return to the boil and cook for ½-1 minute. They should be just tender and flexible. Drain thoroughly and transfer to a warmed serving dish, curling the strips a little. Keep warm.
3 Reboil the water and cook the carrots in the same way. Drain and pile in the centre of the courgettes (zucchini). Serve immediately.

Stir-Fried Vegetables

The secrets of a good stir-fry are: to have all the vegetables prepared before starting, to cut them all the same size, and to have the pan very hot before adding them.

SERVES 4
15 ml (1 tbsp) sunflower oil
1 medium onion, skinned and thinly sliced
2 celery sticks, trimmed and cut into matchsticks
2 carrots, scrubbed and cut into matchsticks
1 red pepper, cored, seeded and cut into matchsticks
50 g (2 oz) mangetout (snow peas)
50 g (2 oz) mushrooms, thinly sliced
225 g (8 oz) beansprouts
10 ml (2 tsp) soya sauce
pepper, to taste

NUTRITIONAL ANALYSIS
90 kcals/376 kJ
4.4 g Protein
9.3 g Carbohydrate
4.2 g Fat ★★
0.6 g Saturated Fat ★★★★
4.5 g Fibre ★★★★
No Added Sugar ★★★★
213 mg Salt ★★

1 Heat the oil in a wok or large non-stick frying pan and fry the onion over a high heat for 1 minute. Add the celery, carrots, pepper and mangetout (snow peas) and stir-fry for 3-4 minutes, stirring and tossing constantly.
2 Add the mushrooms and beansprouts and stir-fry for a further 2 minutes.
3 Sprinkle over the soya sauce, season to taste and serve immediately.

NUTRITIONAL ANALYSIS
38 kcals/159 kJ
1.3 g Protein
1.5 g Carbohydrate
3.1 g Fat ★
0.6 g Saturated Fat ★★★
4.3 g Fibre ★★★★
No Added Sugar ★★★★
91 mg Salt ★★

Green Beans with Lime Juice

The lime juice adds freshness and flavour to the green beans here.

SERVES 4

450 g (1 lb) cut green beans
15 g (1/2 oz) polyunsaturated margarine
juice of 1 lime
pepper, to taste
30 ml (2 tbsp) chopped fresh parsley, to garnish

1 Put the beans in a saucepan containing the minimum of boiling water. Cook for about 5 minutes until just tender. Drain well.
2 Melt the margarine in a large non-stick frying pan and gently cook the beans until they begin to lose their bright green colour. Pour over the lime juice and sprinkle with pepper. Serve garnished with the parsley.

NUTRITIONAL ANALYSIS
132 kcals/550 kJ
2.4 g Protein
23.4 g Carbohydrate
3.9 g Fat ★★★
0.5 g Saturated Fat ★★★★
2.4 g Fibre ★★★★
No Added Sugar ★★★★
20 mg Salt ★★★★

Oven Chips

Tuck into these lower fat chips as an occasional alternative to jacket or boiled potatoes.

SERVES 4

450 g (1 lb) potatoes, scrubbed
15 ml (1 tbsp) sunflower oil

1 Cut the potatoes into 1 cm (½ inch) strips. Put the strips in a large saucepan of boiling water. Return to the boil and simmer for 3 minutes. Drain and allow them to dry in the air.
2 Spoon the oil into a large polythene bag and add the potatoes. Shake gently to coat all sides. Remove and arrange the potatoes on a non-stick baking sheet.
3 Bake at 240°C (475°F) mark 9 for 15-20 minutes, turning occasionally, or until the chips are golden brown on all sides.

NUTRITIONAL ANALYSIS
31 kcals/128 kJ
1.4 g Protein
4.3 g Carbohydrate
1 g Fat ★★★
0.2 g Saturated Fat ★★★★
2.7 g Fibre ★★★★
No Added Sugar ★★★★
657 mg Salt ★

Marrow with Orange Juice

Delicate tasting marrow is best when under 30 cm (12 inches) long and weighing about 1 kg (2 lb). Flavoured with orange and nutmeg, it makes an excellent accompaniment to fish.

SERVES 4

1 medium marrow, peeled, quartered lengthways and deseeded
5 ml (1 tsp) salt
5 ml (1 tsp) polyunsaturated margarine
1/4 nutmeg, grated
grated rind and juice of 1 orange
pepper, to taste
60 ml (4 tbsp) chopped fresh parsley, to garnish

1 Cut the marrow into 2 cm (¾ inch) slices and spread out on a wire rack. Sprinkle with salt and leave to drain for 30 minutes. Rinse off all the salt, drain and pat dry.
2 Melt the margarine in a non-stick frying pan and cook the marrow for about 5 minutes until just cooked and beginning to brown on both sides.
3 Sprinkle the marrow with the nutmeg, grated orange rind and juice. Season to taste and garnish with chopped parsley. Serve immediately.

Seasonal Salads

Salads play an important part in any healthy diet, and they can be eaten all year round. Combine different grains, pulses, nuts, fruits and herbs for maximum variety of tastes and textures, and ring the changes by mixing them with small amounts of meat or fish.

If you're mixing up your own salad, use the recipe on page 114 for a good tasting, low-fat dressing. Add herbs or garlic according to taste and what you're wanting to serve it with. If you're using an oil-based dressing, make sure it's monounsaturated and polyunsaturated (see page 000), and add it just before serving so that the salad maintains its crispness and doesn's absorb too much of the oil.

NUTRITIONAL ANALYSIS
130 kcals/543 kJ
2.1 g Protein
4.5 g Carbohydrate
11.7 g Fat ★
1.7 g Saturated Fat ★★★
2.4 g Fibre ★★★★
No Added Sugar ★★★★
100 mg Salt ★★★★

Wilted Salad

This is a delicious way to serve nutritious raw vegetables. The salad is 'wilted' by the warm dressing but the vegetables remain crisp.

SERVES 4

1 round lettuce, torn into pieces
1 punnet mustard and cress
1 bunch watercress, trimmed
1 bunch spring onions, trimmed
1 bunch radishes, trimmed and sliced

FOR THE DRESSING

juice of 1/2 lemon
5 ml (1 tsp) Dijon mustard
1 garlic clove, skinned and crushed
45 ml (3 tbsp) olive oil
pepper, to taste
30 ml (2 tbsp) low-fat natural yogurt

1 Put the salad vegetables into a serving bowl. Put the lemon juice, mustard and garlic into another bowl.
2 Put the oil into a small saucepan and warm gently for about 3 minutes, then add to the lemon juice mixture, whisking well. Season to taste.
3 Add the warm dressing to the salad and toss well. Add the yogurt, gently toss through and serve at once.

NUTRITIONAL ANALYSIS
133 kcals/555 kJ
4 g Protein
12.3 g Carbohydrate
7.8 g Fat ★
1.1 g Saturated Fat ★★★★
3.8 g Fibre ★★★★
No Added Sugar ★★★★
107 mg Salt ★★★★

Mixed Spring Salad

This refreshing, tangy salad has an interesting combination of flavours and textures.

SERVES 4

100 g (4 oz) spinach, washed, stalks removed and finely sliced
225 g (8 oz) Chinese cabbage, sliced
1 green pepper, cored, seeded and thinly sliced
2 large oranges, peeled and segmented
1 grapefruit, peeled, segmented and cut in half crossways
1 bunch of watercress, trimmed and coarsely chopped

FOR THE CITRUS DRESSING

juice of 2 lemons
juice of 1 large orange
30 ml (2 tbsp) olive oil
pepper, to taste

1 Put the spinach, Chinese cabbage, green pepper, orange and grapefruit segments and watercress into a large bowl.
2 For the dressing, whisk together the lemon and orange juices and oil in a bowl. Season to taste. Pour over the salad, toss well and serve immediately.

Crab and Fennel Salad

The aniseed flavour of fennel combines particularly well with crab.

SERVES 4
½ crisp lettuce, finely shredded
1 fennel bulb, weighing about 225 g (8 oz), sliced, feathery leaves chopped and reserved
½ cucumber, thinly sliced
15 ml (1 tbsp) finely chopped fresh mint
225 g (8 oz) crab meat, thawed if frozen
FOR THE DRESSING
30 ml (2 tbsp) sunflower oil
15 ml (1 tbsp) lemon juice
15 ml (1 tbsp) low-fat natural yogurt
pepper, to taste

NUTRITIONAL ANALYSIS
135 kcals/565 kJ
13 g Protein
2.8 g Carbohydrate
8.1 g Fat ★
1 g Saturated Fat ★★★★
2.2 g Fibre ★★★★
No Added Sugar ★★★★
767 mg Salt ★

1 Spread the lettuce over the base of a serving dish and arrange the fennel and cucumber on top. Sprinkle over the mint.
2 Flake the crab meat, discarding all shell and cartilage. Place on top of the salad.
3 For the dressing, whisk together the oil, lemon juice, yogurt, and pepper in a bowl until smooth.
4 Pour the dressing over the crab and vegetables and sprinkle with the chopped fennel leaves. Serve immediately.

Salad of New Season's Vegetables

Just the salad to make when the new season's vegetables first appear in the shops.

SERVES 4
175 g (6 oz) cauliflower, divided into florets
175 g (6 oz) carrots, scrubbed and cut lengthways if large
225 g (8 oz) tiny new potatoes, scrubbed
2 medium thin courgettes (zucchini), trimmed and sliced
100 g (4 oz) tiny French beans
450 g (1 lb) broad beans, shelled
100 g (4 oz) mangetout (snow peas)
FOR THE DRESSING
20 ml (4 tsp) sunflower oil
15 ml (1 tbsp) water
10 ml (2 tsp) wine vinegar
2.5 ml (½ tsp) Dijon mustard
pepper, to taste

NUTRITIONAL ANALYSIS
187 kcals/781 kJ
8.8 g Protein
26.3 g Carbohydrate
6 g Fat ★★★
0.8 g Saturated Fat ★★★★
10.4 g Fibre ★★★★
No Added Sugar ★★★★
243 mg Salt ★★★

1 Steam each vegetable individually until just cooked (a microwave is excellent for this). Cool the vegetables a little, then arrange them on a very large serving platter.
2 For the dressing, beat all the ingredients together in a screw-top jar and brush over the vegetables while still warm. Serve at room temperature.

NUTRITIONAL ANALYSIS
93 kcals/389 kJ
4 g Protein
5 g Carbohydrate
6.5 g Fat ★
1.2 g Saturated Fat ★★★
5.5 g Fibre ★★★★
No Added Sugar ★★★★
221 mg Salt ★★

Celeriac Salad

Celeriac has a tangy, pronounced celery flavour. Choose celeriac that is firm and heavy for its size. If light in weight, the flesh will be airy and spongy.

SERVES 4

juice of 1 lemon
450 g (1 lb) celeriac, peeled

FOR THE DRESSING

2.5 ml (½ tsp) Dijon mustard
150 ml (¼ pint) low-fat natural yogurt
30 ml (2 tbsp) mayonnaise
pepper, to taste

1 Mix the lemon juice with 300 ml (½ pint) water.
2 Grate the celeriac on the coarsest grater, then rinse in the lemon water. Drain well.
3 For the dressing, stir together the mustard, yogurt and mayonnaise in a large bowl. Season to taste.
4 Add the celeriac and toss lightly with a fork.

NUTRITIONAL ANALYSIS
99 kcals/412 kJ
2.9 g Protein
22.3 g Carbohydrate
0.4 g Fat ★★★★
0.1 g Saturated Fat ★★★★
2.4 g Fibre ★★★★
No Added Sugar ★★★★
156 mg Salt ★★★

New Potato Salad

British grown new potatoes are available from May to August. For the dressing in this salad, yogurt is substituted for soured cream to reduce the fat content.

SERVES 4

450 g (1 lb) new potatoes, scrubbed
15 ml (1 tbsp) snipped fresh chives, to garnish

FOR THE DRESSING

75 ml (5 tbsp) low-fat yogurt or Greek strained yogurt
2.5 ml (½ tsp) Dijon mustard
10 ml (2 tsp) wine vinegar
pepper, to taste

1 Put the potatoes in a saucepan of water and cook for about 15 minutes until tender. Drain and cool.
2 For the dressing, mix together the yogurt, mustard, wine vinegar and pepper in a bowl.
3 Leave the potatoes whole if they are very small, or cut them into small pieces if large. Toss in the dressing. Transfer to a serving dish and garnish with chives.

Red and Green Bean Salad with Corn

This is an excellent salad to make when awaiting the arrival of the new season's vegetables. Since the beans and corn are canned with salt, no additional salt is needed.

NUTRITIONAL ANALYSIS
233 kcals/973 kJ
11.3 g Protein
35 g Carbohydrate
6.3 g Fat ★★★
0.9 g Saturated Fat ★★★★
14.1 g Fibre ★★★★
No Added Sugar ★★★★
44 mg Salt ★★★★

SERVES 4

225 g (8 oz) frozen whole green beans

400 g (14 oz) can red kidney beans, drained

326 g (11½ oz) can sweetcorn, drained

45 ml (3 tbsp) very finely chopped Spanish onion

FOR THE DRESSING

1.25 ml (¼ tsp) Dijon mustard

7.5 ml (1½ tsp) wine vinegar

15 ml (1 tbsp) sunflower oil

pepper, to taste

1 Put the green beans in a saucepan of boiling water and cook for about 5 minutes. Drain and plunge them into cold water, then drain again.
2 For the dressing, put the mustard into a salad bowl, stir in the vinegar, oil and pepper. Add the green beans, kidney beans, sweetcorn and onion, then toss lightly to coat the vegetables with the dressing.

Chick-Pea Salad

A sweet and sour tasting salad, using fibre- and protein-rich chick-peas.

NUTRITIONAL ANALYSIS
129 kcals/541 kJ
6 g Protein
21.4 g Carbohydrate
2.8 g Fat ★★★
0.2 g Saturated Fat ★★★★
4.9 g Fibre ★★★★
No Added Sugar ★★★★
48 mg Salt ★★★★

SERVES 4

100 g (4 oz) dried chick-peas, soaked overnight

5 ml (1 tsp) sunflower oil

1 medium onion, skinned and finely chopped

1 red pepper, cored, seeded and chopped

fresh thyme sprig

50 g (2 oz) raisins

30 ml (2 tbsp) wine vinegar

1 Drain the chick-peas and rinse. Put into a saucepan with plenty of fresh water. Bring to the boil and boil for 10 minutes. Lower the heat and simmer for 1 hour or until tender.
2 Heat the oil in a non-stick saucepan and cook the onion for 5-8 minutes until golden brown. Add the pepper and cook for 5 minutes. Drain the chick-peas and add to the pan with the thyme and raisins.
3 Cook for a further 5 minutes, stirring occasionally and making sure that the chick-peas do not become mushy.
4 Transfer the chick-pea mixture to a serving bowl and add the vinegar while still hot. Allow to cool, uncovered, then serve.

NUTRITIONAL ANALYSIS
27 kcals/114 kJ
2.1 g Protein
3.8 g Carbohydrate
0.5 g Fat ★★★★
0.1 g Saturated Fat ★★★★
1.3 g Fibre ★★★★
No Added Sugar ★★★★
32 mg Salt ★★★

Spiced Courgette (Zucchini) Salad

The spicy dressing could be made in advance to allow the flavours to blend; add it to the vegetables just before serving the salad.

SERVES 4

225 g (8 oz) courgettes (zucchini), trimmed and thinly sliced

½ yellow pepper, cored, seeded and cut into thin strips

½ red pepper, cored, seeded and cut into thin strips

100 g (4 oz) button mushrooms, thinly sliced

FOR THE DRESSING

60 ml (4 tbsp) cider vinegar

30 ml (2 tbsp) tomato purée

pinch of sugar

1.25 ml (¼ tsp) chilli powder

1.25 ml (¼ tsp) mustard powder

1 small garlic clove, skinned and crushed

1.25 ml (¼ tsp) paprika

1 For the dressing, put the vinegar, tomato purée, sugar, chilli powder, mustard, garlic and paprika into a bowl and mix well.

2 Add the courgettes (zucchini), pepper and mushrooms and toss together lightly. Serve the same day.

NUTRITIONAL ANALYSIS
105 kcals/438 kJ
2.6 g Protein
4.8 g Carbohydrate
8.4 g Fat ★
1.2 g Saturated Fat ★★★
2.1 g Fibre ★★★★
No Added Sugar ★★★★
36 mg Salt ★★★★

Salad Bowl with Tofu Mayonnaise

Traditional mayonnaise is high in fat. The tofu mayonnaise in this recipe is a good low-fat alternative.

SERVES 4

1 lettuce, shredded

1 medium onion, skinned and thinly sliced

1 grapefruit or 2 oranges, peeled and segmented

100 g (4 oz) button mushrooms, thinly sliced

FOR THE TOFU MAYONNAISE

50 g (2 oz) tofu

15 ml (1 tbsp) low-fat natural yogurt

30 ml (2 tbsp) olive oil

15 ml (1 tbsp) lemon juice

1 garlic clove, skinned (optional)

2.5 ml (½ tsp) chopped fresh tarragon or 1.25 ml (¼ tsp) dried

10 ml (2 tsp) chopped fresh parsley

1 For the mayonnaise, purée the tofu, yogurt, oil, lemon juice, garlic and tarragon in a blender or food processor until smooth. Spoon into a bowl, add the parsley and set aside.

2 Put the lettuce, onion, grapefruit segments and mushrooms into a bowl and toss well together. Serve at once, accompanied with the tofu mayonnaise.

Chicken Salad

This colourful and crunchy salad is a useful way to use left-over chicken.

SERVES 4-6
700 g (1½ lb) cooked chicken, skinned, boned and shredded
425 g (15 oz) can red kidney beans, drained and rinsed
2 oranges, peeled and segmented, with rind cut into strips
100 g (4 oz) button mushrooms, sliced
3 spring onions, trimmed and finely chopped
50 g (2 oz) walnut halves
pepper, to taste
225 g (8 oz) spinach leaves, washed and shredded
½ crisp lettuce, shredded
½ green pepper, cored, seeded and sliced
FOR THE DRESSING
½ cucumber, grated and drained
150 ml (¼ pint) low-fat natural yogurt
15 ml (1 tbsp) lemon juice
little paprika

NUTRITIONAL ANALYSIS
332 kcals/1387 kJ
38.6 g Protein
19.3 g Carbohydrate
11.7 g Fat ★★★
2.8 g Saturated Fat ★★★
9.3 g Fibre ★★★★
No Added Sugar ★★★★
506 mg Salt ★★★

1 Mix the chicken and beans in a bowl. Add the orange segments, rind, mushrooms, onions, walnuts and seasoning.
2 Mix the spinach, lettuce and green pepper in a large serving bowl and place the chicken mixture on top.
3 For the dressing, mix together the cucumber, yogurt, lemon juice, paprika and seasoning. Serve the dressing separately.

Fennel and Tomato Salad

This salad is delicious served with pasta dishes or a selection of cold meats; the sunflower seeds add a crunchy texture to the dish.

SERVES 4
15 g (½ oz) sunflower seeds
350 g (12 oz) tomatoes, sliced
¼ bulb fennel, finely chopped
20 ml (1½ tbsp) olive oil
pepper, to taste

NUTRITIONAL ANALYSIS
100 kcals/417 kJ
1.5 g Protein
4.1 g Carbohydrate
8.7 g Fat ★
1.1 g Saturated Fat ★★★
1.7 g Fibre ★★★★
No Added Sugar ★★★★
51 mg Salt ★★★★

1 Place the sunflower seeds in a small heavy-based frying pan. Heat gently, turning frequently so the seeds do not burn, until lightly golden brown. Set aside to cool.
2 Arrange the tomatoes and fennel in a shallow bowl. Spoon over the olive oil and season to taste. Gently mix until well coated. Add the sunflower seeds and gently toss. Serve at once.

NUTRITIONAL ANALYSIS
177 kcals/740 kJ
5.5 g Protein
31.2 g Carbohydrate
4.2 g Fat ★★★
0.7 g Saturated Fat ★★★★
3.4 g Fibre ★★★★
0.1 g Added Sugar ★★★★
27 mg Salt ★★★★

Tabbouleh

Tabbouleh is a fresh herby salad made from burghul or cracked wheat. It makes a particularly good accompaniment to grilled meat.

SERVES 4

150 g (5 oz) burghul wheat, soaked for 1 hour in cold water

1 bunch spring onions, trimmed and finely chopped

50 g (2 oz) fresh parsley, finely chopped

25 g (1 oz) fresh mint, finely chopped

juice of 2 lemons

15 ml (1 tbsp) olive oil

lettuce, to serve

1 Drain the burghul wheat and pile it in the centre of a clean tea-towel. Twist the cloth and squeeze out the water. Spread the burghul wheat out over the cloth to dry for about 30 minutes.
2 Transfer the burghul wheat to a large bowl and mix in the remaining ingredients.
3 Line a salad bowl with lettuce leaves and pile in the wheat salad.

NUTRITIONAL ANALYSIS
79 kcals/330 kJ
2 g Protein
5.1 g Carbohydrate
5.9 g Fat ★
0.8 g Saturated Fat ★★★
1.9 g Fibre ★★★★
No Added Sugar ★★★★
11 mg Salt ★★★★

Pepper Salad

Peppers can now be found in several different colours which will give you the opportunity of creating exciting visual effects with this salad. Don't bother buying the black peppers as they turn green when cooked.

SERVES 4

1 kg (2 lb) peppers, red, green, yellow or mixed

FOR THE DRESSING

20 ml (1½ tbsp) olive oil

1 garlic clove, skinned and crushed

fresh mixed herbs like basil and thyme

pepper, to taste

1 Cook the peppers on all sides under the grill until the skin is charred. Put them in a polythene bag and leave for 15 minutes. Strip off the skins.
2 Cut the peppers in half lengthways and remove the seeds and cores. Arrange the peppers in a dish, cut sides down.
3 For the dressing, mix together the oil, garlic, herbs and seasoning.
4 Pour the dressing over the peppers. Cover and leave to marinate overnight.

NUTRITIONAL ANALYSIS
104 kcals/434 kJ
3.8 g Protein
4.5 g Carbohydrate
8 g Fat ★
1 g Saturated Fat ★★★
1.6 g Fibre ★★★★
No Added Sugar ★★★★
45 mg Salt ★★★★

Beansprout Salad

This light salad goes well with most meats, yet is just as delicious on its own too as a separate course.

SERVES 4

275 g (10 oz) beansprouts, trimmed and roughly chopped

1 bunch watercress, trimmed and roughly chopped

100 g (4 oz) button mushrooms, sliced

FOR THE DRESSING

30 ml (2 tbsp) sunflower oil

5 ml (1 tsp) prepared English mustard

15 ml (1 tbsp) wine vinegar

pepper, to taste

1 Mix together the beansprouts, watercress and mushrooms in a large salad bowl.
2 For the dressing, mix together all the ingredients. Pour over the salad, toss well and leave to stand for 15 minutes before serving.

Raw Beetroot Salad

Beetroot is usually cooked, cooled and served in vinegar. This salad proves beetroot is also delicious raw.

SERVES 4
150 g (5 oz) baby beetroots, trimmed, scrubbed and cut into thin sticks
15 ml (1 tbsp) lemon juice
10 ml (2 tsp) caraway seeds
1 small lettuce
1 radicchio
150 g (5 oz) celeriac, mooli or turnip, peeled and cut into thin sticks
150 g (5 oz) carrots, scrubbed and cut into thin sticks
FOR THE DRESSING
150 ml (¼ pint) low-fat natural yogurt
10 ml (2 tsp) Dijon mustard

NUTRITIONAL ANALYSIS
68 kcals/283 kJ
4.2 g Protein
10 g Carbohydrate
1.7 g Fat ★★★
0.4 g Saturated Fat ★★★★
4.3 g Fibre ★★★★
No Added Sugar ★★★★
320 mg Salt ★

1 Mix together the beetroot, lemon juice and 5 ml (1 tsp) of the caraway seeds.
2 Arrange the lettuce and radicchio leaves on an oval serving platter. Place the beetroot, celeriac and carrots attractively on top.
3 For the dressing, mix together the yogurt, mustard and remaining caraway seeds in a bowl. Serve separately.

Lebanese Salad

This refreshing, versatile accompanying salad is excellent with curries or cold meats. Alternatively, serve as a starter with wholemeal pitta bread.

SERVES 4 AS A STARTER; 6 AS AN ACCOMPANIMENT
1 large cucumber, diced
2.5 ml (½ tsp) salt
225 ml (8 fl oz) low-fat natural yogurt
1 garlic clove, skinned and crushed
30 ml (2 tbsp) finely chopped fresh mint
pepper, to taste

NUTRITIONAL ANALYSIS
41 kcals/171 kJ
3.5 g Protein
5.7 g Carbohydrate
0.7 g Fat ★★★★
0.4 g Saturated Fat ★★★
0.4 g Fibre ★★★
No Added Sugar ★★★★
142 mg Salt ★

1 Place the cucumber into a sieve and sprinkle lightly with salt. Leave to drain for 30 minutes. Rinse off the salt and drain again. Pat dry on absorbent kitchen paper.
2 Mix 30 ml (2 tbsp) of the yogurt with the garlic, add the mixture to the rest of the yogurt, combining well. Stir in the cucumber and mint and season to taste.

NUTRITIONAL ANALYSIS
283 kcals/1183 kJ
15.2 g Protein
27.7 g Carbohydrate
13.2 g Fat ★★
3.2 g Saturated Fat ★★★
5.4 g Fibre ★★★★
No Added Sugar ★★★★
1047 mg Salt ★

Chicory Waldorf Salad

The unusual dressing in this salad is made from cottage cheese, orange and watercress. It can be made up to a day in advance. Store in a screw-topped jar in the refrigerator.

SERVES 4

2 heads chicory, chopped
4 red dessert apples, cored and diced
50 g (2 oz) raisins
lettuce leaves, to serve
75 g (3 oz) walnut halves, roughly chopped
orange twists, to garnish

FOR THE CHEESY ORANGE DRESSING

350 g (12 oz) cottage cheese
finely grated rind and juice of 1 large orange
½ small bunch watercress, stalks removed
pepper, to taste

1 For the dressing, purée the cottage cheese, orange rind and juice and watercress leaves in a blender or food processor until smooth and creamy. Season to taste. Cover and chill until ready to serve.
2 Mix together the chicory, apples and raisins in a bowl. Add the dressing and gently mix until all the ingredients are well coated.
3 To serve, line 4 plates with the lettuce leaves. Divide the salad between the plates and sprinkle the chopped walnuts on top. Garnish with orange twists and serve at once.

NUTRITIONAL ANALYSIS
122 kcals/510 kJ
6.6 g Protein
9.3 g Carbohydrate
6.8 g Fat ★★★
0.9 g Saturated Fat ★★★★
4.9 g Fibre ★★★★
No Added Sugar ★★★★
111 mg Salt ★★★★

Cauliflower and Walnut Salad

A crunchy side salad that would provide a welcome element of texture to a smoother main course.

SERVES 4

1 green eating apple, cored and chopped
15 ml (1 tbsp) lemon juice
1 cauliflower, weighing about 700 g (1½ lb), divided into florets
150 ml (¼ pint) low-fat natural yogurt
pepper, to taste
50 g (2 oz) walnut halves, roughly chopped

1 Put the apple and lemon juice in a bowl and toss together. Add the cauliflower, yogurt and seasoning. Transfer to a salad bowl, cover and chill for 1 hour.
2 Stir in the walnuts just before serving.

Artichoke and Mushroom Salad

Canned artichoke hearts are a great standby, and make an unusual salad ingredient.

SERVES 4
400 g (14 oz) can artichoke hearts, drained and quartered
100 g (4 oz) button mushrooms, halved
1 small fennel bulb, finely shredded
endive leaves, to serve
FOR THE HERB DRESSING
30 ml (2 tbsp) olive oil
30 ml (2 tbsp) tarragon vinegar
1 garlic clove, skinned and crushed
grated rind of ½ lemon
15 ml (1 tbsp) chopped fresh parsley
pepper, to taste

NUTRITIONAL ANALYSIS
92 kcals/384 kJ
2.2 g Protein
3.6 g Carbohydrate
7.7 g Fat ★
1.1 g Saturated Fat ★★★
1.8 g Fibre ★★★★
No Added Sugar ★★★★
187 mg Salt ★★★

1 Place the artichoke hearts in a shallow dish with the mushrooms and fennel.
2 For the dressing, mix together all the ingredients in a bowl. Spoon over the vegetables, cover and chill for 1 hour.
3 Gently toss the chilled vegetables so they are well coated. Arrange a bed of endive leaves on 4 individual serving plates. Spoon the salad on top and serve.

Red Cabbage Slaw

Dates, orange and apple are included in this colourful salad. The dressing is spiced with cumin.

SERVES 4
1 green skinned apple, cored and cut into small cubes
225 g (8 oz) red cabbage, finely shredded
1 small carrot, scrubbed and coarsely grated
½ green pepper, cored, seeded and finely shredded
1 orange, peeled and cut into small cubes
25 g (1 oz) dried stoned dates, finely chopped
FOR THE DRESSING
2.5 ml (½ tsp) Dijon mustard
1.25 ml (¼ tsp) freshly ground cumin
10 ml (2 tsp) sunflower oil
30 ml (2 tbsp) orange juice
pepper, to taste

NUTRITIONAL ANALYSIS
83 kcals/347 kJ
1.8 g Protein
13.8 g Carbohydrate
2.7 g Fat ★★★
0.4 g Saturated Fat ★★★★
4.1 g Fibre ★★★★
No Added Sugar ★★★★
86 mg Salt ★★★★

1 For the dressing, put the mustard into a large bowl and stir in the cumin, oil and orange juice. Season to taste.
2 Add the apple and toss, then add the cabbage, carrot, pepper, orange and dates. Toss well, cover and leave in a cool place for 1 hour. Toss again before serving.

NUTRITIONAL ANALYSIS
149 kcals/621 kJ
3.7 g Protein
18.5 g Carbohydrate
7.3 g Fat ★★
0.9 g Saturated Fat ★★★★
4.6 g Fibre ★
No Added Sugar ★★★★
353 mg Salt ★★

Beetroot and Celery Salad

Choose small, undamaged beetroot as they will be tender and sweet. The salad is flavoured with dill, reminiscent in taste to caraway.

SERVES 4

225 g (8 oz) cooked beetroot, skinned and diced
2 apples, cored and chopped
4 celery sticks, trimmed and diced
1 small onion, skinned and finely chopped
1 small cooked potato, peeled and diced
1 dill cucumber, diced
25 ml (1½ tbsp) chopped fresh dill or 10 ml (2 tsp) dried dill weed
30 ml (2 tbsp) white wine vinegar
2.5-5 ml (½–1 tsp) prepared mustard
15 ml (1 tbsp) olive oil
45 ml (3 tbsp) low-fat natural yogurt
25 g (1 oz) walnut halves, chopped
few large lettuce leaves
watercress sprigs, to garnish

1 Mix together the beetroot, apples, celery, onion, potato and dill cucumber in a bowl.
2 Mix 15 ml (1 tbsp) fresh dill, or all the dried dill, with 15 ml (1 tbsp) of the vinegar, pour over the salad and toss together.
3 Mix the mustard to taste with the remaining vinegar, the oil and yogurt. Stir in the walnuts. Pour over the salad and mix lightly. Cover and chill for at least 2 hours.
4 Arrange lettuce leaves in a bowl or platter, spoon the salad on top and sprinkle with the remaining chopped fresh dill. Garnish with watercress sprigs and serve.

NUTRITIONAL ANALYSIS
254 kcals/1061 kJ
9.5 g Protein
42 g Carbohydrate
6.5 g Fat ★★★
1.2 g Saturated Fat ★★★★
6.2 g Fibre ★★★★
No Added Sugar ★★★★
337 mg Salt ★★★

Barley Salad

Pot barley provides a delicious nutty taste to this salad.

SERVES 4

175 g (6 oz) pot barley, rinsed
5 ml (1 tsp) sunflower oil
100 g (4 oz) mushrooms, sliced
pepper, to taste
25 g (1 oz) flaked almonds
100 g (4 oz) watercress, roughly chopped
100 g (4 oz) cottage cheese
1 large orange, grated, peeled and roughly chopped

1 Put the barley in a saucepan containing 450 ml (¾ pint) cold water and bring to the boil. Cover and simmer for about 45 minutes or until tender, adding a little more water during cooking, if needed. Place in a salad bowl.
2 Heat the oil in a large non-stick frying pan and cook the mushrooms, covered, for 3 minutes. Remove the lid to let the mushrooms brown as the liquid evaporates. Add to the cooked barley and season to taste.
3 Add the almonds to the pan and brown lightly over a very low heat.
4 Add the watercress, cottage cheese and orange to the salad bowl, and toss lightly to mix. Scatter over the almonds and garnish with the grated orange rind.

Provençal-Style Tart (PAGE 134)

Sprouted Salad

Mung or aduki beans, alfalfa and chick-peas can be bought ready sprouted at reputable health food stores and some of the larger supermarkets. Also available are sprouters; if you have a bought sprouter, follow the instructions given.

SERVES 4	FOR THE TAHINI DRESSING
50 g (2 oz) alfalfa seeds	30 ml (2 tbsp) tahini
50 g (2 oz) mung or aduki beans	45 ml (3 tbsp) low-fat natural yogurt
50 g (2 oz) chick-peas	1 garlic clove, skinned and crushed (optional)
1 punnet mustard and cress	15-30 ml (1-2 tbsp) lemon juice, to taste
½ red pepper, cored, seeded and diced	1.25 ml (¼ tsp) ground cumin
2 tomatoes, sliced	pepper, to taste

NUTRITIONAL ANALYSIS
160 kcals/669 kJ
10.7 g Protein
19.3 g Carbohydrate
5.1 g Fat ★★★
1 g Saturated Fat ★★★★
8.7 g Fibre ★★★★
No Added Sugar ★★★★
63 mg Salt ★★★★

1 Before the sprouting, check all pulses for broken beans or pods which will not sprout.
2 Soak the pulses for 10-15 hours to enable germination to start. Rinse well.
3 To sprout the pulses use a glass jar with a piece of muslin held with a rubber band over the mouth to enable you to pour in and drain out water. Keep the sprouting pulses in a warm dark place, rinsing twice a day. Alfalfa will take 5-6 days to sprout, mung or aduki beans will take 3-6 days and chick-peas 2-3 days. Place in daylight just before the sprouts have reached their full length.
4 Rinse and drain the sprouts well, then mix with the remaining salad ingredients in a bowl.
5 For the dressing, stir together the ingredients, adding a little more yogurt if the dressing is too thick. Pour over the centre of the salad and toss just before serving.

Bean Salad

Part of the staple diet in Central and Southern America, black beans have a sweet taste and are very tender.

SERVES 4	FOR THE GARLIC AND PARSLEY DRESSING
175 g (6 oz) dried black beans, soaked overnight	60 ml (4 tbsp) chopped fresh parsley
400 g (14 oz) can flageolet beans, drained	30 ml (2 tbsp) sunflower oil
1 yellow pepper, cored, seeded and chopped	45 ml (3 tbsp) lemon juice
1 red pepper, cored, seeded and chopped	3 garlic cloves, skinned and crushed
1 green pepper, cored, seeded and chopped	
chopped fresh parsley, to garnish	pepper, to taste

NUTRITIONAL ANALYSIS
304 kcals/1270 kJ
18.4 g Protein
39.6 g Carbohydrate
9.2 g Fat ★★★
1.2 g Saturated Fat ★★★★
21.1 g Fibre ★★★★
No Added Sugar ★★★★
106 mg Salt ★★★★

1 Drain the beans and rinse. Put in a saucepan with plenty of fresh water. Bring to the boil and boil for 10-15 minutes. Reduce the heat and simmer for 1 hour or until tender. Drain and leave to cool.
2 Mix the black beans with the remaining salad ingredients in a large bowl.
3 For the dressing, combine together the ingredients and pour over the salad. Toss gently together and leave to stand for 1 hour before serving to allow flavours to blend.

Barbecued Red Mullet (PAGE 142)

NUTRITIONAL ANALYSIS
342 kcals/1431 kJ
5.9 g Protein
47.7 g Carbohydrate
15.6 g Fat ★★
1.8 g Saturated Fat ★★★★
5.8 g Fibre ★★★★
No Added Sugar ★★★★
85 mg Salt ★★★★

Almond, Raisin and Rice Salad

In rice salads, pour the dressing over the hot rice for maximum flavour absorption.

SERVES 4

175 g (6 oz) brown rice
50 g (2 oz) raisins
50 g (2 oz) flaked almonds, toasted
2 spring onions, trimmed and sliced
½ small red pepper, cored, seeded and diced
1 small green eating apple, cored and diced
1 celery stick, trimmed and chopped
fresh coriander leaves, to garnish

FOR THE MUSTARD DRESSING

30 ml (2 tbsp) sunflower oil
15 ml (1 tbsp) cider vinegar
2.5 ml (½ tsp) prepared English mustard
1 garlic clove, skinned and crushed
pepper, to taste

1 Put the rice in a saucepan with 450 ml (¾ pint) boiling water. Cover and gently simmer for 30 minutes or until tender and all the liquid has been absorbed.
2 Meanwhile for the dressing, put the ingredients into a screw-topped jar or bowl and shake or whisk vigorously until thoroughly blended. Set aside.
3 Shake the dressing again and pour over the hot rice. Mix gently with a fork until the rice is well coated, then set aside to cook completely.
4 Add the raisins, almonds, spring onions, red pepper, apple and celery to the rice and mix well together. Serve garnished with coriander leaves.

NUTRITIONAL ANALYSIS
8 kcals/32 kJ
0.6 g Protein
1.1 g Carbohydrate
0.2 g Fat ★★★★
0.1 g Saturated Fat ★★★
0 g Fibre ★★★★
No Added Sugar ★★★★
22 mg Salt ★★

Salad Dressing

This basic oil-free salad dressing can be varied by adding spices, fresh herbs, garlic or shallots.

SERVES 4

45 ml (3 tbsp) low-fat natural yogurt
15 ml (1 tbsp) lemon juice
pepper, to taste

1 Mix together the yogurt, lemon juice and seasoning in a bowl.
2 To the basic dressing any of the following can be added: cumin, paprika, crushed garlic, mustard, chopped shallot and chopped fresh herbs such as parsley, mint etc.

8

Entertaining

Because many people don't understand exactly what healthy eating means, there is a generally held assumption that it is not possible to entertain with flair when you are being sensible about your diet. As this chapter will prove, it is quite possible to provide delicious, filling, elegant and appealing recipes that will satisfy guests without damaging their health!

To take the strain out of entertaining, the recipes in this section are given as complete menus, each with a starter, a main course and a pudding.

MENU 1

NUTRITIONAL ANALYSIS
129 kcals/537 kJ
10.5 g Protein
22 g Carbohydrate
0.5 g Fat ★★★★
0.2 g Saturated Fat ★★★★
1.6 g Fibre ★★★★
7.9 g Added Sugar ★
777 mg Salt ★

Sweet Pepper Sorbets

Peppers are combined with quark, low-fat soft cheese, to make these unusual two-coloured savoury sorbets.

SERVES 4

225 g (8 oz) red pepper, cored, seeded and diced

10 ml (2 tsp) Worcestershire sauce

30 ml (2 tbsp) sugar

225 g (8 oz) low-fat quark or other low-fat soft cheese

225 g (8 oz) green pepper, cored, seeded and diced

15 ml (1 tbsp) finely chopped fresh mint

2 egg whites

mint sprigs, to garnish (optional)

1 Purée the red pepper in a blender or food processor with the Worcestershire sauce and 15 ml (1 tbsp) of the sugar.
2 Sieve into a bowl, pressing to extract about 175 ml (6 fl oz) purée. Whisk 100 g (4 oz) of the quark into the purée until evenly mixed, then transfer to a freezer-proof container.
3 Purée the green pepper with the remaining sugar and sieve as for the red pepper. Whisk in the remaining quark and the mint, then transfer to a freezerproof container. Freeze both purées for 4 hours or until ice crystals begin to form around the edge.
4 Turn the half-frozen purées into separate bowls and break up with a fork. Whisk the egg whites until stiff, then fold half into each purée. Return the sorbets to the freezer containers, cover and freeze for at least 12 hours.
5 To serve, leave the sorbets at a cool room temperature to soften slightly for about 20 minutes, then scoop 2 balls of each colour on to individual plates. Garnish with mint sprigs, if using, and serve immediately.

NUTRITIONAL ANALYSIS
373 kcals/1559 kJ
38 g Protein
5 g Carbohydrate
22.7 g Fat ★
8.2 g Saturated Fat ★★
3.3 g Fibre ★★
No Added Sugar ★★★★
394 mg Salt ★★★

Middle Eastern Style Lamb

Tahini is a paste made from ground sesame seeds. There are pale and dark varieties available; the pale paste has a milder, creamier flavour.

SERVES 4

2 rack of lamb (6 bones on each), trimmed of all excess fat

15 ml (1 tbsp) chopped fresh mint

15 ml (1 tbsp) chopped fresh coriander

2 garlic cloves, skinned and crushed

juice of 2 limes

1 aubergine, thinly sliced

15 ml (1 tbsp) sunflower oil

pepper, to taste

30 ml (2 tbsp) tahini

lime wedges and mint sprigs, to garnish

1 Place the lamb in a shallow dish. Scatter the chopped mint, coriander and garlic over the top and sprinkle with lime juice. Cover and leave to chill for 4 hours.
2 Spread the sliced aubergine out on a non-stick baking sheet, brush with oil and season to taste. Bake at 190°C (375°F) mark 5 for 5 minutes, then reduce the oven temperature to 180°C (350°F) mark 4.
3 Put the marinated lamb in a roasting tin, standing each piece on its broad bones and interlocking the cutlet bones to form an arch at the top. Roast for 45 minutes.
4 Spread the tahini over the outside of the meat, season and press the aubergine slices on to the tahini. Roast for a further 15 minutes. Garnish the lamb with lime wedges and mint sprigs. Accompany with boiled rice or burghul wheat.

Apricot and Orange Fools

This colourful pudding is quick and easy to make. Use no-soak dried apricots as they only take 10 minutes to cook.

SERVES 4	
225 g (8 oz) no-soak dried apricots, rinsed	150 ml (1/4 pint) dry white wine
juice of 2 oranges	225 ml (8 fl oz) Greek strained yogurt
finely grated rind of 1/2 orange	2 large oranges, peeled and segmented, to decorate

1 Put the apricots, half the orange juice, the rind and wine in a saucepan. Cover and simmer gently for 12-15 minutes or until tender.
2 Purée in a blender or food processor. Stir in the remaining orange juice and chill for 1-2 hours or until cold.
3 Put alternate spoonfuls of the mixture and the yogurt into 4 tall stemmed glasses. Gently draw them together with a knife to create a marbled effect. Decorate with orange segments and serve.

NUTRITIONAL ANALYSIS
236 kcals/987 kJ
6.9 g Protein
35.9 g Carbohydrate
5.6 g Fat ★★★
3.6 g Saturated Fat ★★★
15 g Fibre ★★★★
No Added Sugar ★★★★
156 mg Salt ★★★★

MENU 2

Courgette (Zucchini) Soup

When selecting courgettes (zucchini), choose ones about 10-15 cm (4-6 inches) long and a good deep green colour.

SERVES 4	
450 g (1 lb) courgettes (zucchini), trimmed and sliced	900 ml (1 1/2 pints) chicken stock
1 medium onion, skinned and chopped	15 ml (1 tbsp) chopped fresh mint or parsley
1 medium potato, peeled and roughly chopped	pepper, to taste
	60 ml (4 tbsp) low-fat natural yogurt

1 Put the courgettes (zucchini), onion, potato and stock in a saucepan. Bring to the boil, cover and simmer for 20 minutes or until the vegetables are soft.
2 Allow to cool slightly, then purée in a food processor or blender until smooth. Stir in the mint, seasoning and yogurt. Reheat gently and serve hot or cold.

NUTRITIONAL ANALYSIS
67 kcals/279 kJ
3.3 g Protein
13.3 g Carbohydrate
0.4 g Fat ★★★★
0.1 g Saturated Fat ★★★★
2 g Fibre ★★★★
No Added Sugar ★★★★
76 mg Salt ★★★

Salmon Parcels

The salmon is cooked with vegetables and lemon juice, all packaged together in foil or parchment paper. The result is a moist, delicately flavoured fish.

SERVES 4	
4 salmon or sea-trout steaks, each weighing about 225 g (8 oz)	60 ml (4 tbsp) lemon juice
4 spring onions, trimmed and cut into matchstick strips	15 ml (1 tbsp) chopped fresh parsley
175 g (6 oz) button mushrooms, sliced	pepper, to taste
	parsley sprigs and lemon wedges, to garnish

1 Cut 4 pieces of foil or parchment paper large enough to enclose the steaks, then lay a steak on each piece. If using foil, place the fish on the shiny side.
2 Equally divide the spring onions, mushrooms and lemon juice over the steaks, sprinkle with parsley and season. Wrap the paper or foil around, sealing the edges.
3 Cook at 190°C (375°F) mark 5 for 25-30 minutes or until the salmon is cooked and the flesh flakes easily.
4 Serve in the foil or paper, garnished with sprigs of parsley and lemon wedges. Open at the table. Accompany with new potatoes. (*Menu 2 continued overleaf*)

NUTRITIONAL ANALYSIS
421 kcals/1758 kJ
42.6 g Protein
1.1 g Carbohydrate
27.3 g Fat ★
5.5 g Saturated Fat ★★★
2.1 g Fibre ★★★
No Added Sugar ★★★★
577 mg Salt ★★★

NUTRITIONAL ANALYSIS
81 kcals/339 kJ
2.9 g Protein
14.8 g Carbohydrate
1.5 g Fat ★★★★
1 g Saturated Fat ★★★
7.4 g Fibre ★★★★
No Added Sugar ★★★★
28 mg Salt ★★★★

Figs with Raspberry Sauce

Fresh figs look nothing like the dried ones, and they taste much better. They have a green or purple skin with pale juicy flesh, enclosing a luscious pink centre.

SERVES 4	*60 ml (4 tbsp) Greek strained yogurt*
8 fresh ripe figs	*extra raspberries and fresh mint leaves, to decorate*
225 g (8 oz) raspberries, thawed if frozen	

1 Make 4 cuts in each fig, from the stalk end almost down to the rounded end. Open each fig to resemble a flower and set aside.
2 Purée the raspberries in a blender or food processor until smooth or rub through a nylon sieve. Pour the purée into a bowl and add the yogurt. Mix well.
3 Place the prepared figs in individual dishes. Pour a little raspberry sauce on to one side of each dish. Decorate with raspberries and mint leaves. Serve the remaining sauce separately.

MENU 3

NUTRITIONAL ANALYSIS
172 kcals/720 kJ
14.7 g Protein
6.8 g Carbohydrate
9.7 g Fat ★★
3 g Saturated Fat ★★
1.3 g Fibre ★★
No Added Sugar ★★★★
1368 mg Salt ★

Chilled Fish Terrine

This elegant no-cook fish terrine is made up of layers of salmon and crab.

SERVES 4	*pepper, to taste*
40 g (1½ oz) polyunsaturated margarine	*200 g (7 oz) can red salmon, drained and flaked*
large bunch fresh parsley, finely chopped	*4-6 very thin slices wholemeal bread, crusts removed*
275 g (10 oz) low-fat soft cheese	
finely grated rind and juice of ½ lemon	*175 g (6 oz) can crab meat in brine, well rinsed, drained and flaked*
7.5 ml (½ tbsp) chopped fresh dill or 2.5 ml (½ tsp) dried dill	*dill sprig, to garnish*

1 Melt 25 g (1 oz) of the margarine in a saucepan and mix in one-third of the parsley. Spoon into the base of a 450g (1 lb) non-stick loaf tin, pressing well into the corners of the tin. Set aside.
2 Beat the cheese with the lemon rind and juice, dill and seasoning until well blended and soft. Melt the remaining margarine, add to the cheese and beat until light and fluffy.
3 Put half the cheese mixture in a separate bowl and beat in the salmon until well blended. Spoon into the tin, pressing into the corners and smoothing the surface.
4 Top with half the remaining parsley. Cut 2 or 3 bread slices to fit neatly over the parsley, covering the entire surface in a smooth layer.
5 Beat the crab meat into the remaining cheese mixture, then spoon into the tin on top of the bread, pressing into the corners and smoothing the surface. Top with the remaining parsley and a final layer of bread, forming a smooth surface.
6 Press down slightly and cover. Chill for at least 4 hours in the coldest part of the refrigerator. To serve, run a knife along the inside edge of the tin. Quickly dip the base into hot water and invert the terrine on to a serving dish. Garnish and serve sliced.

Duckling with Apple and Ginger

To lower the fat content considerably, the duckling is skinned. The tartness of the apple complements the richness of the duck meat.

SERVES 4
3 cooking apples
2 kg (4½ lb) oven-ready duckling, skinned and fat removed
50 g (2 oz) fresh root ginger, peeled and sliced
15 ml (1 tbsp) clear honey
15 ml (1 tbsp) cider vinegar
5 ml (1 tsp) ground ginger
watercress, to garnish

NUTRITIONAL ANALYSIS
247 kcals/1032 kJ
28.6 g Protein
19.1 g Carbohydrate
6.9 g Fat ★★★
1.9 g Saturated Fat ★★★★
4 g Fibre ★★★★
2.9 g Added Sugar ★★★★
416 mg Salt ★★★

1 Cut one of the apples into wedges, core and place in the duckling cavity with the root ginger. Place the duckling, breast-side down, in a roasting tin and pour over 10 ml (2 tsp) honey and 300 ml (½ pint) water.
2 Cover with foil and roast at 180°C (350°F) mark 4 for 1¼ hours or until almost cooked, turning the duckling over halfway through cooking and basting occasionally.
3 Peel and core the remaining apples and cut into rings. When the duckling is almost cooked, uncover and place the apple rings around the bird. Increase the oven temperature to 230°C (450°F) mark 8 and roast for a further 10-15 minutes or until the duckling and apples are tender and golden brown, basting frequently.
4 Place the duckling on a carving dish, arrange the apple rings across the breast and keep warm. Skim any fat from the juices, then pour the juices into a small saucepan. Add the remaining honey, vinegar and ground ginger. Boil rapidly for 2-3 minutes, then serve with the duckling. Garnish and accompany with new potatoes and mangetout.

Chilled Lemon Custards

These light and refreshing whips contain very little added sugar; they are flavoured by lemon rind and freshly squeezed juice.

SERVES 4
300 ml (½ pint) skimmed milk
1 egg, separated
30 ml (2 tbsp) sugar
finely grated rind and juice of 1 lemon
10 ml (2 tsp) powdered gelatine
1 egg white
lemon slices, to decorate

NUTRITIONAL ANALYSIS
86 kcals/361 kJ
7 g Protein
11.9 g Carbohydrate
1.6 g Fat ★★★★
0.5 g Saturated Fat ★★★★
0 g Fibre ★
7.9 g Added Sugar ★
179 mg Salt ★★★

1 Put the milk, egg yolk and sugar in a saucepan and heat gently until very slightly thickened, but not boiling. Stir in the lemon rind and set aside for about 10 minutes.
2 Put the lemon juice in a small heatproof bowl and sprinkle over the gelatine. Leave for 5 minutes to soften. Place the bowl over a saucepan of gently simmering water and stir until the gelatine dissolves. Cool slightly, then whisk into the cold custard.
3 Whisk the egg white until stiff, then fold into the custard. Divide the mixture between 4 glass dishes and chill for 2-3 hours. Decorate with lemon slices.

MENU 4

Stuffed Globe Artichokes

NUTRITIONAL ANALYSIS
140 kcals/585 kJ
19.5 g Protein
9.7 g Carbohydrate
2.7 g Fat ★★★
0.4 g Saturated Fat ★★★★
1.8 g Fibre ★★★★
No Added Sugar ★★★★
2639 mg Salt ★

Tofu is a soya bean curd made from curdling warmed soya bean milk. There are three varieties, firm, silken and soft. Silken is more lightly pressed than the firm type.

SERVES 4

- *4 globe artichokes*
- *½ lemon*
- *½ bunch watercress, trimmed*
- *150 g (5 oz) silken tofu*
- *2 garlic cloves, skinned and crushed*
- *finely grated rind and juice of 1 lime*
- *pepper, to taste*
- *225 g (8 oz) peeled cooked prawns, thawed if frozen, roughly chopped if large*
- *1 large ripe pear, peeled, cored and diced*
- *4 lime slices and 8 unpeeled cooked prawns (optional), to garnish*

1 Pull away and discard any discoloured leaves from the outside of each artichoke. Break off each artichoke stalk to level the base.
2 With a sharp, stainless steel knife, cut off the top quarter of each artichoke, then snip off the tips of the leaves with kitchen scissors. Rub the cut surfaces of the artichokes with the lemon.
3 Plunge the artichokes into a large saucepan of lightly salted boiling water. Cover tightly and simmer for 30-40 minutes or until tender and a leaf comes away easily when pulled. Drain, run under cold water, then cool and drain upside down.
4 Reserve a few sprigs of watercress for the garnish. Finely chop the remainder and place in a bowl.
5 Purée the tofu, garlic, lime rind and juice, and seasoning in a blender or food processor until smooth. Add to the watercress. Stir in the prawns and pear.
6 Carefully peel back the leaves of each artichoke and scoop out the hairy choke in the centre. Remove some leaves from the centre to make room for the filling.
7 Stand the artichokes on individual serving plates and spoon in the filling. Garnish with the reserved watercress sprigs, lime slices and unpeeled prawns, if using. Serve as soon as possible.

Sole (Flounder) in Filo Pastry

NUTRITIONAL ANALYSIS
287 kcals/1199 kJ
30.1 g Protein
34.9 g Carbohydrate
4 g Fat ★★★★
0.6 g Saturated Fat ★★★★
1.6 g Fibre ★★
No Added Sugar ★★★★
1656 mg Salt ★

Filo pastry is time-consuming and fairly difficult to make. Ready-made filo pastry is available from good delicatessens and large supermarkets.

SERVES 4

- *8 lemon sole (flounder) fillets, each weighing about 75 g (3 oz), skinned and cut into thin strips*
- *30 ml (2 tbsp) lemon or lime juice*
- *pepper, to taste*
- *3 courgettes (zucchini), trimmed and grated*
- *2 shallots, skinned and chopped*
- *8 sheets filo pastry*

1 Combine the fish, juice, seasoning, courgettes (zucchini) and shallots in a bowl. Mix well, then divide into 8 equal portions.
2 Work with one sheet of filo pastry at a time, keeping the remainder covered with a damp cloth. Fold the filo in half lengthways. Place one-eighth of the fish mixture in one corner and pat out lightly. Fold the filo over the filling at right angles to make a triangle. Continue folding the filo strip over to form a neat triangular-shaped parcel. Repeat with the remaining filo and fish mixture.
3 Arrange the 8 parcels on a lightly greased baking sheet. Cook at 190°C (375°F) mark 5 for 25 minutes or until golden and cooked through. If necessary, cover the pointed ends of the parcels with foil during cooking to prevent overbrowning. Serve hot. Accompany with spinach, tossed in low-fat natural yogurt.

Chilled Vanilla Soufflé

The use of low-fat yogurt makes this dish much lower in fat than traditional soufflés.

SERVES 4

3 eggs, separated

50 g (2 oz) sugar

5 ml (1 tsp) vanilla essence

10 ml (2 tsp) powdered gelatine

150 ml (1/4 pint) low-fat natural yogurt

25 g (1 oz) pistachio nuts, skinned and finely chopped, and 1 large kiwi fruit, peeled and thinly sliced, to decorate

1 Prepare a 600 ml (1 pint) soufflé dish with a greaseproof collar tied round the outside of the dish to stand about 5 cm (2 inches) above the rim.
2 Place the egg yolks, sugar and vanilla essence in a bowl over a pan of simmering water. Whisk till thick and pale and the whisk leaves a trail. Remove from the heat.
3 Sprinkle the gelatine over 30 ml (2 tbsp) cold water in a heatproof bowl and leave for 1 minute to soften. Place the bowl over a saucepan of gently simmering water and stir until the gelatine dissolves. Stir into the vanilla mixture with the yogurt. Chill for about 30 minutes or until the mixture begins to thicken.
4 Whisk the egg whites until stiff, then fold into the soufflé mixture. Pour into the prepared dish and chill for 2-3 hours or until set.
5 Carefully peel off the paper collar. Using a palette knife, press the nuts around the side of the soufflé. Decorate the top with the sliced kiwi fruit. Served chilled.

NUTRITIONAL ANALYSIS
186 kcals/777 kJ
10.5 g Protein
19.1 g Carbohydrate
8 g Fat ★★
2.1 g Saturated Fat ★★★
0.3 g Fibre ★
13.1 g Added Sugar ★
222 mg Salt ★★★

MENU 5

Pesto Stuffed Tomatoes

Basil and pine nuts are the classic ingredients of an Italian pesto sauce.

SERVES 4

50 g (2 oz) burghul wheat

4 beefsteak tomatoes

30 ml (2 tbsp) chopped fresh basil

1 garlic clove, skinned and crushed

15 ml (1 tbsp) pine nuts

15 ml (1 tbsp) freshly grated Parmesan cheese

30 ml (2 tbsp) sunflower oil

pepper, to taste

shredded endive and cucumber slices, to serve

fresh basil sprigs, to garnish

1 Cover burghul with boiling water and soak for 15 minutes.
2 Meanwhile, cut a slice from the base of each tomato. Scoop out the flesh and put in a sieve to remove the excess moisture, then finely chop. Set shells aside.
3 Place the basil, garlic, pine nuts and Parmesan cheese in a mortar or in a blender. Pound or blend until a fine paste is formed, then add the oil a little at a time.
4 Drain the burghul, pressing out excess water. Add the basil sauce, tomato flesh and seasoning and mix well. Pile into the tomato shells. Serve on a bed of shredded endive and cucumber slices, garnished with basil sprigs. (*Menu 5 continued overleaf*)

NUTRITIONAL ANALYSIS
174 kcals/725 kJ
5 g Protein
14.8 g Carbohydrate
11.1 g Fat ★
1.8 g Saturated Fat ★★★
3.2 g Fibre ★★★★
No Added Sugar ★★★★
93 mg Salt ★★★★

NUTRITIONAL ANALYSIS
241 kcals/1005 kJ
31.2 g Protein
14.4 g Carbohydrate
6.1 g Fat ★★★
1.8 g Saturated Fat ★★★★
2.3 g Fibre ★★★
No Added Sugar ★★★★
465 mg Salt ★★★

Roast Guinea Fowl with Bread Sauce

Guinea fowl is a lean meat. Using skimmed milk and low-fat yogurt reduces the overall fat content of the dish.

SERVES 4

1 orange

1 guinea fowl, weighing about 1.1 kg (2 lb)

sunflower oil, for brushing

orange slices and watercress, to garnish

FOR THE BREAD SAUCE

300 ml (½ pint) skimmed milk

1 medium onion, skinned

3 cloves

1 bay leaf

4 black peppercorns

50 g (2 oz) fresh wholemeal breadcrumbs

pepper, to taste

45 ml (3 tbsp) low-fat natural yogurt

1 Grate the orange rind and set aside. Cut the orange into halves or quarters and place in the cavity of the guinea fowl. Brush the bird with a little oil and put into a roasting tin. Roast at 200°C (400°F) mark 6 for 1 hour.

2 Meanwhile for the sauce, put the milk, onion studded with the cloves, bay leaf and peppercorns in a saucepan. Bring almost to the boil. Remove from the heat, leave to infuse for 30 minutes.

3 Strain the milk and return to the pan. Add the breadcrumbs, orange rind and seasoning. Cook over a low heat for 10-15 minutes until thick, stirring occasionally. Stir in the yogurt. Garnish the guinea fowl with orange slices and watercress and serve with the bread sauce. Accompany with new potatoes and broccoli.

NUTRITIONAL ANALYSIS
100 kcals/416 kJ
1 g Protein
19.3 g Carbohydrate
0 g Fat ★★★★
0 g Saturated Fat ★★★★
3.5 g Fibre ★★★★
No Added Sugar ★★★★
13 mg Salt ★★★★

Pears and Peaches in Wine

Buy pears before fully ripe as they can change from rock hard to overripe very quickly.

SERVES 4

3 large firm pears, peeled, cored and cut into 12 slices

150 ml (¼ pint) dry white wine

thinly pared rind and juice of ½ lemon

thinly pared rind and juice of ½ orange

2.5 cm (1 inch) piece cinnamon stick

3 peaches, skinned, stoned and sliced

1 Put the pears, wine, lemon and orange juices and the cinnamon stick in a saucepan. Simmer gently for about 8 minutes, then add the peach slices. Simmer for a further 5 minutes or until both fruits are just tender.

2 Using a slotted spoon, transfer the fruit to a shallow serving dish. Remove the cinnamon stick from the juices in the pan.

3 Cut the citrus rind into fine strips and add to the juices. Bring to the boil and cook over high heat until the juice has reduced by half. Pour over the fruit and allow to cool, then chill for about 1 hour. Serve chilled.

MENU 6

Tomato Ice in Fennel Cups

This attractive starter is surprisingly low in calories.

SERVES 4	5 ml (1 tsp) Worcestershire sauce
two 400 g (14 oz) cans tomatoes	5 ml (1 tsp) sugar
5 ml (1 tsp) dried basil	2 fennel bulbs
5 ml (1 tsp) dried oregano	curly endive, radicchio and fennel fronds, to garnish

1 Purée the tomatoes and their juice in a blender or food processor until smooth. Pour into a saucepan, add the basil, oregano, Worcestershire sauce and sugar. Bring to the boil and simmer for 5 minutes.
2 Strain the mixture into a freezerproof container. Cool, then place in the freezer for at least 1½ hours or until the mixture is completely frozen.
3 Cut the base from the fennel and carefully pull away the cup-shaped pieces. Trim the pieces, leaving the green stem on. Cook the fennel 'cups' in a saucepan of boiling water for 5 minutes, then drain and refresh under cold water. Chill until ready to use.
4 Remove the tomato ice from the freezer 5-10 minutes before serving. Fill each fennel cup with the tomato ice. Garnish with endive, radicchio and fennel fronds, then serve immediately.

NUTRITIONAL ANALYSIS
38 kcals/160 kJ
3.1 g Protein
6.9 g Carbohydrate
0 g Fat ★★★★
0.1 g Saturated Fat ★★★★
3.5 g Fibre ★★★★
1.3 g Added Sugar ★★
500 mg Salt ★

Chicken Véronique

Using skinned chicken pieces and low-fat yogurt helps to reduce the fat content of this dish.

SERVES 4	pared rind and juice of 1 lemon
15 ml (1 tbsp) sunflower oil	150 ml (¼ pint) chicken stock
4 chicken pieces, each weighing 100-175 g (4-6 oz), skinned	150 ml (¼ pint) dry white wine
	pepper, to taste
1 medium onion, skinned and sliced	175 g (6 oz) seedless green grapes
	15 ml (1 tbsp) cornflour
100 g (4 oz) button mushrooms	30 ml (2 tbsp) low-fat natural yogurt

1 Heat the oil in a non-stick frying pan and cook the chicken for about 2 minutes or until lightly browned on both sides. Put into a large casserole.
2 Add the onion and mushrooms to the pan and cook for 3 minutes until the onion is soft. Add the lemon rind and juice, stock, wine and pepper. Bring to the boil and simmer for 2 minutes, then pour over the chicken.
3 Cover and cook at 190°C (375°F) mark 5 for 40 minutes until the juices run clear when the thickest part of the chicken is pierced. Add 100 g (4 oz) of the grapes and continue cooking for 5 minutes. Using a slotted spoon, transfer the chicken, onion, mushrooms and grapes to a serving dish and keep hot.
4 Strain off 300 ml (½ pint) of the cooking liquid and put in a pan, skimming off any fat. Blend the cornflour with a little water, then stir in a little of the hot cooking liquid. Add to the pan and cook for about 2 minutes, stirring, until thickened. Remove from the heat and stir in the yogurt. Pour over the chicken and garnish with the remaining grapes. Accompany with new potatoes and French beans.

NUTRITIONAL ANALYSIS
234 kcals/978 kJ
21.9 g Protein
12.5 g Carbohydrate
8.4 g Fat ★★★
2 g Saturated Fat ★★★
1.5 g Fibre ★★
No Added Sugar ★★★★
248 mg Salt ★★★

NUTRITIONAL ANALYSIS
70 kcals/292 kJ
1 g Protein
17.7 g Carbohydrate
0 g Fat ★★★★
0 g Saturated Fat ★★★★
9.2 g Fibre ★★★★
No Added Sugar ★★★★
16 mg Salt ★★★★

Rosy Pears

Vitamin C rich blackcurrants are made into a strongly coloured and flavoured sauce to coat the pears.

MAKES 4

4 cooking pears, peeled, but with stalks left intact
225 g (8 oz) frozen blackcurrants
25 g (1 oz) sugar (optional)

1 Put the pears, blackcurrants, sugar and 100 ml (4 fl oz) water in a saucepan. Bring slowly to the boil, cover and simmer about 25 minutes, turning once, until the pears are soft but not mushy.
2 Gently remove the pears and place on to 4 individual plates.
3 Increase the heat and boil the blackcurrants rapidly for 3-4 minutes or until the liquid has reduced slightly. Press through a fine sieve and pour a little sauce over each pear. Serve at once or chill.

MENU 7

NUTRITIONAL ANALYSIS
183 kcals/764 kJ
5.5 g Protein
8.2 g Carbohydrate
14.5 g Fat ★
1.5 g Saturated Fat ★★★
3.7 g Fibre ★★★★
No Added Sugar ★★★★
136 mg Salt ★★★★

Chilled Curried Almond and Apple Soup

Serve this refreshing summer soup with crisp Indian poppadoms. Instead of frying them, grill the poppadoms for 5-10 seconds on each side or until bubbles appear on the surface.

SERVES 4

15ml (1 tbsp) sunflower oil
1 small onion, skinned and chopped
1 eating apple, cored and chopped
10 ml (2 tsp) garam masala
2.5 ml (½ tsp) ground turmeric
75 g (3 oz) blanched almonds, split or flaked
1.1 litres (2 pints) vegetable stock
pepper, to taste
150 ml (¼ pint) low-fat natural yogurt

1 Heat the oil in a large non-stick saucepan and gently cook the onion and apple, stirring, for about 10 minutes until soft and lightly coloured.
2 Sprinkle in the garam masala and turmeric and cook, stirring, for a further 2 minutes or until the mixture gives off a spicy aroma.
3 Reserve a few almonds for the garnish. Add the remainder to the pan and cook over moderate heat until the nuts are lightly coloured, stirring constantly.
4 Pour in the stock, bring to the boil and add pepper to taste. Cover and simmer for 40 minutes.
5 Allow to cool slightly, then purée in a blender or food processor, breaking up the nuts well. Sieve into a large bowl. Cool, then chill in the refrigerator overnight.
6 Before serving, toast the reserved almonds under the grill until light and golden in colour, then cool. Whisk the yogurt until smooth and creamy. Divide the soup between 4 chilled soup bowls. Swirl in the yogurt and sprinkle with the toasted almonds. Serve well chilled.

Vegetable Biryani

This spicy high fibre dish contains a selection of vegetables which may be varied according to availability and personal taste.

SERVES 4	175 g (6 oz) cauliflower florets
30 ml (2 tbsp) sunflower oil	2 carrots, scrubbed and cubed
4 cloves	1 large green pepper, cored, seeded and sliced
seeds of 4 cardamoms	50 g (2 oz) French beans, trimmed and cut into 2.5 cm (1 inch) lengths
5 ml (1 tsp) cumin seeds	
2.5 cm (1 inch) piece cinnamon stick	2 large tomatoes, roughly chopped
175 g (6 oz) brown rice	100 g (4 oz) fresh or frozen peas
2 garlic cloves, skinned	50 g (2 oz) button mushrooms, halved
2.5 cm (1 inch) piece fresh root ginger, peeled	150 ml (¼ pint) low-fat natural yogurt
1 medium onion, skinned and chopped	30 ml (2 tbsp) chopped fresh coriander
2.5 ml (½ tsp) chilli powder	2 green chillies, seeded and finely chopped
5 ml (1 tsp) coriander seeds	25 g (1 oz) cashew nuts
2.5 ml (½ tsp) ground turmeric	45 ml (3 tbsp) lemon or lime juice
15 ml (1 tbsp) poppy seeds	onion rings and fresh coriander, to garnish
2 potatoes, scrubbed and cubed	

NUTRITIONAL ANALYSIS
458 kcals/1915 kJ
13 g Protein
64 g Carbohydrate
18.3 g Fat ★★
2.7 g Saturated Fat ★★★★
12.1 g Fibre ★★★★
No Added Sugar ★★★★
222 mg Salt ★★★★

1 Heat 15 ml (1 tbsp) of the oil in a large non-stick saucepan and gently cook the cloves, cardamom, cumin and cinnamon for 1 minute. Add the rice and stir to coat in the spice mixture. Add 450 ml (¾ pint) water and bring to the boil, then cover and simmer for 30 minutes or until all the liquid has been absorbed.

2 Meanwhile, blend the garlic, ginger, onion, chilli powder, coriander seeds, turmeric and poppy seeds in a blender or food processor with about 15 ml (1 tbsp) water until smooth.

3 Heat the remaining oil in a flameproof casserole and cook the spice paste for 3-4 minutes, stirring frequently to prevent the mixture from sticking.

4 Add the potatoes, cauliflower, carrots, green pepper and French beans and cook, stirring, for 2 minutes. Cover and cook for 10 minutes. Add the tomatoes, peas, mushrooms and 15 ml (1 tbsp) hot water.

5 Gradually stir in the yogurt, 15 ml (1 tbsp) at a time, stirring continuously until the yogurt is absorbed. Add the chopped coriander.

6 Spoon the rice over the vegetable mixture. Sprinkle with the chillies and cashew nuts and pour over the lemon juice. Do not stir. Cover and cook at 180°C (350°F) mark 4 for 30 minutes or until the rice is tender.

7 Remove from the oven and leave in the dish to stand for 5 minutes. Fluff up the rice with a fork and garnish with onion rings and coriander. Accompany with low-fat natural yogurt and a tomato and cucumber salad. (*Menu 7 continued overleaf*)

NUTRITIONAL ANALYSIS
98 kcals/411 kJ
2.4 g Protein
20 g Carbohydrate
0.1 g Fat ★★★★
0 g Saturated Fat ★★★★
11.2 g Fibre ★★★★
No Added Sugar ★★★★
54 mg Salt ★★★★

Berry and Tropical Fruit Salad

Tropical fruits such as papaya and passion fruit are sold in specialist fruiterers' and some larger supermarkets. If these fruits are not available, substitute sweet, orange-fleshed melon such as cantaloupe for the papaya and kiwi fruit for the passion fruit.

SERVES 4

100 g (4 oz) strawberries, hulled
100 g (4 oz) raspberries
2 nectarines, stoned and sliced
1 papaya, peeled, seeded and sliced
3 passion fruit, halved
75 ml (5 tbsp) sweet white wine

1 Halve the strawberries if they are large and mix them with the raspberries, nectarines and papaya.
2 Scoop out the flesh and seeds from the passion fruit and mix with the wine. Pour over the fruit. Mix well and chill for 30 minutes before serving.

MENU 8

NUTRITIONAL ANALYSIS
88 kcals/367 kJ
3.9 g Protein
14.8 g Carbohydrate
1.9 g Fat ★★★
0.4 g Saturated Fat ★★★★
3.2 g Fibre ★★★★
2.4 g Added Sugar ★★
716 mg Salt ★

Gazpacho

This colourful iced Spanish soup can be made using 450 g (1 lb) fresh tomatoes, skinned and roughly chopped

SERVES 4

400 g (14 oz) can tomatoes
3 garlic cloves, skinned and crushed
1 small Spanish onion, skinned and cut into chunks
1 small green pepper, cored, seeded and cut into chunks
½ cucumber, cut into chunks
30 ml (2 tbsp) wine vinegar
300 ml (½ pint) tomato juice
pepper, to taste
few ice cubes

ACCOMPANIMENT

1 red pepper, cored, seeded and cut into chunks
1 yellow pepper, cored, seeded and cut into chunks
½ cucumber, cut into chunks
1 hard-boiled egg, cut into pieces

1 Purée the tomatoes, garlic, onion, green pepper and cucumber in a blender or food processor until very smooth. Add the vinegar and tomato juice. Season to taste. Pour the soup into a soup tureen, cover and chill for several hours.
2 Add the ice cubes to the soup just before serving. Hand the vegetables and egg separately.

Paella

This colourful seafood and chicken rice dish from Spain is coloured golden by the saffron. Saffron is one of the most expensive spices.

SERVES 4	
pinch of saffron	*1 small onion, skinned and chopped*
15 ml (1 tbsp) chopped fresh parsley	*200 g (7 oz) Italian brown rice*
2 garlic cloves, skinned and crushed	*500 ml (17 fl oz) mussel and chicken stock (see method)*
100 g (4 oz) mussels, cleaned and scrubbed	*100 g (4 oz) firm white fish, cut into large cubes*
30 ml (2 tbsp) olive oil	*200 g (7 oz) can red pimentos, drained and cut into strips, a few reserved for garnish*
2-3 squid, heads removed, cut into rings	*75 g (3 oz) peeled prawns*
175 g (6 oz) chicken, cubed	*4 large prawns in their shells*
1 small green pepper, cored, seeded and chopped	

1 Mix the saffron with 30 ml (2 tbsp) boiling water. Cool and add the parsley and garlic. Set aside.
2 Put the mussels in a saucepan with about 1 cm (½ inch) water. Cook for about 5 minutes until the shells open. Drain the mussels through a sieve lined with absorbent kitchen paper into a measure jug. Make up the mussel liquid to 500 ml (17 fl oz) with hot chicken stock.
3 Heat the oil in a paella pan or large non-stick frying pan and gently cook the squid and chicken for 5 minutes. Add the pepper and onion and gently cook for a further 5 minutes.
4 Mix in the rice and add the hot stock, stirring well. Stir in the fish, peas, pimento, peeled prawns and crushed garlic mixture. Arrange the large prawns and mussels over the rice.
5 Cook over a low heat for 35-45 minutes or until the liquid is absorbed and the rice is soft but not dry. As paella is cooked without a lid, evaporation will take place as the rice cooks and it will be necessary to add extra boiling water from time to time during cooking. Accompany with a green or mixed leaf salad.

NUTRITIONAL ANALYSIS
448 kcals/1873 kJ
41.4 g Protein
43.7 g Carbohydrate
13.2 g Fat ★★★
2.2 g Saturated Fat ★★★★
3.4 g Fibre ★★
No Added Sugar ★★★★
3065 mg Salt ★

Fruit-Stuffed Pears

Filled with nuts and raisins, these pears are spiced with cinnamon. Available in ground and stick form, both kinds are used here.

SERVES 4	
25 g (1 oz) raisins	*150 ml (¼ pint) red wine*
15 g (½ oz) walnuts, chopped	*1 small stick cinnamon*
2.5 ml (½ tsp) ground cinnamon	*4 cloves*
	4 ripe pears, peeled

1 Combine the raisins, walnuts and ground cinnamon in a bowl.
2 Put the wine, 100 ml (3½ fl oz) water, cinnamon stick and cloves into a small saucepan and bring to the boil. Set aside.
3 Cut a 2.5 cm (1 inch) piece from the stem end of the pears and set aside. Using a small teaspoon, scoop out the cores and sufficient flesh to leave room for the filling. Spoon in the raisin filling, replace the tops and arrange the pears in an ovenproof dish just large enough to accommodate them.
4 Pour over the wine mixture. Cover and bake at 180°C (350°F) mark 4 for 40-50 minutes or until the pears are cooked.
5 Arrange the pears on a serving dish. Return the juice to the pan and boil rapidly to reduce it to a thick syrup. Pour over the pears and chill before serving.

NUTRITIONAL ANALYSIS
106 kcals/442 kJ
0.9 g Protein
16.1 g Carbohydrate
2 g Fat ★★★★
0.2 g Saturated Fat ★★★★
3.3 g Fibre ★★★★
No Added Sugar ★★★★
25 mg Salt ★★★★

MENU 9

Provençal Fish Soup

This fish soup from the South of France can be made from any white fish. Ask your fishmonger to provide you with the fish trimmings for the soup.

NUTRITIONAL ANALYSIS
238 kcals/993 kJ
38.3 g Protein
4.2 g Carbohydrate
4.1 g Fat ★★★★
0.7 g Saturated Fat ★★★★
2.2 g Fibre ★★★
No Added Sugar ★★★★
498 mg Salt ★★

SERVES 4

FOR THE FISH STOCK:

450 g (1 lb) fish trimmings from crustaceans and white fish such as prawn shells, cod head

100 ml (4 fl oz) dry white wine

1 medium onion, skinned and cut in half

1 medium carrot, scrubbed and chopped

sprig of fennel

1 bay leaf

parsley stalks

FOR THE SOUP:

10 ml (2 tsp) sunflower oil

1 medium onion, skinned and chopped

1 celery stalk, chopped

4 tomatoes, skinned and diced

100 ml (4 fl oz) dry white wine

2 garlic cloves, skinned and crushed

30 ml (2 tbsp) chopped fresh parsley

15 ml (1 tbsp) grated orange rind

a few threads of saffron

800 g (1¾ lb) fillets of white fish

pepper, to taste

1 Make the fish stock. Put all the ingredients into a large saucepan. Add 1.1 litres (2 pints) of water and bring to the boil. Simmer for 30 minutes, remove any scum and sieve.
2 Heat the oil in a non-stick pan and fry the onions and celery until soft. Add the tomatoes, wine, garlic, parsley, orange rind, saffron and stock. Simmer for 20 minutes.
3 Cut the fish into 2.5 cm (1 inch) pieces and add to the soup. Bring to the boil, add pepper and cook for a further 10 minutes.

Turkey Marsala

Marsala is an Italian aperitif which complements turkey well. If you are unable to find it, substitute sweet vermouth.

NUTRITIONAL ANALYSIS
147 kcals/614 kJ
20.9 g Protein
3.2 g Carbohydrate
4.8 g Fat ★★★
0.8 g Saturated Fat ★★★★
0.4 g Fibre ★
0.5 g Added Sugar ★★★★
101 mg Salt ★★★★

SERVES 4

350 g (12 oz) skinless, boneless turkey breast steaks

pepper, to taste

15 g (½ oz) wholemeal flour

15 ml (1 tbsp) sunflower oil

juice of ½ lemon

30 ml (2 tbsp) Marsala

90 ml (6 tbsp) chicken stock

1 Cut the turkey breast vertically into 25 g (1 oz) slices and beat them out wafer-thin between 2 sheets of greaseproof paper. Sprinkle with pepper and dust lightly with flour.
2 Heat the oil in a non-stick frying pan and quickly brown the turkey slices for 2-3 minutes on each side. Add the lemon juice and Marsala, allow to bubble, then add the chicken stock. Simmer for 1-2 minutes or until the sauce begins to turn syrupy. Serve with carrots and mangetout.

Indian Saffron Yogurt (PAGE 155)

Light Prune Mousse

In this delicate prune mousse, the sweetness is provided by the fruit

SERVES 4	
200 g (7 oz) no-soak dried prunes	*200 ml (7 fl oz) low-fat natural yogurt*
15 g (½ oz) powdered gelatine	*2 egg whites*
	15 g (½ oz) toasted hazelnuts, chopped, to decorate

1 Place the prunes in a saucepan with 175 ml (6 fl oz) water. Bring to the boil and simmer for 1-2 minutes. Cool.
2 Put the gelatine in a small heatproof bowl with 45 ml (3 tbsp) cold water. Leave for 1 minute to soften. Place the bowl over a saucepan of simmering water and stir until the gelatine dissolves. Leave to cool.
3 Purée the prunes and cooking water in a food processor or blender. Transfer to a bowl and stir in the gelatine mixture and yogurt.
4 Whisk the egg whites until stiff but not dry, and fold into the prune mixture.
5 Divide the mousse between 4 wine glasses and chill. Decorate with the chopped nuts.

NUTRITIONAL ANALYSIS
138 kcals/578 kJ
8.4 g Protein
23.5 g Carbohydrate
1.9 g Fat ★★★★
0.4 g Saturated Fat ★★★★
8.3 g Fibre ★★★★
No Added Sugar ★★★★
178 mg Salt ★★★

MENU 10

Salade Niçoise

Serve this colourful tuna and vegetable salad with wholemeal bread and lemon quarters.

SERVES 4	
4 anchovy fillets	*1 egg, hard-boiled and quartered*
50 ml (2 fl oz) skimmed milk	*8 black olives, stoned and well rinsed*
3 medium potatoes, scrubbed	*100 g (3½ oz) can tuna, drained and cut into chunks*
100 g (4 oz) French beans, trimmed	FOR THE DRESSING
few lettuce leaves, torn into small pieces	*30 ml (2 tbsp) olive oil*
2 celery sticks, trimmed and cut into small strips	*15 ml (1 tbsp) wine vinegar*
3 tomatoes, cut into quarters	*2.5 ml (½ tsp) Dijon mustard*
1 large pepper, cored, seeded and finely sliced	*pepper, to taste*

1 Rinse the anchovies under cold running water and put them to soak in the milk.
2 Put the potatoes in their skins in a saucepan of water and cook for about 20 minutes until tender. Peel and slice. Put the French beans in a saucepan of boiling water and cook for about 5 minutes until just cooked. Drain, plunge them into cold water then drain again. Cut into slices.
3 Drain the anchovies, rinse again under cold running water, then dry on absorbent kitchen paper.
4 For the dressing, mix together the oil, vinegar, mustard and pepper, then set aside.
5 Arrange the potato slices, French beans, lettuce, celery, tomatoes and pepper in layers in a salad bowl. Finish with the egg quarters, anchovies, olives and tuna.
6 Pour the dressing over the salad and toss well just before serving.

NUTRITIONAL ANALYSIS
264 kcals/1102 kJ
13.3 g Protein
31 g Carbohydrate
10.6 g Fat ★★
1.8 g Saturated Fat ★★★★
5.3 g Fibre ★★★★
No Added Sugar ★★★★
1007 mg Salt ★

Dried Apricot Roulade (PAGE 158)

NUTRITIONAL ANALYSIS
370 kcals/1546 kJ
25.9 g Protein
53 g Carbohydrate
4.8 g Fat ★★★★
0.8 g Saturated Fat ★★★★
4.8 g Fibre ★★★★
No Added Sugar ★★★★
3569 mg Salt ★

Scampi Provençal

Popular scampi is usually fried. In this healthy dish, it is lightly cooked in a white wine mixture.

SERVES 4	
225 g (8 oz) brown rice	*300 ml (1/2 pint) chicken stock*
1 small onion, skinned and very finely chopped	*350 g (12 oz) peeled scampi or large prawns*
150 ml (1/4 pint) dry white wine	*5 ml (1 tsp) sunflower oil*
1 bouquet garni	*150 g (5 oz) button mushrooms, very finely sliced*
15 ml (1 tbsp) tomato purée	*2 medium tomatoes, skinned and chopped*
1 garlic clove, skinned and crushed	*pepper, to taste*
2.5 ml (1/2 tsp) dried herbes de provence or basil	*chopped fresh parsley, to garnish*

1 Put the rice in a saucepan of boiling salted water and cook for 30-35 minutes or until tender.
2 Meanwhile, put the onion into a saucepan with the wine and bouquet garni and simmer until the liquid is reduced by half. Discard the bouquet garni.
3 Put the tomato purée, garlic, herbs, stock and reduced wine into a saucepan and bring to the boil, stirring vigorously. Simmer very gently for 10 minutes. Add the scampi and simmer for a further 2 minutes. Keep warm.
4 Heat the oil in a non-stick frying pan and gently cook the mushrooms, covered, for about 5 minutes. When almost cooked, add the tomatoes and fry for 1 minute. Season to taste.
5 Arrange the rice on a warmed serving dish and pour over the scampi mixture. Spoon over the tomatoes and mushrooms. Garnish with parsley. Accompany with broccoli.

NUTRITIONAL ANALYSIS
235 kcals/983 kJ
5.4 g Protein
25.6 g Carbohydrate
13 g Fat ★★
3.4 g Saturated Fat ★★★
10 g Fibre ★★★★
No Added Sugar ★★★★
293 mg Salt ★★★

Raspberry Flan

Serve your guests this seemingly rich fruit flan. They will never know it is a healthier alternative to the full fat variety.

SERVES 4-6	
	pinch of salt
50 g (2 oz) white flour	FOR THE FILLING
50 g (2 oz) wholemeal flour	*150 ml (1/4 pint) Greek strained yogurt*
50 g (2 oz) polyunsaturated margarine	*450 g (1 lb) fresh or frozen rasbperries*

1 Put the flours and salt into a bowl. Add the margarine and work with a fork until the mixture resembles breadcrumbs. Add 15 ml (1 tbsp) water and mix to form a dough. Chill for 30 minutes.
2 Roll out the pastry and use to line a 23 cm (9 inch) flan dish or ring. Prick with a fork and line with greaseproof paper weighed down with dried beans. Bake blind at 200°C (400°F) mark 6 for 10 minutes. Remove paper and beans and bake for a further 5 minutes. Leave to cool.
3 Spoon the yogurt into the flan case. Fill with the raspberries and serve immediately.

9

Picnics

Most children love picnics so it is the ideal time to encourage them to eat healthily. The picnics here include dishes that will appeal to the whole family, and include a mixture of dishes – some needing forks and plates, others that can be eaten easily with fingers.

If you want to make the picnic go even further, pack some fresh figs and grapes; mandarin oranges or passion fruit as well as a more traditional selection of fruits, and bring along a large piece of medium-to-low fat cheese for people to nibble at.

MENU 1

NUTRITIONAL ANALYSIS
344 kcals/1436 kJ
14.6 g Protein
53.1 g Carbohydrate
9.6 g Fat ★★★
1.5 g Saturated Fat ★★★★
10.9 g Fibre ★★★★
No Added Sugar ★★★★
59 mg Salt ★★★★

Chick-Pea and Macaroni Salad

Using wholewheat pasta increases the fibre content of this salad.

SERVES 4

175 g (6 oz) wholewheat macaroni

450 g (1 lb) canned chick-peas, drained and rinsed

1/4 cucumber, diced

2 tomatoes, diced

1/2 red pepper, cored, seeded and diced

1/2 green pepper, cored, seeded and diced

FOR THE MUSTARD DRESSING

15 ml (1 tbsp) sunflower oil

30 ml (2 tbsp) olive oil

25 ml (1 1/2 tbsp) white wine vinegar

2.5 ml (1/2 tsp) Dijon mustard

1 garlic clove, skinned and crushed

5 ml (1 tsp) Greek strained yogurt

pepper, to taste

1 Put the macaroni in a saucepan of boiling water and cook for about 10 minutes or until just tender. Drain and cool.
2 Meanwhile for the dressing, put the ingredients into a screw-topped jar or bowl and shake or whisk until well mixed. Set aside until required.
3 Place the chick-peas in a large bowl with the cucumber, tomatoes, red and green peppers and macaroni. Toss well.
4 Shake the dressing, then pour over the salad and gently mix until all the ingredients are well coated.

NUTRITIONAL ANALYSIS
91 kcals/380 kJ
12.4 g Protein
2.4 g Carbohydrate
3.6 g Fat ★★
1.1 g Saturated Fat ★★★
0.3 g Fibre ★
No Added Sugar ★★★★
377 mg Salt ★

Spicy Chicken Drumsticks

These lightly curried chicken pieces are a tasty and nourishing treat for adults and children alike.

MAKES 8

60 ml (4 tbsp) sugarless tomato ketchup

15 ml (1 tbsp) mild curry powder or to taste

30 ml (2 tbsp) lemon juice

8 chicken drumsticks, skinned

1 Mix the ketchup with the curry powder and blend in the lemon juice. Rub over the drumsticks and leave to marinate for at least 30 minutes.
2 Place the drumsticks on a rack in a roasting tin. Bake at 180°C (350°F) mark 4 for 30 minutes or until golden brown. Leave to cool.

Marinated Mushrooms

The sweet and spicy flavours of this marinade combine well with the raw button mushrooms. Serve with slices of wholemeal bread or pitta bread.

SERVES 4	*4 black peppercorns, crushed*
4 large oranges	*30 ml (2 tbsp) olive oil*
2 lemons	*350 g (12 oz) button mushrooms*
10 ml (2 tsp) coriander seeds, crushed	*30 ml (2 tbsp) chopped fresh coriander*
10 ml (2 tsp) cumin seeds, crushed	

1 Grate the rind from 2 of the oranges and 1 lemon; set the rind aside. Squeeze the juice from all the oranges and lemons. Strain the orange and lemon juice into a heavy-based saucepan. Add the crushed spices, then pour in the olive oil. Bring to the boil and simmer for about 10 minutes until reduced, stirring frequently.
2 Put the mushrooms in a bowl. Pour over the hot marinade, then add the grated orange and lemon rinds, the chopped coriander and salt. Gently mix. Cover and marinate for at least 4 hours, turning occasionally. Chill before serving.

NUTRITIONAL ANALYSIS
131 kcals/547 kJ
3.2 g Protein
12.3 g Carbohydrate
8 g Fat ★
1.2 g Saturated Fat ★★★
6.9 g Fibre ★★★★
No Added Sugar ★★★★
39 mg Salt ★★★★

Garlic Herb Breadsticks

These yeasted bread sticks, made with wholemeal flour, make an interesting alternative to bread rolls.

MAKES 24	*150 ml (¼ pint) skimmed milk*
225 g (8 oz) plain wholemeal flour	*15 g (½ oz) polyunsaturated margarine*
pinch of salt	*10 g (¼ oz) fresh yeast, or 5 ml (1 tsp) dried yeast and 1.25 ml (¼ tsp) sugar*
2 garlic cloves, skinned and crushed	*skimmed milk, to glaze*
15 ml (1 tbsp) chopped fresh herbs, such as chives, parsley, tarragon, or 5 ml (1 tsp) dried mixed herbs	*poppy seeds, to decorate*

1 Sift the flour and salt into a bowl, adding any bran remaining in the sieve. Add the garlic and herbs.
2 Gently heat the milk in a pan until tepid, add the margarine and allow to melt. Blend the fresh yeast with a little of the warmed milk and add the remaining milk, then add to the flour mixture. If using dried yeast, sprinkle it into the milk with the sugar and leave in a warm place for 15 minutes until frothy, before adding to the flour. Mix to a dough and knead on a floured work surface for about 5 minutes until smooth.
3 Place the dough in a clean bowl, cover with a damp cloth and leave to rise in a warm place for about 1 hour until doubled in size.
4 Turn out the dough on to a lightly floured work surface and knead for 3 minutes. Roll into a sausage shape and divide into 24 equal portions. Roll each portion into a stick about 20 cm (8 inches) long. Place on 2 or 3 lightly greased baking sheets and leave to prove for 10 minutes.
5 Brush the breadsticks with a little milk and sprinkle with poppy seeds. Bake at 180°C (350°F) mark 4 for 20 minutes. Reduce the oven temperature to 110°C (225°F) mark ¼ and leave the sticks to crisp for about 30-40 minutes so that they will snap when broken. Leave to cool on a wire rack. (*Picnic 1 continued overleaf*)

NUTRITIONAL ANALYSIS
40 kcals/168 kJ
1.8 g Protein
6.7 g Carbohydrate
0.9 g Fat ★★★
0.1 g Saturated Fat ★★★★
1.1 g Fibre ★★★★
No Added Sugar ★★★★
35 mg Salt ★★★★

NUTRITIONAL ANALYSIS
31 kcals/131 kJ
0.5 g Protein
5.2 g Carbohydrate
1 g Fat ★★★
0.6 g Saturated Fat ★★
1.8 g Fibre ★★★★
No Added Sugar ★★★★
8 mg Salt ★★★★

Nutted Fruits

The dried fruit provides all the sweetness you need plus additional fibre, vitamins and minerals.

MAKES ABOUT 16
75 g (3 oz) dried fruit, such as dates, prunes or figs, stoned
75 g (3 oz) dried fruit, such as dried apricots, pineapple or mango
15 g (½ oz) nuts
15 g (½ oz) desiccated coconut, or 2 sheets of rice paper

1 Using the medium cutter of a hand mincer or a food processor, grind all the fruit and nuts. Mash together with a fork to blend well.
2 Roll into about 16 small balls using the palms of your hands. Place the coconut in a bag and toss each ball to coat all over.
3 Alternatively, place the mixture between 2 sheets of rice paper and roll out to about 0.5 cm (¼ inch) thick. Using sharp scissors or a knife, cut into pieces, retaining the rice paper which can be eaten.

MENU 2

NUTRITIONAL ANALYSIS
203 kcals/850 kJ
5.3 g Protein
15.7 g Carbohydrate
13.7 g Fat ★
2.2 g Saturated Fat ★★★
3.5 g Fibre ★★★★
No Added Sugar ★★★★
1786 mg Salt ★

Provençal-Style Tart

This healthy variation on a Provençal tart is delicious served hot or cold. Soaking the anchovy fillets in milk for at least 10 minutes draws out the saltiness.

SERVES 6
100 g (4 oz) wholemeal flour
50g (2 oz) polyunsaturated margarine
FOR THE PROVENCAL FILLING
20 ml (1½ tbsp) sunflower oil
450 g (1 lb) onions, skinned and thinly sliced
1 garlic clove, skinned and crushed
2.5 ml (½ tsp) dried thyme
2.5 ml (½ tsp) dried tarragon
2 tomatoes, sliced
50 g (2 oz) can anchovy fillets, soaked in milk, drained and patted dry
16 black olives

1 For the pastry, put the flour in a bowl and rub in the margarine until the mixture resembles fine breadcrumbs. Add enough cold water to make a soft dough. Wrap in foil and chill for 30 minutes.
2 Meanwhile for the filling, heat the oil in a non-stick frying pan and cook the onions, garlic, thyme and tarragon, covered with a tight-fitting lid, over a very low heat for 20 minutes, stirring occasionally, until the onions are very soft.
3 Roll out the dough on a lightly floured work surface and use to line a 20 cm (8 inch) flan tin or four 7.5 cm (3 inch) tins. Line with greaseproof paper and half fill with baking beans. Bake blind at 200°C (400°F) mark 6 for 15 minutes. Remove the beans and paper and bake for a further 5 minutes.
4 Using a slotted spoon, remove the onions from the saucepan, pressing out the oil, and spoon them into the pastry case. Cover with the tomato slices. Arrange the anchovies in a lattice pattern and place the olives in the middle of the squares. Bake for 15-20 minutes until lightly browned.

Tomato Broad Beans

If using older, larger broad beans, slip them out of their outer skins once cooked and use only the tender green beans inside.

SERVES 4
15 ml (1 tbsp) sunflower oil
30 ml (2 tbsp) finely chopped onion
1 garlic clove, skinned and crushed
7.5 ml (1½ tsp) ground coriander
400 g (14 oz) can tomatoes
450 g (1 lb) broad beans
pepper, to taste

NUTRITIONAL ANALYSIS
114 kcals/478 kJ
5.8 g Protein
10.8 g Carbohydrate
5.7 g Fat ★★
0.8 g Saturated Fat ★★★★
5.7 g Fibre ★★★★
No Added Sugar ★★★★
133 mg Salt ★★★

1 Heat the oil in a non-stick saucepan and cook the onion for 2 minutes, stirring. Add the garlic and coriander and stir for 1 minute. Stir in the tomatoes and continue cooking for 5 minutes, stirring occasionally.
2 Meanwhile, put the broad beans in a saucepan of boiling water and cook for about 5 minutes or until tender.
3 Drain the broad beans and add to the sauce. Cook for a further 3-5 minutes, stirring, until piping hot. Season to taste.

Chicory Salad with Lemon

To make spring onion tassels, first trim off the roots and include only a little of the green. Cut narrow strips down the length of the onion almost to the root end. Put into iced water to open out and curl.

SERVES 4
1 Cos lettuce
1 endive
2 heads chicory
225 g (8 oz) French beans, thawed if frozen, trimmed and cut into 4 cm (1½ inch) lengths
watercress sprigs and spring onion tassels, to garnish
FOR THE LEMON DRESSING
grated rind and juice of 2 lemons
30 ml (2 tbsp) sunflower oil
1 garlic clove, skinned and crushed

NUTRITIONAL ANALYSIS
90 kcals/377 kJ
2.4 g Protein
3 g Carbohydrate
7.8 g Fat ★
1.1 g Saturated Fat ★★★
4.2 g Fibre ★★★★
No Added Sugar ★★★★
42 mg Salt ★★★★

1 Slice the Cos lettuce into 1 cm (½ inch) pieces crossways and place in a large bowl. Pick off the leaves of the endive, tearing them into bite-size pieces. Separate the chicory leaves and mix them with the endive and the lettuce.
2 Put the beans in a saucepan of boiling water and cook for about 3 minutes until just tender. Drain and rinse in cold water. Drain again, then sprinkle over the lettuce, endive and chicory leaves.
3 For the dressing, mix together the lemon rind, juice, oil and garlic. Pour the dressing over the salad. Garnish with watercress sprigs and spring onion tassels. (*Picnic 2 continued overleaf*)

NUTRITIONAL ANALYSIS
198 kcals/829 kJ
25 g Protein
6.6 g Carbohydrate
8.2 g Fat ★★
2.3 g Saturated Fat ★★★
3 g Fibre ★★★★
No Added Sugar ★★★★
299 mg Salt ★★★

Chef's Salad

You can vary the ingredients in this recipe to suit your own taste. If preferred, use one variety of meat, increasing the quantity accordingly.

SERVES 4	175 g (6 oz) cooked chicken meat, skinned and cut into strips
1 Cos lettuce	FOR THE YOGURT DRESSING
1 curly endive or Iceberg lettuce	225 g (8 fl oz) low-fat natural yogurt
2 tomatoes, quartered	15 ml (1 tbsp) sunflower oil
1 carrot, scrubbed and thinly sliced	5 ml (1 tsp) wholegrain mustard
2 spring onions, finely chopped	5 ml (1 tsp) white wine vinegar
175 g (6 oz) cooked lean beef, cut into strips	pepper, to taste

1 Break the Cos lettuce and curly endive or Iceberg lettuce into bite-sized pieces and place in a large bowl. Add the tomato quarters, sliced carrot, chopped spring onion, strips of beef and chicken.
2 To make the yogurt dressing, mix the yogurt, oil, mustard, vinegar and seasoning together until smooth. Pour over the salad and toss until all the ingredients are well coated.

NUTRITIONAL ANALYSIS
38 kcals/160 kJ
0.9 g Protein
9.3 g Carbohydrate
0 g Fat ★★★★
0 g Saturated Fat ★★★★
2.4 g Fibre ★★★★
No Added Sugar ★★★★
19 mg Salt ★★★★

Sparkling Fruit Crush

Carry this refreshing drink in a vacuum flask for a summer picnic.

SERVES 4	600 ml (1 pint) mineral water
2 oranges, unpeeled and roughly chopped	ice cubes
175 g (6 oz) apricots, stoned	orange slices, to decorate

1 Purée the oranges, apricots and 300 ml (½ pint) of the mineral water in a blender or food processor.
2 Divide the purée between 4 tall glasses and top up with the remaining mineral water and ice cubes. Decorate with slices of orange.

MENU 3

NUTRITIONAL ANALYSIS
114 kcals/476 kJ
2.5 g Protein
8.5 g Carbohydrate
8.1 g Fat ★
1.2 g Saturated Fat ★★★
3.3 g Fibre ★★★★
No Added Sugar ★★★★
26 mg Salt ★★★★

Pepper Starter

If yellow peppers are difficult to find, red peppers can be substituted in this colourful starter.

SERVES 4	2 garlic cloves, skinned and crushed
15 ml (1 tbsp) sunflower oil	450 g (1 lb) small tomatoes, halved
1 large onion, skinned and thinly sliced	pepper, to taste
2 green peppers, cored, seeded and cut into thin strips	15 ml (1 tbsp) chopped fresh mint or 7.5 ml (½ tbsp) dried
1 yellow pepper, cored, seeded and cut into thin strips	

1 Heat the oil in a non-stick saucepan and gently cook the onion, peppers and garlic for 5 minutes until soft but not coloured.
2 Add the tomatoes, pepper and mint. Cover and cook very gently for about 15 minutes or until just tender.

Broccoli and Pasta Salad

This colourful high fibre salad is ideal to serve in summer and winter.

SERVES 4	
175 g (6 oz) wholewheat pasta spirals	*20 ml (4 tsp) sunflower oil*
275 g (10 oz) broccoli florets and chopped stems	*1 orange, peeled, segmented and chopped, with any juice reserved*
15 ml (1 tbsp) sesame seeds	*pepper, to taste*

1 Put the pasta in a saucepan half-filled with boiling water. Bring back to the boil and place the broccoli in a sieve over the pan. Cover and cook for about 8 minutes or until the pasta and broccoli are tender. Drain and place in a large bowl.
2 Place the sesame seeds in an ungreased heavy-based frying pan and cook over a low heat for 2-3 minutes or until the seeds are just beginning to jump. Remove the seeds and crush them in a pestle and mortar or grind them in a coffee grinder.
3 Mix together the sesame seeds, oil, orange pieces and any remaining orange juice in serving bowl. Add the broccoli and pasta, season to taste and toss gently. Cover and chill before serving.

NUTRITIONAL ANALYSIS
238 kcals/996 kJ
9.3 g Protein
34.5 g Carbohydrate
8.3 g Fat ★★★
1.1 g Saturated Fat ★★★★
7.6 g Fibre ★★★★
No Added Sugar ★★★★
71 mg Salt ★★★★

Chicken and Cheese Salad

This is an ideal way to use up leftover chicken. Toasting and roasting nuts or seeds enhances their flavour.

SERVES 4	
50 g (2 oz) blanched almonds, chopped	*30 ml (2 tbsp) finely chopped fresh parsley*
450 g (1 lb) cooked chicken meat, skinned	*pepper, to taste*
225 g (8 oz) low-fat cottage cheese	*lettuce leaves, to serve*

1 Put the almonds on a sheet of foil and cook under a hot grill, stirring continuously, for 1-2 minutes or until lightly golden brown. Set aside to cool.
2 Meanwhile, finely dice or shred the chicken and put in a bowl with the cottage cheese, parsley and seasoning. Add the almonds and gently mix together. Serve on a bed of lettuce.

NUTRITIONAL ANALYSIS
276 kcals/1153 kJ
38.1 g Protein
1.6 g Carbohydrate
13 g Fat ★★
2.7 g Saturated Fat ★★★
2.5 g Fibre ★★★
No Added Sugar ★★★★
884 mg Salt ★

Oaty Bars

These high fibre oaty bars are ideal packed in a picnic basket for a day out. They can also be used as a lunch box filler.

MAKES 18	
75 g (3 oz) polyunsaturated margarine	*75 g (3 oz) wholemeal flour*
30 ml (2 tbsp) skimmed milk	*2.5 ml (½ tsp) bicarbonate of soda*
15 ml (1 tbsp) clear honey	*2.5 ml (½ tsp) sugar*
	75 g (3 oz) rolled oats

1 Melt the margarine with the milk and honey in a saucepan.
2 Put the flour, bicarbonate of soda, sugar and oats in a bowl. Mix together, then make a well in the centre. Pour in the melted margarine mixture and combine well.
3 Divide the mixture into 18 portions and mould each portion into a bar about 6.5 cm (2½ inches) long. Place on 2 non-stick paper lined baking sheets. Bake at 170°C (325°F) mark 3 for 20 minutes or until golden. Leave to cool for 2-3 minutes, then transfer to wire racks to cool completely. *(Picnic 3 continued overleaf)*

NUTRITIONAL ANALYSIS
64 kcals/268 kJ
1.1 g Protein
6.7 g Carbohydrate
3.8 g Fat ★
0.6 g Saturated Fat ★★★
0.7 g Fibre ★★★
0.8 g Added Sugar ★★★
91 mg Salt ★★★

NUTRITIONAL ANALYSIS
11 kcals/47 kJ
0.6 g Protein
2.4 g Carbohydrate
0 g Fat ★★★★
0 g Saturated Fat ★★★★
3.9 g Fibre ★★★★
No Added Sugar ★★★★
11 mg Salt ★★★★

Still Lemonade

Refreshing home-made lemonade is the perfect drink on a summer's day.

SERVES 4

3 large lemons, scrubbed

25 ml (1½ tbsp) clear honey (optional)

1 Finely grate the lemon rind, then carefully peel the lemons, ensuring that all the bitter white pith is removed. Discard any pips and coarsely chop the flesh.
2 Blend the lemon rind and flesh, honey and 600 ml (1 pint) cold water in a blender or food processor for 1 minute.
3 Strain the lemonade into a jug and chill for at least 30 minutes before serving.

MENU 4

NUTRITIONAL ANALYSIS
29 kcals/122 kJ
1.2 g Protein
4.2 g Carbohydrate
1 g Fat ★★★
0.2 g Saturated Fat ★★★★
0.8 g Fibre ★★★★
No Added Sugar ★★★★
32 mg Salt ★★★

Falafel

Serve these healthy spiced wheat and chick-pea nuggets with salad. For those who like a hot flavour, add extra chilli.

MAKES 30

50 g (2 oz) burghul wheat

400 g (14 oz) can chick-peas, drained and rinsed

50 g (2 oz) fresh granary or wholemeal breadcrumbs

3 garlic cloves, skinned and crushed

5 ml (1 tsp) chilli powder

5 ml (1 tsp) coriander seeds

5 ml (1 tsp) cumin seeds

45 ml (3 tbsp) lemon juice

pepper, to taste

sunflower oil, for brushing

1 Pour 75 ml (3 fl oz) water over the burghul wheat and soak for a few minutes until absorbed.
2 Blend all the ingredients, except the seasoning and oil, in a food processor or blender until a fairly smooth paste, but do not let it become too smooth. Turn the mixture out into a bowl and season to taste.
3 Mould the mixture with your hands into 30 balls with your hands. To cook, place the balls close together in a lightly greased baking tin and brush with oil. Cook at 220°C (425°F) mark 7 for 20 minutes, brushing with oil once more during cooking.

Chillied Potato Salad

This is a potato salad with a difference – the skins are left on the potatoes for maximum nutritional benefit.

SERVES 4
900 g (2 lb) potatoes, scrubbed
100 g (4 oz) spring onions, trimmed and chopped
5 ml (1 tsp) sunflower oil
5 ml (1 tsp) chilli powder or to taste
100 ml (4 fl oz) low-fat natural yogurt
pepper, to taste

1 Cut the potatoes into 5 cm (2 inch) cubes and place in a saucepan containing 1.25 cm (½ inch) boiling water. Cover and cook for about 20 minutes or until tender. Drain and set aside to cool.
2 Meanwhile, mix the spring onions with the oil and chilli powder in a saucepan. Cook for just 3 minutes. Set aside to cool.
3 When the potatoes are cooled, place them in a bowl. Mix the yogurt into the spring onion mixture, then pour the yogurt mixture over the potatoes. Combine well and season to taste.

NUTRITIONAL ANALYSIS
233 kcals/976 kJ
6.4 g Protein
51.3 g Carbohydrate
2 g Fat ★★★★
0.4 g Saturated Fat ★★★★
5.8 g Fibre ★★★★
No Added Sugar ★★★★
129 mg Salt ★★★★

Tomato and Chicory Salad

Chicory is grown in darkness to produce its crisp white leaves. A greeny tinge at the tip of the leaves usually indicates bitterness. Do not use very bitter chicory for salads.

SERVES 4
½ onion, skinned and finely chopped
15 ml (1 tbsp) sunflower oil
15 ml (1 tbsp) red wine vinegar
1 garlic clove, skinned and crushed
15 ml (1 tbsp) chopped fresh basil or 30 ml (2 tbsp) chopped fresh parsley
pepper, to taste
4 tomatoes, sliced
2 heads chicory, thinly sliced

1 Mix together the onion, oil, vinegar, garlic, herbs and seasoning in a serving bowl.
2 Add the tomatoes and chicory and stir gently until well coated. Cover tightly. Set aside to marinate for at least 1 hour before serving. (*Picnic 4 continued overleaf*)

NUTRITIONAL ANALYSIS
53 kcals/223 kJ
1.5 g Protein
3.6 g Carbohydrate
3.8 g Fat ★
0.5 g Saturated Fat ★★★
2.2 g Fibre ★★★★
No Added Sugar ★★★★
23 mg Salt ★★★★

NUTRITIONAL ANALYSIS
73 kcals/305 kJ
0.7 g Protein
19 g Carbohydrate
0 g Fat ★★★★
0 g Saturated Fat ★★★★
3.1 g Fibre ★★★★
No Added Sugar ★★★★
10 mg Salt ★★★★

Minty Fruit Salad

If mint is unavailable use ground cinnamon or freshly grated nutmeg.

SERVES 4

100 ml (4 fl oz) unsweetened apple juice
1 red eating apple, cored and sliced
1 green eating apple, cored and sliced
2 ripe pears, sliced
3 satsumas, peeled and segmented
15 ml (1 tbsp) chopped fresh mint
fresh mint sprigs, to decorate

1 Put the apple juice in a bowl and add the remaining ingredients.
2 Toss gently so all the ingredients are coated in the apple juice. Cover and chill before serving.

NUTRITIONAL ANALYSIS
116 kcals/485 kJ
2.4 g Protein
27.6 g Carbohydrate
0.2 g Fat ★★★★
0 g Saturated Fat ★★★★
6.5 g Fibre ★★★★
No Added Sugar ★★★★
36 mg Salt ★★★★

Tropical Nectar

Papayas or paw paws are ripe when the skin turns from green to yellow and the flesh feels slightly soft.

SERVES 4

2 passion fruit
1 papaya, peeled, seeded and chopped
1 large orange, peeled and segmented
450 ml (¾ pint) unsweetened pineapple juice
10 ml (2 tsp) lime juice
8 orange slices, to decorate

1 Halve the passion fruit, remove the pulp and seeds and sieve. Discard the seeds. Put the juice in a blender or food processor.
2 Add the papaya, orange and pineapple juice to the passion fruit juice and blend until smooth.
3 Add the lime juice and orange slices. Chill before serving.

Barbecues

In the summer months, with long, balmy evenings, there is nothing better than a barbecue as a means of preparing food. If you want to add variety to the usual fare of barbecues, try one of the special fish dishes included here or try a different marinade on the food you usually cook. The barbecued fruits (page 140) provide a novel end to a summer meal.

NUTRITIONAL ANALYSIS
420 kcals/1754 kJ
49.1 g Protein
1 g Carbohydrate
22.9 g Fat ★★
4.1 g Saturated Fat ★★★
0 g Fibre ★
0.5 g Added Sugar ★★★★
548 mg Salt ★★★

Barbecued Red Mullet

Red mullet are perfect for barbecues – small and compact, they are easy to cook and serve.

SERVES 4

4 red mullet, cleaned and scaled
pepper, to taste
rosemary sprigs
juice of 1 lemon
30 ml (2 tbsp) red wine vinegar
10 ml (2 tsp) Worcestershire sauce
5 ml (1 tsp) clear honey
45 ml (3 tbsp) sunflower oil
10 ml (2 tsp) chopped fresh rosemary

1 Sprinkle the inside of each fish with pepper and put 1 sprig of rosemary in each. Arrange in a dish.
2 Put the lemon juice, vinegar, Worcestershire sauce, honey, oil and chopped rosemary into a small saucepan and bring to the boil. Pour over the fish, cover and leave to marinate for 30 minutes, turning once.
3 Drain the fish, reserving the marinade, and place in a grill basket on top of the barbecue. Barbecue over medium heat for 10-15 minutes, turning carefully once and brushing with the reserved marinade.
4 Discard the cooked rosemary sprigs and use fresh sprigs to garnish. Serve hot.

NUTRITIONAL ANALYSIS
228 kcals/951 kJ
33.1 g Protein
3.1 g Carbohydrate
8.9 g Fat ★★
1.9 g Saturated Fat ★★★★
1.2 g Fibre ★★
No Added Sugar ★★★★
899 mg Salt ★

Fish Kebabs

Fish is generally very low in fat, particularly saturated fat. Marinating the fish in lemon juice, parsley and mint gives it plenty of flavour so there is no need to add salt.

SERVES 4

700 g (1½ lb) firm-fleshed white fish, trimmed and cubed
juice of 2 lemons
15 ml (1 tbsp) chopped fresh mint or 7.5 ml (½ tbsp) dried
30 ml (2 tbsp) chopped fresh parsley

FOR THE LEMON AND MINT SAUCE

150 ml (¼ pint) low-fat natural yogurt
juice of 2 lemons
15 ml (1 tbsp) chopped fresh mint or 7.5 ml (½ tbsp) dried
25 g (1 oz) cucumber, finely diced
lemon slices, to garnish

1 Thread the fish on to 4 skewers and put in a shallow dish. Mix together the lemon juice, mint and parsley and pour over the fish. Leave to marinate for 1 hour, turning frequently.
2 For the sauce, mix together the yogurt, lemon juice, mint and cucumber.
3 Put the kebabs on the grill rack. Barbecue for 10-15 minutes, turning several times, until cooked through. Garnish the kebabs with lemon and serve hot with the sauce handed separately in a bowl.

Tandoori Prawns

For this recipe, it really is best to use the large-size or 'jumbo' prawns.

SERVES 4
16 raw jumbo prawns, legs removed, shelled and deveined
150 ml (¼ pint) low-fat natural yogurt
2.5 cm (1 inch) piece fresh root ginger, peeled and chopped
2 large garlic cloves, skinned and crushed
juice of ½ a lemon
10 ml (2 tsp) freshly ground cumin
1.25 ml (¼ tsp) cayenne
2.5 ml (½ tsp) paprika
lettuce leaves and lemon wedges, to garnish

NUTRITIONAL ANALYSIS
180 kcals/754 kJ
28.1 g Protein
5.6 g Carbohydrate
5.5 g Fat ★★★
1 g Saturated Fat ★★★★
0.6 g Fibre ★
No Added Sugar ★★★★
4723 mg Salt ★

1 Put the prawns in a bowl. Blend the yogurt, ginger, garlic, lemon juice, cumin, cayenne and paprika in a food processor or blender until smooth. Pour the marinade over the prawns, mixing well to coat. Marinate in the refrigerator for at least 4 hours.

2 Thread the prawns on to 4 skewers. Put the skewers on the grill rack. Barbecue for about 5 minutes on each side or until the flesh has turned white and opaque, brushing occasionally with oil.

3 When cooked, push the prawns off the skewers with a fork and serve on a bed of lettuce leaves, garnished with lemon wedges.

Barbecued Fish Cutlets

Fish is a good choice for trouble-free healthy barbecue meals because it cooks so quickly. However, it is fragile so use firm-fleshed fish and a hinged grill basket for easy handling.

SERVES 4
1 small onion, skinned and minced
1 garlic clove, skinned and minced
¼ red pepper, cored, seeded and minced
100 ml (4 fl oz) passata or other sieved tomatoes
50 ml (2 fl oz) unsweetened apple juice
10 ml (2 tsp) Worcestershire sauce
4 firm-fleshed white fish cutlets, at least 2.5 cm (1 inch) thick

NUTRITIONAL ANALYSIS
122 kcals/509 kJ
26.3 g Protein
1.8 g Carbohydrate
1.1 g Fat ★★★★
0.2 g Saturated Fat ★★★★
0.2 g Fibre ★
No Added Sugar ★★★★
334 mg Salt ★★

1 Put the onion, garlic, pepper, tomato sauce, apple juice and Worcestershire sauce in a saucepan and simmer for 5 minutes. Cool.

2 Arrange the cutlets in a dish just large enough to accommodate them in one layer. Pour over the sauce, cover and marinate at room temperature for 30 minutes-1 hour.

3 Put the cutlets in a lightly oiled hinged grill basket or on the grill rack. Barbecue over a moderately hot heat for 5-10 minutes on each side, basting with the marinade from time to time, or until the fish flakes when pierced with the point of a knife near the bone.

NUTRITIONAL ANALYSIS
133 kcals/557 kJ
27.6 g Protein
0.9 g Carbohydrate
1.5 g Fat ★★★★
0.3 g Saturated Fat ★★★★
2.4 g Fibre ★★★★
No Added Sugar ★★★★
331 mg Salt ★★

Fish Barbecued in Foil

Wrap fillets of fish in foil for a moist succulent result. Serve them straight from the foil packet.

SERVES 4

20 ml (4 tsp) dry sherry

4 fillets of any firm-fleshed white fish, each weighing 150 g (5 oz)

4 large mushrooms, thinly sliced

4 thin lemon slices

½ large carrot, scrubbed and cut into very thin matchsticks

pepper, to taste

1 Cut four 25 cm (10 inch) squares of foil. Spread 5 ml (1 tsp) sherry over the centre of each and place a fish fillet on top. Arrange the remaining ingredients attractively over the fish. Season to taste. Bring the sides of the foil together and fold them over twice to make a firm seal. Seal the ends.
2 Put the parcels on the grill rack. Barbecue over a medium heat for 7-10 minutes.

NUTRITIONAL ANALYSIS
244kcals/1020 kJ
31.9 g Protein
2.8 g Carbohydrate
11.9 g Fat ★★
3 g Saturated Fat ★★★
0.2 g Fibre ★
No Added Sugar ★★★★
445 mg Salt ★★★

Spatchcock Chicken

Flattening the birds will ensure even cooking all the way through. Inserting the seasoning under the skin intensifies the flavour and helps keep the flesh moist. However, to make sure the overall fat content of what you eat remains low, don't eat the skin of the bird.

SERVES 4

10 ml (2 tsp) green peppercorns

25 g (1 oz) polyunsaturated margarine

1 garlic clove, skinned and crushed

finely grated rind of 1 orange

2 poussins, each weighing about 700 g (1½ lb)

orange slices, to garnish

1 Crush the peppercorns and mix with the margarine, garlic and orange rind.
2 Put the poussins on a chopping board, breast side down. With a sharp knife, cut right along each side of the backbone of each bird through the skin and flesh. Cut out the backbone with scissors and open out the birds as much as possible. Turn the birds over and crush the breastbones with the heel of the hand so that the poussins will lie flat on the grill rack when cooking. Trim the knobs off the ends of the legs.
3 Loosen the skin over the breast with the fingers and insert the seasoned margarine under the skin. From the outside, smooth the seasoned margarine to the shape of the bird. Cover and leave in the refrigerator for 4 hours to absorb the flavourings.
4 Put the poussins, skin side down, on the grill rack. Barbecue for 5 minutes, then turn the birds over and barbecue for 25-30 minutes or until the juices run clear when pierced in the thigh with the point of a knife.
5 When cooked, cut the poussins into serving pieces and garnish with orange slices.

Spicy Charcoal Chicken

Prepare this marinated chicken dish the day before and simply cook on the barbecue about 30 minutes before serving.

SERVES 4
30 ml (2 tbsp) low-fat natural yogurt
25 g (1 oz) fine plain wholemeal flour
15 ml (1 tbsp) red wine vinegar
30 ml (2 tbsp) sunflower oil
60 ml (4 tbsp) lemon juice
1 garlic clove, skinned and crushed
5 ml (1 tsp) grated fresh root ginger
5 ml (1 tsp) paprika
5 ml (1 tsp) black peppercorns, lightly crushed
4 chicken portions, skinned
lemon wedges, to serve

NUTRITIONAL ANALYSIS
207 kcals/864 kJ
24.4 g Protein
4.8 g Carbohydrate
10.2 g Fat ★★
2.4 g Saturated Fat ★★★
0.6 g Fibre ★
No Added Sugar ★★★★
267 mg Salt ★★★

1 Mix together the yogurt, wholemeal flour, vinegar, oil, 30 ml (2 tbsp) of the lemon juice, the garlic, ginger, paprika and peppercorns.
2 Make parallel cuts through the chicken meat almost to the bone, about 1 cm (½ inch) apart. Sprinkle with remaining lemon juice.
3 Place the chicken in a bowl and cover with the yogurt mixture. Leave in a cool place for several hours or overnight, turning occasionally.
4 Put the chicken on the grill rack. Barbecue for 10-15 minutes on each side or until the juices run clear when pierced with the point of a knife. Serve hot or cold with lemon wedges.

Turkey Breasts with Mint

Marinating the turkey in a spicy mint yogurt flavours and keeps them moist during barbecuing.

SERVES 4
4 turkey or chicken breasts, each weighing about 150 g (5 oz)
300 ml (½ pint) low-fat natural yogurt
½ small onion, skinned and grated
2 garlic cloves, skinned and crushed
75 ml (5 tbsp) chopped fresh mint
5 ml (1 tsp) freshly ground cumin
lemon slices and mint sprigs, to garnish

NUTRITIONAL ANALYSIS
209 kcals/872 kJ
39.9 g Protein
6.8 g Carbohydrate
2.8 g Fat ★★★★
1.2 g Saturated Fat ★★★★
2.3 g Fibre ★★★
No Added Sugar ★★★★
390 mg Salt ★★★

1 Cut each turkey breast in half crossways and place each half between sheets of greaseproof paper. Beat well until the breasts measure about 10×15 cm (4×6 inches). Put the turkey breasts in a shallow dish.
2 Mix together the yogurt, onion, garlic, mint and cumin. Pour the marinade over the turkey breasts and mix well to coat. Cover and leave in the refrigerator for at least 4 hours or overnight.
3 Place the breasts on the grill rack. Barbecue for about 10 minutes or until cooked through, turning once. Serve garnished with lemon slices and mint sprigs.

NUTRITIONAL ANALYSIS
179 kcals/750 kJ
19.1 g Protein
12 g Carbohydrate
6.5 g Fat ★★★
2.4 g Saturated Fat ★★★
1.5 g Fibre ★★★
No Added Sugar ★★★★
187 mg Salt ★★★★

Pineapple and Pork Kebabs

Using lean pork fillet and a non-oil marinade keeps the fat content of these colourful kebabs low.

SERVES 4

225 g (8 oz) can unsweetened pineapple chunks, drained with juice reserved

15 ml (1 tbsp) wine vinegar

5 ml (1 tsp) ground cloves

5 ml (1 tsp) finely chopped fresh root ginger or 2.5 ml (½ tsp) ground

350 g (12 oz) lean pork fillet, cut into 2.5 cm (1 inch) cubes

12 small onions, skinned

½ red pepper, cored, seeded and cut into 2.5 cm (1 inch) cubes

½ green pepper, cored, seeded and cut into 2.5 cm (1 inch) cubes

1 Combine the pineapple juice, vinegar, cloves and ginger in a bowl. Add the pork cubes and marinate for at least 2 hours, turning occasionally. Drain well, reserving the marinade.
2 Thread 4 large skewers, alternating the pork with the pineapple, onions and pepper cubes. Brush with a little of the marinade.
3 Place the kebabs on the grill rack. Barbecue for 20 minutes or until the meat is browned and cooked through, turning and brushing occasionally with the remaining marinade. Serve immediately.

NUTRITIONAL ANALYSIS
37 kcals/154 kJ
6.6 g Protein
0.1 g Carbohydrate
1.2 g Fat ★★★
0.2 g Saturated Fat ★★★★
0 g Fibre ★
No Added Sugar ★★★★
41 mg Salt ★★★

Souvlakia

These mini kebabs cook quickly on the barbecue and go well with a drink while waiting for the main dish to cook. Serve in halved wholemeal pitta breads. The skewers, called satay sticks, can be found at good kitchen shops and specialist grocers.

MAKES 15 KEBABS

450 g (1 lb) skinless turkey fillet

15 ml (1 tbsp) sunflower oil

juice of 1 lemon

10 ml (2 tsp) chopped fresh thyme or 5 ml (1 tsp) dried

10 ml (2 tsp) chopped fresh oregano or 5 ml (1 tsp) dried

pepper, to taste

1 Cut the turkey into 2 cm (¾ inch) squares and thread on to fifteen 15 cm (6 inch) thin wooden skewers. Put into a dish.
2 Mix together the remaining ingredients and pour over the turkey. Cover and refrigerate for several hours, turning occasionally.
3 Place the kebabs on the grill rack. Barbecue over a medium heat for about 8 minutes, turning occasionally, until they are beginning to brown and are no longer pink inside.

Lamb and Vegetable Kebabs

Fresh coriander is a tall, flat-leaved herb with delicately scented leaves. Bunches are often available in supermarkets or specialist grocers.

SERVES 4

700 g (1½ lb) boneless lamb fillet or leg, trimmed of excess fat and cut into small cubes

30 ml (2 tbsp) sunflower oil

30 ml (2 tbsp) lemon juice

1 large garlic clove, skinned and crushed

30 ml (2 tbsp) chopped fresh coriander

30 ml (2 tbsp) chopped fresh parsley

pepper, to taste

8 small mushrooms

1 red pepper, cored, seeded and cut into 2.5 cm (1 inch) pieces

2 courgettes (zucchini), trimmed and cut into 2.5 cm (1 inch) pieces

NUTRITIONAL ANALYSIS
336 kcals/1405 kJ
38.2 g Protein
2.5 g Carbohydrate
19.4 g Fat ★★
7.8 g Saturated Fat ★★
2.2 g Fibre ★★
No Added Sugar ★★★★
412 mg Salt ★★

1 Put the lamb in a large bowl. Mix together the oil, lemon juice, garlic, coriander, parsley and pepper. Reserve a little for coating the vegetables, then pour the rest over the lamb cubes. Mix thoroughly to coat.
2 Cover and leave to marinate in the refrigerator for at least 8 hours.
3 Prepare the vegetables just before cooking. Pour over the reserved marinade, mixing well to coat.
4 Thread the lamb cubes on to 8 medium skewers, alternating with a selection of each type of vegetable.
5 Put the kebabs on the grill rack. Barbecue for 20-25 minutes, turning frequently and basting with any remaining marinade.

Jumbo Burgers

Lean minced beef is essential for healthy hamburgers. Ideally, mince chuck steak yourself or buy the best mince available.

SERVES 4

450 g (1 lb) lean minced beef

100 g (4 oz) fresh wholemeal breadcrumbs

1 small onion, skinned and grated

100 g (4 oz) carrots, scrubbed and grated

30 ml (2 tbsp) chopped fresh parsley

1 egg, beaten

4 wholemeal buns, lettuce leaves, tomato slices and Spanish onion rings, to serve

NUTRITIONAL ANALYSIS
331 kcals/1384 kJ
32.5 g Protein
32.7 g Carbohydrate
8.7 g Fat ★★★
3 g Saturated Fat ★★★
9.2 g Fibre ★★★★
No Added Sugar ★★★★
1331 mg Salt ★

1 Mix together the beef, breadcrumbs, onion, carrots, parsley and egg in a bowl. Divide into 4 patties.
2 Put the burgers on the grill rack. Barbecue for 15 minutes, turning once during cooking, or until cooked according to personal preference. Serve in wholemeal buns with lettuce, tomato and onion.

Minced Beef Kebabs

NUTRITIONAL ANALYSIS
206 kcals/860 kJ
21.4 g Protein
8.4 g Carbohydrate
9.8 g Fat ★★
2.7 g Saturated Fat ★★★
1.9 g Fibre ★★★
No Added Sugar ★★★★
231 mg Salt ★★★

A food processor will make this a very quick dish to prepare, but the traditional method is very simple too. Warm the oil very slightly before brushing the kebabs to make it go further.

SERVES 4

1 small onion, skinned

350 g (12 oz) beef, all fat removed

1 egg

40 g (1½ oz) wholemeal flour

15 ml (1 tbsp) chopped fresh parsley

5 ml (1 tsp) freshly ground cumin

7.5 ml (1½ tsp) freshly ground coriander

1.25 ml (¼ tsp) chilli powder

10 ml (2 tsp) garam masala

pepper, to taste

15 ml (1 tbsp) sunflower oil for brushing

lemon slices, tomatoes and thin Spanish onion slices, to garnish

1 Purée the onion in a food processor. Add the beef and work until fine. Add the egg, 25 g (1 oz) of the flour, parsley, cumin, coriander, chilli powder, garam masala and salt and work until the mixture sticks together.
2 Alternatively, use lean minced beef and put into a bowl. Grate the onion and add it to the meat with the flour and lightly beaten egg. Add the herbs and spices and knead until the mixture becomes sticky.
3 Divide the beef mixture into twelve and shape each portion with the hands, on a work surface sprinkled with the remaining flour, into a sausage, 10 cm (4 inches) long. Thread lengthways on to 4 skewers. Cover and refrigerate until required.
4 Brush the meat with only enough oil to prevent it sticking to the grill rack. Barbecue for 15-20 minutes, turning frequently, or until the meat is very well cooked through. Garnish and serve hot with bread.

Barbecued Lamb's Liver

NUTRITIONAL ANALYSIS
191 kcals/797 kJ
18.6 g Protein
7.5 g Carbohydrate
9.8 g Fat ★★
2.8 g Saturated Fat ★★★
0 g Fibre ★
No Added Sugar ★★★★
180 mg Salt ★★★★

Liver is a rich source of the B vitamins, in particular vitamin B12 which is essential for healthy red blood cells. Timing of this dish will depend on the thickness of the liver and, of course, the heat of the barbecue. Serve with onions barbecued in foil and barbecued jacket potatoes.

SERVES 4

20 ml (4 tsp) Dijon mustard

20 ml (4 tsp) semi-skimmed milk

350 g (12 oz) lamb's liver, trimmed and cut into 4 slices

1 Mix together the mustard and milk in a dish.
2 Coat the liver on all sides with the marinade. Cover and set aside for about 1 hour.
3 Place the liver on the grill rack. Barbecue 7.5 cm (3 inches) above the heat for 3-4 minutes on each side or until the juices run clear when the liver is pierced with the point of a knife.

Summer Vegetable Kebabs

Choose vegetables carefully for size, cutting the peppers, courgettes (zucchini) and aubergine into similar sized chunks for a really stunning effect. Blanching the vegetables before cooking ensures that they remain brightly coloured and juicy.

NUTRITIONAL ANALYSIS
41 kcals/173 kJ
2.3 g Protein
4.7 g Carbohydrate
1.7 g Fat ★★
0.3 g Saturated Fat ★★★★
3.2 g Fibre ★★★★
No Added Sugar ★★★★
25 mg Salt ★★★★

SERVES 4

8 pickling onions, skinned

2 thin courgettes (zucchini), trimmed and cut into thick slices

1 small aubergine, cut into chunks

1 green pepper, cored, seeded and cut into chunks

1 red pepper, cored, seeded and cut into chunks

12 firm button mushrooms

1 small aubergine, cut into chunks

15 ml (1 tbsp) sunflower oil

juice of ½ lemon

1 garlic clove, skinned and crushed

2.5 ml (½ tsp) dried basil

pepper, to taste

4 cherry tomatoes

1 Put the onions in a saucepan of boiling water and blanch for 5 minutes. Drain and plunge into a bowl of ice cold water, then drain again. Blanch the courgettes (zucchini) in the same way for 3 minutes, the peppers and mushrooms for 1 minute, then the aubergine for ½ minute.
2 Thread the vegetables on to 4 large kebab skewers, arranging them attractively.
3 Mix together the oil, lemon, garlic and basil and brush over the kebabs. Sprinkle with the pepper.
4 Put the kebabs on the grill rack. Barbecue for 10-15 minutes, turning occasionally. Just before kebabs are ready, add the cherry tomatoes and continue to cook until they are heated through.

Tofu and Vegetable Kebabs

Tofu provides protein in these vegetable kebabs. It has a relatively low carbohydrate and fat content and is an ideal way of providing tasty food for vegetarian guests.

NUTRITIONAL ANALYSIS
134 kcals/561 kJ
12.2 g Protein
6.1 g Carbohydrate
6.5 g Fat ★★
0.9 g Saturated Fat ★★★★
2 g Fibre ★★★★
No Added Sugar ★★★★
389 mg Salt ★★

SERVES 4

100 ml (4 fl oz) sugarless tomato ketchup

100 ml (4 fl oz) dry cider

1 garlic clove, skinned and crushed

10 ml (2 tsp) Dijon mustard

5 ml (1 tsp) dried oregano

pepper, to taste

two 285 g (10 oz) blocks firm tofu, cut into 18 cubes

8 pickling onions, skinned

2 thin courgettes (zucchini), trimmed and cut into 2.5 cm (1 inch) slices

12 button mushrooms

1 Mix together the tomato ketchup, cider, garlic, mustard, oregano and pepper in a large bowl. Put in the tofu, toss lightly to cover all surfaces with the marinade. Cover and refrigerate for several hours.
2 Put the onions into a saucepan of boiling water and blanch for 5 minutes. Drain, plunge them into cold water and drain again. Blanch the courgettes (zucchini) in the same way for 3 minutes, then the mushrooms for 1 minute.
3 Thread the vegetables and tofu on to long skewers, alternating them attractively. Brush with the marinade.
4 Put the kebabs on the grill rack. Barbecue for about 5 minutes on each side, brushing occasionally with any remaining marinade.

Fruit Kebabs

NUTRITIONAL ANALYSIS
185 kcals/774 kJ
1.6 g Protein
23.5 g Carbohydrate
10.1 g Fat ★★
3 g Saturated Fat ★★★
4.2 g Fibre ★★★★
No Added Sugar ★★★★
213 mg Salt ★★★

Fruits is an excellent source of dietary fibre. Select fruits that will not disintegrate when heated such as plums, apple and pears.

SERVES 4

juice of 2 oranges

30 ml (2 tbsp) lemon juice

4 apricots, stoned and cut into quarters

2 bananas, peeled and cut into quarters

½ medium pineapple, peeled, cored and cut into 2.5 cm (1 inch) cubes

40 g (1½ oz) polyunsaturated margarine, melted

shredded coconut, to decorate

1 Combine the orange juice and lemon juice in a bowl. Add the fruit pieces and marinate for at least 1 hour, turning occasionally. Drain well, reserving the marinade.
2 Thread the fruit on to 4 large skewers, including a selection of all the fruits on each skewer. Brush the kebabs with the melted margarine.
3 Put the kebabs on the grill rack. Barbecue for 10 minutes, brushing with the melted margarine and turning frequently so that the fruit does not burn.
4 Gently heat the reserved marinade in a small saucepan. To serve the kebabs, push the fruit off the skewers with a fork, decorate with shredded coconut and accompany with the warmed marinade.

Hot Fruit Salad Parcels

NUTRITIONAL ANALYSIS
77 kcals/322 kJ
0.8 g Protein
19.7 g Carbohydrate
0.1 g Fat ★★★★
0 g Saturated Fat ★★★★
3.3 g Fibre ★★★★
No Added Sugar ★★★★
10 mg Salt ★★★★

This is a good recipe for first-time barbecue cooks because although it is particularly delicious hot but crisp, it really doesn't matter if the fruit does cook a little. Don't leave the parcels too long though, or the fruit will become a pulp. Open the fruit parcels with care as they become very hot.

SERVES 4

juice of ½ lemon

juice of 1 orange

1 red skinned eating apple, cored and cut into thick slices

1 green skinned eating apple, cored and cut into thick slices

1 large pear, cored and cut into thick slices

12 cherries, stoned

1 large banana, peeled and cut into 8 chunks

15 g (½ oz) brown sugar (optional)

2.5 ml (½ tsp) ground mixed spice

1 Cut out four 25 cm (10 inch) squares of foil and lay them on a work surface.,
2 Pour the lemon and orange juices into a large bowl. Add the prepared fruit and toss in the juice.
3 Place an equal amount of fruit in the centre of each piece of foil. Mix the sugar with the juice and spice and spoon it over the fruit. Bring the sides of the foil up over the apples and bunch it together firmly, draw-string purse style.
4 Put the parcels on the grill rack, folded side up, taking care not to break the foil. Barbecue over a medium heat for 15-20 minutes.

Puddings

Healthy puddings that are low in fat and added sugar are usually based on fresh fruit. Use whatever is in season or, alternatively, make the most of your freezer and use those fruits that freeze well out of season. The recipes included here are all low in added sugar and you will quickly begin to appreciate the true flavour of these dishes as opposed to the over-riding one of sweetness so often found in puddings.

Blackberry and Apple Jellies

Make this light, pretty dessert when blackberries are in season. Full of flavour, blackberries provide the attractive colour of the jellies.

NUTRITIONAL ANALYSIS
115 kcals/482 kJ
6.8 g Protein
22.6 g Carbohydrate
0.4 g Fat ★★★★
0.2 g Saturated Fat ★★★★
3.5 g Fibre ★★★★
No Added Sugar ★★★★
84 mg Salt ★★★★

SERVES 4

20 ml (4 tsp) powdered gelatine
450 ml (¾ pint) unsweetened apple juice
175 g (6 oz) blackberries
25 g (1 oz) sugar (optional)
150 ml (¼ pint) low-fat natural yogurt
½ eating apple, thinly sliced, to decorate

1 Mix 5 ml (1 tsp) of the gelatine and 150 ml (¼ pint) of the apple juice in a heatproof bowl and leave to soften for about 1 minute. Put the bowl over a saucepan of gently simmering water and stir until the gelatine dissolves. Leave to cool.
2 Reserve 4 blackberries for decoration and arrange 50 g (2 oz) of the remaining berries in the base of 4 glasses. Pour the apple jelly into the glasses and chill for 30 minutes or until set.
3 Meanwhile, put the remaining berries in a saucepan with 200 ml (⅓ pint) of the remaining apple juice. Cover and simmer gently until the fruit is tender. Cool a little, then purée in a blender or food processor. If liked, rub through a fine nylon sieve to remove the seeds. Add sugar to taste.
4 Dissolve the remaining gelatine in the remaining apple juice as before. Add to the blackberry and apple purée and make up to 450 ml (¾ pint) with cold water if necessary. Chill for 30 minutes or until thick.
5 Lightly whisk the jelly, then fold in the yogurt. Pour into the glasses over the set apple jelly, cover and chill for 1 hour. Serve decorated with the reserved blackberries and apple slices.

Italian Marsala Cheesecakes

These individual cheesecakes are lower in fat than most traditional cheesecakes. Ricotta cheese is a medium-fat cheese, which is preferable to using high-fat cream cheese.

NUTRITIONAL ANALYSIS
310 kcals/1298 kJ
12.4 g Protein
28.4 g Carbohydrate
15.9 g Fat ★★
5.2 g Saturated Fat ★★
2.3 g Fibre ★★
7.8 g Added Sugar ★★
489 mg Salt ★★★

SERVES 4

25 g (1 oz) raisins
30 ml (2 tbsp) Marsala
75 g (3 oz) plain wholemeal flour
40 g (1½ oz) polyunsaturated margarine
225 g (8 oz) ricotta cheese
2 eggs
25 g (1 oz) sugar
1 slice orange, quartered, to decorate
low-fat natural yogurt, to serve

1 Put the raisins and Marsala into a bowl, cover and set aside to soak for 30 minutes, until the raisins are plump and soft.
2 Put the flour into a bowl and rub in the margarine. Add 15 ml (1 tbsp) chilled water or just enough to form a dough. Divide the pastry into 4, roll out each piece into a circle and use to line 4 individual quiche dishes or Yorkshire pudding tins. Prick with a fork, line with greaseproof foil and baking beans and bake blind at 200°C (400°F) mark 6 for 5 minutes. Remove from the oven. Lower the oven temperature to 180°C (350°F) mark 4.
3 Add the ricotta, eggs and sugar to the raisins and mix well. Divide the mixture among the 4 pastry-lined tins and smooth the tops. Return to the oven and bake for a further 35 minutes, until set and golden brown. Decorate with orange and serve with yogurt.

Flambéed Pineapple

When brandy is flamed the alcohol burns off; the resulting liquor gives a delicious flavour to the fruit.

SERVES 4
1 pineapple, weighing about 900 g (2 lb)
30 ml (2 tbsp) clear honey
100 ml (4 fl oz) brandy
low-fat natural yogurt, to serve

1 Trim about 1 cm (½ inch) from each end of the pineapple. Cut in quarters lengthways. Carefully trim the core away, then cut along the base of each quarter so that the flesh is separated from the skin. Cut the flesh in half lengthways, then 4 times across to give bite-sized pieces of pineapple.
2 Lay the pineapple shell and flesh in an ovenproof dish and spoon the honey over. Cook at 190°C (375°F) mark 5 for 45 minutes, basting occasionally.
3 When the pineapple is golden, remove from the oven. Gently heat the brandy in a small saucepan. Ignite, then pour over the pineapple. After the flames die down, pour the cooking juice over. Serve with yogurt.

NUTRITIONAL ANALYSIS
132 kcals/552 kJ
0.6 g Protein
19.6 g Carbohydrate
0 g Fat ★★★★
0 g Saturated Fat ★★★★
1.4 g Fibre ★★★
5.7 g Added Sugar ★
8 mg Salt ★★★★

Prune and Orange Jelly

Use the no-soak prunes now available. These tenderized prunes are the most convenient and cook in about 10 minutes.

SERVES 4
225 g (8 oz) no-soak prunes
thinly pared rind of 1 orange
150 ml (¼ pint) unsweetened orange juice
15 g (½ oz) powdered gelatine
3 large oranges, peeled and segmented

1 Put the prunes, orange rind and 450 ml (¾ pint) water in a saucepan. Gently cook for 10-15 minutes or until the prunes are tender. Drain, reserving the cooking liquid, and discard the rind. Halve the prunes and remove the stones.
2 Add the orange juice and enough cold water to the prune liquid to make 600 ml (1 pint).
3 Sprinkle the gelatine over 45 ml (3 tbsp) cold water in a heatproof bowl and leave to soften for 1 minute. Put the bowl over a saucepan of gently simmering water and stir until the gelatine dissolves. Leave to cool, then mix into the fruit juices.
4 Place a 1.1 litre (2 pint) jelly mould or dish in a large mixing bowl containing ice cubes. Pour a little of the jelly mixture into the mould to a depth of 2.5 cm (1 inch) and allow to set.
5 Arrange either a layer of halved prunes or orange segments on top. Cover with a little jelly and allow to set. Add more jelly, then more fruit, allowing each layer to set before starting the next. Continue until all the jelly and fruit have been used. Chill for 3 hours or until set.

NUTRITIONAL ANALYSIS
160 kcals/670 kJ
5.7 g Protein
36.8 g Carbohydrate
0 g Fat ★★★★
0 g Saturated Fat ★★★★
11.5 g Fibre ★★★★
No Added Sugar ★★★★
27 mg Salt ★★★★

NUTRITIONAL ANALYSIS
158 kcals/660 kJ
5.3 g Protein
28.4 g Carbohydrate
3.3 g Fat ★★★
0.3 g Saturated Fat ★★★★
13.4 g Fibre ★★★★
0.7 g Added Sugar ★★★★
187 mg Salt ★★★

Dried Fruit Soufflé

The puréed dried fruits are the base for this light soufflé, replacing a traditional flour and fat roux. The dried fruit are interchangeable, so use your favourites. Serve the soufflé immediately from the oven so it is still well risen and light.

SERVES 4
75 g (3 oz) dried figs
75 g (3 oz) no-soak dried apricots
75 g (3 oz) dried mango or peach pieces
juice of 1 orange
25 ml (1½ tbsp) ground almonds
3 egg whites
2.5 ml (½ tsp) icing sugar (optional)

1 Put the dried fruit into a bowl, cover with cold water and leave for 8 hours or overnight.
2 Drain the dried fruit. Purée in a blender or food processor with the orange juice until smooth. Press through a sieve, then mix the ground almonds into the purée.
3 Whisk the egg whites until stiff, then fold into the mixture. Spoon into the four lightly greased 150 ml (¼ pint) individual soufflé dishes. Bake at 190°C (375°F) mark 5 for 20-25 minutes or until well risen and golden. Dust lightly with icing sugar, if liked, and serve immediately.

NUTRITIONAL ANALYSIS
60 kcals/253 kJ
1.5 g Protein
14.7 g Carbohydrate
0 g Fat ★★★★
0 g Saturated Fat ★★★★
2.1 g Fibre ★★★★
2.9 g Added Sugar ★
108 mg Salt ★★★

Melon Granita

A light honey, such as Acacia, is recommended here as a strong honey may mask the flavour of the melon.

SERVES 4
1.4-1.6 kg (3-3½ lb) melon, peeled, seeded and cut into chunks
15 ml (1 tbsp) clear honey
finely grated rind and juice of 1 small orange
finely grated rind and juice of 1 lemon
mint sprigs, to garnish

1 Purée the melon in a blender or food processor, then put in a bowl with the honey, rind and juice and mix well.
2 Transfer to a freezerproof container and freeze for 3 hours or until the mixture is partly frozen and setting around the edges.
3 Turn the mixture into a bowl and whisk well to break up the ice crystals. Freeze for about 4 hours or until frozen.
4 Before serving, soften in the refrigerator for about 45 minutes. Spoon into chilled glasses or dishes and garnish with mint sprigs.

Indian Saffron Yogurt

Saffron and aromatic cardamom pods add flavour to this chilled dessert. The saffron strands also add a subtle golden glow to the yogurt.

SERVES 4

600 ml (1 pint) low-fat natural yogurt

30 ml (2 tbsp) skimmed milk

pinch of saffron strands

4 green cardamom pods, bruised

50 g (2 oz) blanched almonds, finely chopped

10 shelled unsalted pistachio nuts, cut into slivers, to decorate

1 Line a large sieve with muslin or all-purpose kitchen cloth and place the sieve over a bowl. Pour the yogurt into the sieve and leave to drain for 30-40 minutes or until most of the whey has drained off.
2 Meanwhile, put the milk, saffron and cardamoms in a saucepan and bring to the boil. Remove from the heat and leave to infuse until cold.
3 Put the strained yogurt into a bowl and stir in the chopped almonds. Strain in the milk, stirring to mix.
4 Spoon the yogurt into 4 small individual bowls and chill for 8 hours or overnight. Serve decorated with the pistachio nuts.

NUTRITIONAL ANALYSIS
197 kcals/823 kJ
11.4 g Protein
12.1 g Carbohydrate
11.8 g Fat ★
1.9 g Saturated Fat ★★★
1.9 g Fibre ★★★
No Added Sugar ★★★
303 mg Salt ★★★

Grapefruit and Orange Sorbet

This very light refreshing dessert is the perfect finish to a filling meal.

SERVES 4

finely grated rind and strained juice of 1 large grapefruit

finely grated rind and strained juice of 3 oranges

45 ml (3 tbsp) clear honey

2 egg whites

orange slices, to decorate

1 Put the grated grapefruit and orange rinds in a saucepan with 300 ml (½ pint) water. Stir in the honey. Bring to the boil and simmer for 5 minutes. Set aside to cool for about 15 minutes.
2 Strain the cooled syrup and mix well with the grapefruit and orange juices. Pour into a freezerproof container or a 900 g (2 lb) loaf tin and freeze for 1-1½ hours or until mushy in texture.
3 Whisk the egg whites until stiff. Tip the partially frozen ice into a chilled bowl and whisk briefly. Fold in the egg whites and whisk lightly together. Return to the freezerproof container or tin and freeze for at least 2½-3 hours or until frozen.
4 Before serving, soften in the refrigerator for about 10 minutes. Scoop into glasses and decorate with orange slices.

NUTRITIONAL ANALYSIS
63 kcals/263 kJ
1.6 g Protein
15 g Carbohydrate
0 g Fat ★★★★
0 g Saturated Fat ★★★★
0.2 g Fibre ★★★★
8.6 g Added Sugar ★
67 mg Salt ★★★

NUTRITIONAL ANALYSIS
143 kcals/598 kJ
1.1 g Protein
20.8 g Carbohydrate
5.1 g Fat ★★★
0.9 g Saturated Fat ★★★★
3.9 g Fibre ★★★★
5.8 g Added Sugar ★
137 mg Salt ★★★★

Hot Strawberry Compote

Cooked in a flash, this compote makes a pleasant change to the more usual cold fruit salad.

SERVES 4
450 g (1 lb) large strawberries
225 g (8 oz) dark red cherries, stoned
grated rind and juice of 1 lime
15 ml (1 tbsp) sugar
45 ml (3 tbsp) kirsch

1 Hull the strawberries, then halve or quarter. Mix the strawberries and cherries with the lime rind and juice in a bowl.
2 Heat the margarine in a large frying pan. Add the fruits and sugar and stir over a high heat for a few seconds only. The fruits should be really hot and have given out a large amount of juice.
3 Stir in the kirsch, allow to bubble, then serve immediately.

NUTRITIONAL ANALYSIS
250 kcals/1045 kJ
4.7 g Protein
40.4 g Carbohydrate
8.8 g Fat ★★★
1.3 g Saturated Fat ★★★★
4.5 g Fibre ★★★★
10.5 g Added Sugar ★
270 mg Salt ★★★

Lattice Plum Pies

A mouthwatering, spicy, nut pastry is used to top the plums. Choose ripe plums for these pies.

SERVES 4
450 g (1 lb) plums, stoned and quartered
40 g (1½ oz) sugar
5 ml (1 tsp) ground cinnamon
50 g (2 oz) self-raising wholemeal flour
50 g (2 oz) self-raising flour
25 g (1 oz) polyunsaturated margarine
25 g (1 oz) walnuts, finely chopped
30 ml (2 tbsp) low-fat natural yogurt
30 ml (2 tbsp) skimmed milk

1 Put the plums in a saucepan with 25 g (1 oz) of the sugar, 2.5 ml (½ tsp) of the cinnamon and 30 ml (2 tbsp) water. Cover and cook over a gentle heat for 10-15 minutes or until just tender.
2 Spoon the plums and their cooking juices into four 300 ml (½ pint) individual pie dishes and set aside.
3 Put the flours and remaining cinnamon in a bowl. Rub in the margarine until the mixture resembles fine breadcrumbs. Stir in the remaining sugar and half the walnuts. Mix the yogurt with 15 ml (1 tbsp) of the milk and add to the mixture to form a soft dough.
4 Roll out the dough on a lightly floured work surface to 1 cm (½ inch) thick. Cut into wide strips and arrange in a lattice pattern across the top of the pie dishes.
5 Brush the strips with the remaining milk and sprinkle with the remaining chopped nuts.
6 Bake at 220°C (425°F) mark 7 for 10-15 minutes or until cooked and golden. Serve hot.

Strawberry Melba

For a different taste and texture, add fresh orange segments and some whole raspberries to the strawberries.

SERVES 4
450 g (1 lb) fresh strawberries, hulled and quartered if large
225 g (8 oz) raspberries, thawed if frozen
juice of 1 small orange
strawberry leaves, to decorate (optional)

1 Place the strawberries in a serving bowl or 4 individual bowls, cover and chill until required.
2 Purée the raspberries and orange juice in a blender or food processor until smooth. If fresh raspberries are used, it may be necessary to add a little more orange juice or water to thin the sauce. Sieve to remove seeds, if liked.
3 Spoon the sauce over the strawberries, decorate with strawberry leaves, if using, and serve.

NUTRITIONAL ANALYSIS
47 kcals/197 kJ
1.2 g Protein
11.1 g Carbohydrate
0 g Fat ★★★★
0 g Saturated Fat ★★★★
6.6 g Fibre ★★★★
No Added Sugar ★★★★
11 mg Salt ★★★★

Melon Boat Fruit Salad

This fruit salad uses fresh, seasonal fruit for the best flavour and nutritional value.

SERVES 4
½ watermelon, weighing about 1.8 kg (4 lb), or 1 plain melon
2 oranges, peeled, segmented and cut into bite-sized pieces, with juice reserved
1 ripe nectarine, halved, stoned and cut into bite-sized pieces
1 ripe pear, halved, cored and cut into bite-sized pieces
100 g (4 oz) seedless green grapes, halved
few blackberries or raspberries, to decorate

1 If using a watermelon, use a melon baller to scoop out the flesh, discarding the seeds, and place in a bowl.
2 Use a spoon to scoop out any flesh remaining in the melon shell and put into a separate bowl. With a sharp knife, make small diagonal cuts around the top edge of the melon shell to give a zigzag effect.
3 If using a plain melon, cut it in half with a zigzag pattern. Remove the seeds and scoop out the flesh into balls. Use a spoon to scoop out any remaining flesh, setting aside in a separate bowl.
4 Add the oranges, nectarine, pear and grapes to the bowl of melon balls.
5 Purée the remaining flesh in a blender or food processor and strain through a sieve. Add with the reserved orange juice to the prepared fruit in the bowl and stir gently to mix. Put the fruit in the melon shell and decorate with blackberries.

NUTRITIONAL ANALYSIS
114 kcals/479 kJ
2 g Protein
28.4 g Carbohydrate
0 g Fat ★★★★
0 g Saturated Fat ★★★★
5.4 g Fibre ★★★★
No Added Sugar ★★★★
32 mg Salt ★★★★

NUTRITIONAL ANALYSIS
178 kcals/745 kJ
7.6 g Protein
15.7 g Carbohydrate
9.9 g Fat ★★
2.6 g Saturated Fat ★★★
8.1 g Fibre ★★★★
No Added Sugar ★★★★
162 mg Salt ★★★★

Dried Apricot Roulade

This fibre-rich roulade contains no added sugar, as the sweetness is provided by the apricots and orange juice. Using a damp cloth to cover the baked cake helps to keep it moist.

MAKES 8 SLICES
225 g (8 oz) dried apricots
200 ml (1/3 pint) orange juice
4 eggs, separated
45 ml (3 tbsp) ground almonds
150 ml (1/4 pint) Greek strained yogurt
30 ml (2 tbsp) flaked almonds, toasted

1 Soak the apricots in the orange juice overnight. Purée in a blender or food processor.
2 Beat the apricot purée with the egg yolks and mix in the ground almonds. Whisk the egg whites until stiff and fold 15 ml (1 tbsp) lightly but thoroughly into the apricot mixture to soften. Carefully fold in the remaining egg whites.
3 Spread the mixture evenly in a non-stick paper lined Swiss roll tin, 30×20 cm (12×8 inches). Bake at 190°C (375°F) mark 5 for 20 minutes. Remove from the oven and cover with a fresh piece of non-stick paper and a damp clean cloth. Leave to cool.
4 Invert the apricot cake on to the paper and clean cloth and remove the lining paper. Spread with the yogurt and roll up loosely from a long end, like a Swiss roll, then wrap in the paper and clean cloth. Leave to stand for at least 10 minutes.
5 To serve, remove the paper and cloth and sprinkle with the toasted flaked almonds.

NUTRITIONAL ANALYSIS
109 kcals/456 kJ
1.9 g Protein
26.6 g Carbohydrate
0.2 g Fat ★★★★
0 g Saturated Fat ★★★★
8.4 g Fibre ★★★★
No Added Sugar ★★★★
35 mg Salt ★★★★

Fresh Fruit Salad with Mango and Passion Fruit Salad

Mangoes should be eaten when they feel slightly soft and smell sweet and fragrant.

SERVES 4
2 passion fruit
1 large mango, skinned and stoned
juice of 1/2 lime
3 kiwi fruit, peeled and sliced
225 g (8 oz) raspberries
100 g (4 oz) seedless grapes
4 mint sprigs, to decorate

1 Halve the passion fruit and spoon out the pulp. Purée with the mango flesh, lime juice and 30 ml (2 tbsp) water in a food processor or blender. Sieve the purée. Chill while preparing the fruit.
2 Spoon the fruit sauce on to the base of 4 individual plates. Attractively arrange the fruit on top of the sauce. Decorate with a sprig of mint.